Can't You Just Get Over It

Angela Kehler

Copyright © 2023 Angela Kehler

All rights reserved.

ISBN: 9798859418923

WITH GRATITUDE

There are too many people who have appeared in my life—however briefly, profoundly, at the perfect moment, with the right words or a hand to hold, arms to carry me, or the fire to light under my ass when needed—to list them here. But there are a few who I must acknowledge.

My husband, whose story is so intertwined with my own, but who didn't once ask me to censor it on his behalf. It took a great deal of courage for you to quietly support this book, knowing that my vulnerability was also going to be yours. I cannot tell you how grateful I am for that courage. Patrick, you gave me the gift of words, of pen to paper, of speaking before I had a voice, of thinking with ink, those things that I could not say out loud. You unwittingly gave me the gift that helped me become the person I was meant to be. Thank you for that and for teaching me to rebel.

Yahanna, you are my rock and my most relentless cheerleader. My proofreader and memory checker when I was feeling fuzzy. The voice on the other end of the line time and again as I sobbed into the phone, "I'm not sure I can do this. I'm not sure I can be this bare, this vulnerable in front of my past, in front of the whole world." Or texted frantically, "Remind me why I'm doing this? Why did I think this was a good idea?"

And you'd say, "Because you can. Because you wanted to write a book, and you did. You wanted to tell the truth about all the ugliness that you couldn't when you were young. You didn't want to be silenced. You won. You did it. You're telling the truth that has to be told, and you have every right to do it." I love you.

My siblings, who are muted in this book because theirs aren't stories that I have a right to tell, but who share my blood and my childhood bubble. Wanting to be the big sister you all deserve has always driven me, and not any less in the writing of this book. You all are my soul.

My children. I don't care if you read this book or not, but if you do, I hope that what you take away from it is that courage is always worth it. Never stop asking questions and demanding answers. I want nothing more from you or for you than to be true to yourselves, compassionate and kind to yourselves when you struggle, and forever confident in your own inner voice. You inspire me every day.

And finally. The journey of getting this book into the hands of readers hasn't been simple or easy. Thank you to my extended friends and family for believing in me—your confidence and words of support and encouragement have inspired the persistence that got me to this point.

These are the facts of my experience as I remember them. Conversations are not verbatim unless I remember exact words, which is rare. Otherwise, they are written in the manner that they *probably* took place based on my knowledge of and experience with the characters involved. I understand that memories can be tricky and are subjective, and I have told this story as I lived it and as it has survived in me. I have maintained as tight a lens as possible to my story because it is the only one I have the right to tell.

I always knew I had to be perfect.
I knew it was what they wanted.
They told me it was what God wanted.
They told me that I was an example
for the younger kids.
I promised them
that I would tell the world.
This is for the kids.

PROLOGUE

It wasn't an easy decision to write this book—the acrid reality of laying myself bare, walking naked in front of the world, in front of friends and strangers alike. I didn't decide to be a writer. I never imagined I would have the drive, the burning, the need to tell stories, specifically this story. It wasn't until I was in college, fumbling my way through a foreign and intimidating world, that my classmates and teacher planted the seed. During those years, whenever I told just a bit of my story to anyone, they insisted that I should write a book. I'd entertain the idea for a moment but then shrink from it entirely, convinced that writing was for, well, writers, and I was woefully unqualified. Consequently, I have numerous versions of varying lengths, started, and abandoned over the years, tucked away in boxes and baskets.

College was excruciating for me. The phrase that aptly captures my college experience is *paralyzed with fear*. Fear of failure, fear of not measuring up to my peers, many of whom were younger than I but already had a much more impressive educational resume, fear of spending all that time and money and then, in the end, having nothing of substance to show for it.

After I left home, I passed the GED when I was eighteen and moved to Vermont. I was already married when I went to college, so although I was a similar age as the kids around me, I had nothing in common with them, and being part of the "normal" world was still terrifyingly new to me. I was awkward and had little aptitude for nuance and social cues. I also lacked academic skills and have since concluded that my advisors and teachers often just passed me through instead of pushing me to learn the skills I hadn't learned in the high school I had never attended. It's not that I didn't do my best. I did. I'd just been teaching myself for the most part since the sixth grade, piecing my education together the best I could with the limited resources around me. When I'd struggle with something, I'd abandon it and try something else. Resignation was as much a part of me as any desire for achievement.

Twenty years later, it's clear that although I have wrestled with the idea of this book, it never stopped knocking at the back door of my mind, sometimes gently, sometimes with more urgency.

I've changed my mind countless times and come up with all sorts of reasons why I shouldn't write. Why not just go on with my life, close and seal those chapters, and live in the present and the future? I could; lots of people do. But the *knock, knock* was persistent and unrelenting. I can't deny that part of me. It's informed so much of my young adult experience and weighed heavily on me as a mother.

It's held me back and tormented me relentlessly.

I've taken hours upon hours to read through notes from sermons and the letters I wrote to friends throughout my young life. My old letters are cringeworthy. I read the words I wrote and am embarrassed for that girl. Even though I know that I had no choice in the matter at the time, it baffles me how completely I embraced something that felt so wrong because it was all there was. The words that came out of my mouth and pen at the time are so far from who I am now that I can't even reconcile the two. Now that I have a choice, the woman that I have chosen to be is worlds away from that girl, decades from her struggle to survive and make sense of the things that pelted off her scrambled brain in a constant onslaught. I thought that reading those letters would give me insight and put me back into the mind of the girl whose story I needed to tell. But the two versions of me are irreconcilable, and instead, I just felt disjointed.

The purpose of this book is to give a voice to that girl, the one that *was* me, the one that had no voice and no choice, and to give voice to all of the other beautiful, determined, and courageous kids that left with me.

CONTENTS

1 A GOOD GIRL 11
2 IN THE BEGINNING 18
3 MY BIRTH—PHYSICAL AND SPIRITUAL 32
4 UNRIGHTEOUS RELATIONS 45
5 LIVE IN THE WORLD BUT BE NOT OF THE WORLD 58
6 DOING THE RIGHT THING 69
7 SCHOOL 82
8 ANGEL OR DEVIL 91
9 YOU'RE TOO YOUNG TO KNOW ABOUT IT YET 105
10 AND THE PRAYER OF FAITH SHALL SAVE THE SICK 115
11 THE SINS OF THE FATHER 124
12 SECOND CHANCES 134
13 DANIELLE 140
14 BLOOD AND BIRTH 146
15 FASHION IN A FISHBOWL 154
16 FALLING IN LOVE 164
17 TWO WEDDINGS 181
18 PASSOVER 192
19 THE AFTERMATH 214
20 DESPERATE MEASURES 220
21 DAY OF RECKONING 228
22 WALKING THE LINE 239
23 THE AWAKENING 249

24 TURNING POINT 261
25 THE GATHERING STORM 268
26 ENGAGED 276
27 THE LAST STRAW 289
28 VOWS AND GOODBYES 295
29 UNFURLING 304

EPILOGUE 310

1 A GOOD GIRL

It was Sabbath morning, and I stood at the kitchen sink, looking out the window. Those early hours were my hours, especially when, in late spring, the chill of the night persisted, but the bold morning sun and the clear blue sky promised a perfect day ahead. The prairie was fresh and fragrant, and everything was blissfully still. Meadowlarks, whose songs stilled my breath, perched on the barbed wire fence directly in front of me, singing in the crisp sunlight, framed by tough prairie grasses, vibrantly green for only a few weeks, with brave bits of Indian Paintbrush standing tall in fiery oranges and reds, fiercely defiant in the arid soil.

As the sounds of my siblings stumbling out of bed reached my ears, I knew my moment of quiet was over, but I didn't care so much. The sooner they were up and dressed, the sooner we could leave for church, which was why I was out of bed so early anyway. It's not like I *enjoyed* church, not really. The sermons were tales of terror, or they droned on monotonously, or they could be targeted and brutal—in any case, I could do without them. My perfect church day would have been nothing but hanging out with everyone and singing all day. I was eager for church mostly because of Mateo. I hadn't planned to be helplessly in love with him. Still, now that I'd accepted that fact, it hurt more than I could've imagined right in the middle of my chest, that part where the two sides of your ribs meet, that little upside-down V. A ball of pain and longing that wound tightly right in that V. It wasn't always the same size, sometimes it grew, sometimes it shrank, sometimes it bounced around a bit, but it was always there.

People thought I was crazy. At fifteen, they insisted, I was too young to be in love, and that much was true. I didn't understand what it meant or know why it happened. It just—happened. I was supposed to be fighting it, to be learning how to have a clean mind and pure heart and be presentable to YHWH—pronounced: *Yah*weh—how to be a vessel for his plan, but that ball just took up too much space to fit much else. I tried to crush it, tried to send it away. I begged YHWH to take it away, but he didn't seem to want to. I kept telling him I was sorry about it, I knew it was a void he was supposed to fill, but somehow, I wasn't letting him fill it. And I didn't know how to change that. So, that's why I was eager for church, to see Mateo and be in the same room with him for a couple of hours.

I lingered at the window for a few more seconds and closed my eyes, inhaling the cool air blowing through the screen and letting my ears fill with the lonesome sound of a mourning dove in the distance. I loved that sound—tortured, penetrating, and deep, it sounded how I felt.

My brothers ate their cinnamon rolls at a glacial pace, stopping to taunt each other, push and punch at each other, and howl with laughter at stupid jokes, prompting my mom to remind them that it was the Sabbath, a day of rest and worship, and they needed to *settle down*. They would've inhaled their food any other time, but those mornings when I was dying to get out the door, it was the exact opposite.

I was annoyed.

I walked out onto the deck, letting the screen door slam behind me. The deck was worn and unfinished, with greying two-by-fours that were chipped and frayed along the edges and stairs that sagged and wobbled when I stepped on them, another project my father started and then ran out of money and ambition to finish. After a quick peek beneath to confirm there wasn't a rattlesnake napping in their shade, I sat on those wobbly stairs, picked up one of the kittens, and hugged her to me, burying my face in her fur, my fingers wrapped lovingly around her ribs and bony legs. She wiggled and struggled until she succumbed to the fact that I would not put her down and reluctantly surrendered to my snuggles. We had six of them. Sometimes we had more, sometimes less; it depended on how many of them got sick and died or were eaten by owls or coyotes. We weren't allowed to bring them inside. Animals were unclean and would defile our house, so they were at the mercy of the outdoors—the weather and wild animals. They survived mostly. When they didn't, we'd bury them with lots of tears and wait for the next stray to show up or the next litter of kittens to be born.

I sat on the steps with the cats until everyone was finally ready and filing out the door. It slammed indignantly after each exit. The boys pushed and shoved each other, trying to be the first one through the door, the first one down the stairs, and the first one to the end of the driveway. My mom barked a warning. They ignored it. She tried again, "*Settle down now*, and stop pushing or I won't let you walk" (walking to church rather than driving was a privilege revoked if we misbehaved, mainly because when we walked, we'd usually run into other members along the way. In our household, hanging out with other members outside of worship was a rare treat). "It's the Sabbath Day. Show some respect." They conceded, stifling snickers and muttering under their breath.

I wanted to run ahead, too—wanted to walk by myself so she wouldn't be there *right next to me* when we ran into Mateo and the other brothers at the corner. I knew they were on their way. I'd heard their guitars and songs traveling effortlessly across the open space between our trailers. I didn't know what I was hoping for, how my mom being next to me would be any different than me walking by myself. It wouldn't. I just hated being observed and mistrusted all the time. I was a good girl; it had never occurred to me to be any other way. But somehow, since

I'd *developed feelings*, as the grown-ups liked to say, I could never actually be good until I made them go away. And since I couldn't figure out how to do that, they didn't trust me.

I'd built up so much anticipation that by the time we finally met at the corner, with a flash of a smile and a quick, *Praise YHWH, Sister Angie* later, I found myself, rather disappointedly, walking alone next to my mom again. First, Mateo was there, and then he was gone, hurrying ahead with my brothers, and the ball twisted a bit and expanded as it radiated the guilt that was weighing on my mind and churning in my stomach.

What I'd been hoping for, but I couldn't admit, not even in the deepest, most secret places of my heart, was a glimmer, a little glow, a hint of something that would tell me that he felt the same way, that I wasn't alone in my constant state of sin.

There wasn't one. I alone was wrapped up in that world of feelings, the one that wouldn't let me rest, wouldn't let me be holy, and never let me be pure like I was supposed to be.

I was suddenly ready for church, the real thing. I needed the praying and the crying. I needed the fear coming from the pulpit. I needed something to snap me out of the stupor holding me hostage. I hurried up the concrete steps into the church ahead of everyone. I slipped off my shoes by the coat rack and breezed past the wooden pews lined up so precisely on both sides of the room to the front of the church to kneel and beg YHWH to set me free. I chose a spot on the far end, closest to the wall, where I could shrink into as small a ball as possible. I crawled under the bench, wrapped my hands around my head, and cried. I cried because I knew I would never be perfect, I cried because I was lonely, and I cried because no matter how hard I tried to be good, *I was still bad.*

All around me, people made their way reverently to the front of the church and knelt to pray, the drone of supplication growing to a crescendo. The men knelt in front of the two benches on either side of the pulpit, and the women knelt behind the two benches in the space between the pews and the pulpit. Ironically, we all faced east to pray. And although I am sure Laycher would've insisted that they didn't plan it that way (the brothers *did* construct the building, they could have set it up differently), it isn't lost on me now that although worshiping the sun god was blasphemous, ritualistically that is precisely what we were doing.

The praying part of the service usually droned on for what seemed like forever. I'd run out of things to say and get bored with asking YHWH to help me be better, to *make* me better. I'd say thank you for every little thing I could think of to say thank you for because since I was asking for help, YHWH would pay more attention if I offered gratitude first. When I finished with that and when I'd said *sorry,* and cried, and beat myself up sufficiently in the eyes of my Savior, I'd peek out from under my arm and watch other people. I knew I shouldn't, it was their private moment with YHWH, but I couldn't help myself.

They were loud and tortured, yelling at the top of their lungs and throwing themselves back and forth. I heard people speak in tongues, a made-up language of random sounds squished together like words without spaces, and I could tell that some of them *weren't* speaking in tongues at all—they were just speaking Spanish. I knew that because sometimes Laycher preached in Spanish, so I knew what it sounded like. I'd never spoken in tongues because I wasn't good enough yet. You had to be perfect to be baptized by the Spirit, and only after getting baptized by the Spirit could you speak in tongues. It was confusing because there were lots of people who I knew weren't as good as me, definitely not perfect, but they *did* speak in tongues. I figured they were just making it up to feel holy. If tongues were some sort of sacred Holy Spirit language, why were everyone's sounds so different and like baby gibberish? I waited patiently for my tongues to appear, but they never did.

The drone of supplication died down until it was nearly silent. Then we'd wait as long as it took for Laycher to start to sing. We never rose from our knees until *he* decided prayer time was over by haltingly wading into the first line of a song alone:

"You-ou fo-ound meee when I wa-as so lonely..."

He always started off-key, and the rest of us chimed in to help fix it. The brothers would get up and fiddle with their guitars to find the cord that worked.

"You found me when I was so blue
You found me when nothing could help me
And I didn't know just what to do.
So let me walk with you, YHWH
Don't ever leave me alone
For without you, I could never,
No, never make heaven my home."

We'd finish the song, rise piously, and find our way to our benches. My family always sat near the front of the room, which I didn't like, but it's where the holier people sat, so my mom would never sit in the back. I wondered why Laycher's wife sat in the very back since she was, by association, the second holiest, which could mean that sitting in the back didn't affect her. When I was little, I used to have to sit with my mom, but by the time I was in my mid-teens, I got to sit one bench back. I'd hug the edge of the bench near the outside aisle with my mom and brothers in front of me. I liked that spot because Laycher couldn't see me. When he looked at me while he was preaching, I felt like he was burning a hole into my head and seeing every bad thought, every little thing I'd done wrong.

He was always telling us that all things would be revealed to the pastor. "*YHWH will show your secret sins to the pastor,*" he assured us. "*You keep in your sinful ways, and I'm gonna rebuke you before the whole assembly. No one can pass a judgment but me. I have my helpers, and I instruct them, but all that should come through the pastor.*" I'd take a second to wonder if he knew about the walk to church, about the ball in my chest. My hands would

16

grow clammy, my heart would race, and I'd try to disappear. Up until that point, he'd never rebuked me in front of everyone, but I knew it was just a matter of time.

He had rebuked our family, along with a list of others. A rebuking day would go like this. "We've *got to get ready now. John and Frank, get in here or leave. Sister Carol, the same thing. Sister Mary, get out of your house with your daughter or leave.* (Sister Mary was an older woman with mental health and maybe developmental issues. Perhaps she'd had a stroke. I don't know the details. She lived with her daughter because she couldn't live alone. Her daughter took care of her but was not a church member.) *Ron, if you want to stay here, get to Oregon immediately and stay there. You're under Brother Jerry. Your family can follow later. Do this or leave. The single brothers, get in there and overcome now. The single sisters, except Gwen* (he always had a thing for Gwen), *get out of your fighting. Brother Bill and family* (that's us), *get together so that your faith might increase and you might get strong. Sister Lisa, get out of your family and relatives and out of your welfare* (food stamps) *too, or leave. There's more for everyone except Brother David."*

The weird thing was that when he rebuked other people, I still felt like it was me. I'd get hot, I'd feel like I was going to vomit, and I'd want to hide under the bench in front of me. I'd wish that I could step in front of the rebuke and stop it from hitting them. I hated rebuking, and I didn't understand how it helped anyone be better.

2 IN THE BEGINNING

Before I fell in love, I said I would never get married. It was a little game I played with the grown-ups that they seemed to love, and so I pretended to enjoy it too. Even before I was thirteen, people would ask me if I was thinking about boys yet, especially Maxine. Laycher would cluck his tongue, shake his head at his wife—although she never really paid him any mind—and reach out his hand, beckoning to me. "No, she's never getting married, right, Jita? She's going to be my schoolteacher." I would perch myself on his knee and wrap my arms around his neck, nodding in agreement.

"I'm already married," I would say, "to YHWH. And I can't wait to teach school. I might even be able to start before I'm eighteen. I practically teach the little kids on my own already." That was true. For a while, in my early teens, Quinn was the only teacher, and she was stretched thin and cranky, so I would teach first and second grade in the morning and then do my schoolwork in the afternoon.

Laycher would turn to his wife triumphantly beaming his toothless grin, thinking he'd won, and she'd sneer and mutter to no one in particular, "That's what they all say, just you wait." Of course, she knew what she was talking about. She could be vicious, but it's because she was smart and cynical.

I was raised in a cult.

I didn't know it was a cult, and the people I grew up with wouldn't have called it a cult. All I knew was that it was my life, it was the only life, and everyone else in the world was wrong. Our cult was just one of the many that popped up over the years in the American West, and I am just one of the hundreds (probably thousands) of kids that grew up and out of such a place. It wasn't a hippie cult, not one of those, *aliens are coming to save us cults*, not an intentional community of back to the landers' cult, a free-love cult, or a doomsday cult. Ours was a cult of religion, belief, and surrender, a fundamentalist cult. Fundamentalists believe in a strict, literal interpretation of the Bible which forms the foundation for their doctrine, and while we did interpret many parts of the Bible literally, and it absolutely formed the basis for our doctrine, there were some parts of the Old Testament that we did not obey, like stoning sinners to death, or enslaving people, or sacrificing animals. We were pick and choose fundamentalists, as most are. We called ourselves: *The Assembly of YHWHHOSUA* (pronounced: Yaweh-hoshua—like Joshua), not to be confused with the Assemblies of Yahweh, a separate group of churches altogether who we had nothing in common with besides the use of the name Yahweh, our name for God.

Boone, Colorado, was our earthly home, where we both lived and worshipped, two things that were expected to occur simultaneously and continuously. Boone is in the southeastern part of the state, in the arid, tumbleweed-producing, sun-scorched grasslands. There were no mountains in my backyard, although I could see their outline in the distance, and the closest city, Pueblo, was forty minutes away. The building where we worshiped is still there, just over the Huerfano River, off Highway Fifty East, heading toward La Junta. It was a one-story, stuccoed building that resembled a basic ranch—it is a house now—unless you could see the roof. The side of the roof that faces the highway is shingled in brown, with white ones spelling out the word YHWH. The brothers felt quite pleased with themselves the day they executed that clever bit of artistic proselytizing. You can still see it on Google Maps' satellite view. For the life of me, I can't imagine why the new owners, after over twenty years, never re-shingled the roof.

I was the first child born into the church. And when I say I was the first child born into the church, the church I'm talking about is the true church, as they would have said, after embracing the true name of the Savior, which will become apparent in the next few paragraphs. There were lots of other kids there who were older than I was, but they were born before the reinvention of the true church, so I was like a rare bird, the first of its kind, and everyone was waiting patiently (or impatiently, from some perspectives) to see what my colors would be. On the other hand, I was learning to be whatever bird they wanted me to be, in whatever colors they wanted to see.

Laycher (pronounced Lay-shur) Gonzales was our pastor, and any quote from him in this book will be in italics and has been copied directly from old sermon notes. A designated person in the congregation wrote down sermon notes in real time while Laycher was preaching. Luckily, my parents were both note-takers throughout the years, so I have a virtual treasure trove of words directly out of his mouth. It is vital to recognize, when reading his words, that although on the face of them, they may appear benign, to a group of people who believed with their hearts and souls that he was a prophet and that the Almighty spoke through him, who hung onto his words for sustenance, every single word carried the weight of a sledgehammer, the terror of a quaking mountain, the toxin of a viper, or, as the case often was, the comfort of a trusted parent.

Purely based on looks, mannerisms, or first impressions, Laycher was an unassuming, modest man. No taller than five and a half feet with broad shoulders and a solid frame (he worked in construction, specifically, pouring concrete), he spoke softly and smiled easily, his un-trimmed salt-and-pepper beard wagging when he talked, his mustache grown down over his top lip, concealing the four teeth left in his fifty-five-year-old mouth. He had shoulder-length hair the same color as his beard that fell in greased ringlets from a receding hairline. But looks can be deceiving, and although he could be gentle and kind when he wanted to, he spoke of his flock as his children—in fact—he referred to us as his children and grandchildren, like a father or grandfather, he reserved the right to rebuke and chastise us when we needed it. It took knowing him to understand the power he held over us, the absolute finality of his words, the fire, and the righteous anger that flew like daggers from the pulpit when he preached. Of course, he wasn't always fifty-five, but in my memory, he is frozen at that age.

Laycher used to pray to God, Lord, and Jesus just like everyone else in the Pentecostal church where he was raised. In case you don't know anything about the Pentecostal church, it happens to be a perfect launching point for starting a cult. Already primed with extreme views, some of which include an obsession with the wrath of God—fire and brimstone—rather than love and forgiveness, baptism by the Holy Spirit, including speaking in tongues which is understood to be a direct communication with God, and public humiliation through condemnation, this taking on many forms, one being rebuking individuals from the pulpit for wrong-doing. Starting from there, it wasn't a great leap to where he ended up.

Laycher wandered away from the church as a young adult and walked a path of sin. He recounted his story incessantly to remind us how far he'd come. He'd spent his time drinking and smoking, gallivanting and whoremongering. Of course, I had no idea what gallivanting and whoremongering were, but I knew by his tone that they were bad. Now I know that's just church-speak for frequenting strip clubs and bars and womanizing. When he was thirty years old, his wife dragged him into an apostolic church (an extreme interpretation of the Pentecostal movement). The details are a bit fuzzy as stories told over time through a long game of telephone often are, but the most plausible is that the church was pastored by Beauford Salee, a Tennessee transplant who had taken over leadership at the Spanish-speaking, Hispanic, Apostolic church that had been launched and previously pastored by Laycher's father and uncle. That church, to my surprise, had been going strong in Pueblo since the 1930s. I didn't even know the Apostolic movement existed in the 1930s. Laycher's family had roots in Pueblo going back generations, generations of hardworking contractors, laboring in all types of construction, from digging basements by hand to pouring concrete and raising the walls and roofs.

A few months later, Laycher was reborn, baptized by the Holy Spirit and by speaking in tongues. He soon became convinced that Beauford was a hypocrite, preaching one thing and living another, one of his favored lines of instruction, *do as I say, not as I do*, proof of that fact. Laycher believed that one should lead by example. He also felt strongly that the church's doctrines shouldn't be optional or voluntary but compulsory and mandatory, such as the doctrine that taught faith healing but still allowed members to seek medical attention when needed. He promptly decided to stir up trouble in that church, morphing seamlessly from miserable sinner to self-righteous prophet, believing that with his baptism of the Spirit, he was being spoken to by God and that he had the authority to condemn other members of the church for things he believed were sins, like going to the doctor or wearing glasses. The congregation fractured and scattered, most of them moving on to other churches, but some, who were ready and eager to believe in his ordination and follow his doctrine, joined Laycher when he decided to start his own church in a home built by his father on Catalpa Street in Pueblo in the early seventies. He was preaching in the name of God, as they had in his old church until he picked up a hitchhiker who changed his mind.

As the story goes, he was driving late at night when he came across an older man with his thumb out. He pulled his rickety pickup over onto the shoulder of the highway, and when the stranger opened the passenger door to climb in, Laycher greeted him, "Praise the Lord." His eyes would grow misty, standing there at the pulpit looking out at us, and he would grin and chuckle, "And that old man said to me, 'son, that's not his name, his name is YHWH.' And I knew in my heart, right at that moment, that my prayers had been answered. I was searching for the truth, and he (meaning God) had led me right to it. I had been baptized by the Spirit, and the Spirit will lead us to the truth. The next day we were all baptized again, in the name of YHWH, and ask anyone who was there, you could hear the angels rejoicing." I always hoped that someday I could hear the angels rejoicing. The angels didn't rejoice at any of the baptisms I had been to, but I figured it was probably because there weren't so many people getting baptized at once.

All of the baptisms I witnessed throughout my life took place in the Arkansas River, a river that flows from its source in the Rockies across the plains to the Mississippi. In Pueblo, it is wide, deep, and muddy, thanks to several smaller rivers and creeks that empty into it, coming off of the clay-rich soils of the mesas. It was hard to find a place where we could park all our cars and then walk down to the edge. We frequented a few spots throughout my life in the church, but the one I remember the most was the one we used when I was very young, no more than seven years old. It was directly off a hidden turn under an overpass in Pueblo. A narrow dirt road led down a steep bank onto the flat floodplain at the river's edge. The image of that turn is burned into my brain. It often seeps into my dreams and taunts me with foggy flashbacks. For some reason, every time I revisit it in my dreams, I get stuck at the turn and can never see what comes next. Tiny roads made by ATVs wound around the clumps of river grass that were taller than I was. The sand was soft and deep, and someone always got their car stuck, and the brothers would have to push, bounce, and rock the car as the tires dug deeper and deeper each time the driver revved the engine.

We had to be baptized, first in water and then by the Spirit. "If you are not born of the water and the spirit, you cannot enter into the kingdom," Laycher would preach. I never knew how to tell if someone had been baptized by the Spirit. The only person we knew who had been baptized by the Spirit was Laycher. Everyone had to be baptized, especially newborn babies. But because it was winter when I was born, I wasn't baptized until I was three months old. Usually, we dunked the babies when they were two weeks old. I remember those baptisms when mamas handed over their little bundles to Laycher.

I'd automatically hold my breath on behalf of the baby as it was plunged into the dirty, freezing water. It was always so quiet that the sunshine, the rustling leaves, and the gurgle of the river were deafening. I tried to hear angels rejoicing, but no matter how hard I strained, I couldn't. I figured I wasn't worthy; they could keep you from hearing if you weren't worthy.

That river sent shivers all through me, and the terror grew as Laycher stepped off the edge into the muddy current. Sometimes the first step was deeper than he'd expected, and he'd sway and stumble while someone grabbed his arm to steady him. I watched as the water swirled around him, tugging at his robe. One step—up to his knees, two steps—up to his chest. He'd brace against the powerful flow, an impish grin on his face. When my dad stepped in, just a bit, to hand over one of my little brothers (who will be introduced into this story as they're born), I'd squeeze my eyes tightly, sure that someone would drop the baby and he'd go floating away. Laycher would put his hand over the baby's face and submerge him completely under

the water. When the baby came up, he would erupt in a sputtering scream, and I'd open my eyes, relieved that it was over. My mom would hurry to wrap the baby in a thick quilt and rush back to the car to change his wet clothes, and the rest of us would sing:
"Shall we gather at the river
Where bright angel feet have trod
With its crystal tide forever
Flowing by the throne of YHWH."

It was one of our happy songs, one of hope and new beginnings, one that made us clap and sway and made me feel like I was floating. The jitters of fear conjured by the water were replaced by butterflies of excitement and the magic of it all. The significance of those moments was not lost on me, no matter my age.

Baptisms were always on the Sabbath. Sabbath was a holy day, so it made sense. Every week was a journey toward that single day, a culmination of build-up and expectation which peaked on the day of rest. When I was a kid, I loved the Sabbath Day. We observed the Sabbath because the Bible commanded it. It was really the only day I spent time with other people besides my family. I had no friends outside of the church. Church services were in the morning, and after services, I waited anxiously to see where everyone would go and who would decide to have lunch with whom. I hated it when families and singles, brothers, and sisters, would make plans all around us, but we would walk home dejectedly to a long day all on our own. Luckily, that didn't happen often. My dad, despite being inconsequential in the grand scheme of things (more on that later), was the life of the party, and people seemed to relish his company. Think of him as the jester at the king's palace, a nobody earning his place because of his ability to amuse and entertain.

We would eat together, and the hours would fly by as we spent the day playing music and worshipping in each other's homes. When I was little, the grown-ups worshipped, and I played with the other kids— until I was about eleven. Then

I migrated into the living rooms where the grown-ups, engaged in somber and devotional conversations in the soft afternoon light, spoke softly to each other. They lounged on crowded couches or sat in dining room chairs or on the floor—circled 'round. The grown-ups barely noticed me there as I listened in on confessions or advice exchanged in hushed tones. A single woman who was aching with sadness, eyes downcast, her hands folded in her lap, a tear glistening at the corner of her eye, because the husband she left behind to join the church had not yet seen the light, and she was worried that he never would.

"Just keep praying," a brother would encourage her, leaning in close, care and concern written on his face, his voice soothing and sympathetic. "YHWH hears our prayers and answers them if our hearts are pure. Just make sure that your concern is for your husband's soul and not for your own fleshly desires or because you're afraid to be alone."

"That's the hard part, isn't it?" she would say, not looking up. "How can I know that what I want is for his salvation and not just for my own carnal desires and fears?"

"Well, you must search your soul and make yourself presentable before the Savior and trust that he knows best." The answer was always that simple. "Maybe we can pray with you. Would you like that?"

The only acceptable answer to that question was—yes.

Sabbath Days were filled with spontaneous prayer meetings and singing. The prayer meetings were monotonous and cringy. I didn't much like listening to peoples' confessions—it was hard not to when they were saying it right out loud right next to you—but I loved playing guitar and singing. I sang with full-throated conviction and devotion. Songs about YHWH's unfathomable love and forgiveness, songs about temptation, songs about the end of the world, songs about being unworthy. Hours would pass, and I could just keep singing. I loved how it made me feel—flushed and tingly, like teetering on the edge of something huge I didn't understand. I knew it was YHWH working in my soul.

The other thing we looked forward to on the Sabbath was going to City Park to find new souls to save. We, the kids, loved it because we got to be outside with the other kids and run around in the grass. We didn't have grass in our yards. Sod was expensive and nearly impossible to keep alive in that harsh climate, so bare feet in the grass was a treat. And then there was the playground, another super rare treat. We weren't allowed to play on the swings until sunset because playing was work, so we milled around the grown-ups restlessly until then, and they reminded us that we weren't there to play. We were there to witness (witness: to openly profess one's religious faith).

They strategically chose a spot far away from the playground, where we carefully lifted our instruments from their cases—guitars, flutes, violins, mandolins—and then, after a brief tuning session, we sang. People walked slowly and deliberately past us, some alone, some with their families out enjoying the weekend. Most of them didn't stop but turned their heads around as they walked, trained on us as they passed, or sometimes they paused for a brief minute to take in the scene of us from a distance and listen to the music, but eventually kept walking. We were well-known around Pueblo as The YHWHs, but we were, nonetheless, quite the spectacle. Our women and girls were covered in veils and long dresses or skirts, in muted colors like tan, pale blue, or dark brown, mostly chambray or muslin, and our men and little boys dressed in robes that zipped up the front from the waist and covered every last bit of their bodies, except their heads, hands, and feet. We would all sing at the top of our voices, clapping and swaying with our eyes closed in devotion.

I didn't close my eyes; I stared at them, staring at us. If someone decided to stop and talk, they'd usually get more than they'd bargained for. They were generally just curious, and we were happy to gently indulge the curiosity at first, hoping to reel them in.

"Nice music, yous really have pretty voices, and those guitars, you play real good."

"Thank you. Yeah, but it's not about us, really, not for our glorification or edification. We're just grateful to serve the Almighty and strive to be an example of his love. Do you have a minute to talk about the Savior?" We never said YHWH right away because that would confuse them, so we'd say the Almighty or the Savior; most people understood those.

"Well, we're Catholic, sooo…but nice singing, cute kids," and with a wink at us, they'd be on their way.

Some stayed longer. We'd tell them about the love of the Savior, his true name, and they'd say, "Wow, really? I didn't know that."

To which the brothers would smile and nod knowingly, "Most people don't. False prophets abound. All these other churches are lying to the people, leading them astray, and teaching them to worship false gods. The wages of sin are death."

And if they stuck around long enough to indulge in a journey through the doctrine with plenty of scripture references but still stood to leave, curiosity satisfied, we would sometimes more forcefully mention, "The scripture also says, 'repent and be baptized in the name of YHWHHOSHUA for the forgiveness of sins and you will receive the gift of the holy spirit': Acts 2:38. 'But the fearful, and unbelieving, and the abominable, and murderers, and whoremongers, and sorcerers, and idolaters, and all liars, shall have their part in the lake which burneth with fire and brimstone, which is the second death': Revelations 21:8." In other words, if you don't join our church, you'll go to hell, but we didn't say hell because it was a curse word.

The Sabbath was our day to rest. With no work to distract us, we could think about YHWH and devote ourselves entirely to worshipping him with no distractions. Friday was Preparation Day. We'd scour every corner of the house (cleanliness is next to holiness, after all), scrub the bathroom, do the laundry, take showers, and make enough beans and potatoes, enchiladas, or lasagna, cinnamon rolls, and bread for two days of eating. Cooking was work, even with a modern stove that asked nothing of us but the turning of a knob. Everything had to be thoroughly cooked the day before because we were allowed to reheat food with a burner on the stove but not cook food with a burner on the stove. I never understood the difference because the fire was doing all the work, not us. We raced against the sun because as soon as it licked the tips of the mountains in the west with its fiery tongue, everything came to a grinding halt. Guilt-ridden housewives left the casserole or loaf of bread in the oven, hoping it would continue to bake with the oven turned off, or left the pasta in its hot water to finish cooking for a few minutes, although the water was no longer boiling.

Saturday was the Sabbath, but we didn't call it Saturday. We called it Seventh Day. Sunday was First Day, Monday was Second Day, Tuesday—Third Day, etcetera. Those were the only names for the days of the week that I knew until I was a teenager and started snooping through the encyclopedias that were hidden away in cardboard boxes in the closet at school. Because the names of the week originated with the Greek gods, they were blasphemous, violating the first commandment to have no other gods before YHWH and not to bow down and worship them. Uttering the names of the Greek Gods would be the same as worshipping them, so Laycher changed the names, simple as that.

YHWH revealed to Laycher what the rules should be, and he, in turn, imparted them to us, and we followed them with reverence and commitment. His revelations appeared with steady predictability and were powerful and binding— YHWH spoke to him, YHWH chose him, he was just the humble vessel—and we accepted that without question. But it seemed to me that the rules changed depending on his mood. Even from a young age, I noticed that when he was content and happy, the rules were more open and relaxed, but when he was stormy, the rules grew dark and more restrictive. Sometimes it was okay to brush our teeth on the Sabbath. Other times it was a sin because it was work, and we weren't supposed to work from sunset to sunset. Sometimes it was a sin to check the mail on the Sabbath because that would make the mail-lady work; other times, it wasn't a problem because she was going to work anyway. Bathing on the Sabbath was always a sin. I could skip a shower, but I hated the no teeth brushing phases.

Laycher was a prophet of YHWH, like Moses, Solomon, or Peter, so we trusted that his word really was coming to us directly from heaven. He told us that we were the lost tribe of Judah. I wondered how we got lost and if we would ever move back to Israel. Israel was the holy land, the promised land of YHWH's chosen people. After the second coming, we would make our home there when the world was re-made. Laycher preached against war, and murder was an unforgivable sin, but he was wistful when he talked about the six-day war that the Jews fought in 1967, calling it miraculous and saying that "there were angels pointing the soldiers where to shoot. It was a miracle, YHWH bringing his chosen people home again, just like when he brought them home after wandering in the desert for forty years."

I concluded that the Israelites must be the only people allowed to kill. The rules were different for YHWH's chosen people. For everyone else, it was a sin. It's hard to understand now, leaping forward into my adult brain, how we believed that the Jews were YHWH's chosen, but at the same time, we condemned them because they crucified our Savior, YHWHHOSHUA, the son of YHWH. The Jewish nation for sure wasn't ever going to be a part of our church, and they committed all kinds of "sins," including war, their dress, food, and drink—but from what I remember, it was almost like they were the only ones who could commit those sins, simply because they were YHWH's chosen people. They would have to answer to him, just like everyone else in the world, and it wasn't our place to judge, whereas everyone else, we judged unequivocally and without mercy.

3 MY BIRTH—PHYSICAL AND SPIRITUAL

My world was a world of passion and extremes. The people around me lived their lives from a place of deep conviction and devotion. That passion informed my first images and memories and every stage of my development into young adulthood. I lived and breathed the rules set down for me from the moment of consciousness. I believed them, I feared them, and they were as much a part of me as my own flesh. The world outside was a place to run and hide from, be wary of, and never, ever become a part of. I strove with all my heart and soul to follow the path laid out for me. To be that child, I had to fully embrace the responsibility of living up to fragmented, morphing, and contradictory expectations, to quash any doubt and swallow my questions before they could fully form.

Fear drove me.

Fear led me.

Fear consumed me.

In fact, as I've wandered back through the past, I've come to recognize that fear was most often my only emotion. When I felt passion, joy, inspiration, or sadness—they were all inevitably birthed from the deep fear injected into my everyday existence for as long as I can remember.

Of course, I don't remember my birth on the living room

floor, but I know the story. "You came early and you were tiny, so even though I was a little bit scared to have a baby at home, it was easier than I thought." My mom never told me much about my birth until I was grown because children aren't supposed to know about such things. "Your brother had been born in the hospital, and it was awful. They pumped me full of drugs and strapped my legs down. I was so groggy and couldn't really tell what was going on. Having you at home hurt a lot more, but it was better. You were so homely when you were born. I remember one of the brothers saying, *what a beautiful baby* and all I could think was, *really?*"

I was born in an ancient, nearly a century-old adobe farmhouse. It had smooth, curved, plastered corners on the insides of the cramped rooms that numbered five in all, with a single bedroom where the whole family slept. The bedroom led into the dining room that, in turn, opened into the kitchen through a high ceiling arch. The living room was to the left of the dining room, and the tiny bathroom was off the kitchen. Outside the kitchen door, the main door to the house was a fully screened-in porch. The house is still standing today, long since abandoned, with a tree growing through the collapsed roof in the living room, but the walls are as strong as ever, and remnants of the same brown paint from all those years past still cling to the cabinets in the kitchen. It was the first of many houses that our family lived in, all within a ten-mile radius of each other.

They were all a bit different and yet, the same, with cramped rooms, peeling paint, and chipped linoleum, surrounded by corn fields and feed lots, with parched yards full of dust and weeds. My mom could not have birthed me in the hospital because it was a sin. Laycher's wife, Maxine, was the church midwife, having trained with an old Hispanic midwife in her previous church for years before I was born. She constantly bragged about how she'd never lost a child, which, outside of the context of a restrictive environment, is certainly something to be incredibly proud of. Within the context of our lives though, it felt more like flirting with fate. If something went wrong, all we were allowed to do was to pray and beg YHWH to show mercy. If he didn't, it was his will, and we had to accept it. It wasn't our place to understand why, only to believe and trust that there was a reason. He was the only one who could decide who lived and died—taking control of that for ourselves by going to the doctor was blasphemy against him and his will.

"If YHWH wanted to show you your innards, he'd have put a zipper on you."

Laycher would chuckle at his own wit.

I wish I knew what compelled my parents to join the church. I never really asked how it happened until I'd left home. I know that my mom often wishes that the group had survived and could have grown to reflect the place she'd perceived it to be and that my dad blames my mom for everything that went wrong. After all, she was the one who first met the brothers in the park that day in 1975 in Colorado Springs.

"I was sitting on the swings," she told me. "I was so lonely. Your dad was always at work, and I missed my mom and dad like crazy." She hated Colorado. Although she had moved every few years throughout her life as a child in a Navy family, most of her family finally settled in Florida when my grandpa retired, a long way from Colorado. When she married my dad at eighteen, they were immediately shipped off to Fort Carson.

I can imagine her that day, swaying back and forth on the swing, maybe propped a bit sideways, dragging one foot on the ground while the other hung lazily, the only sound in the empty park the creaking of the chain. The cool mountain air, fresh and brisk, flirting with strands of her hair, the sunlight filtering down through leaves of elm trees and cottonwoods, dancing on the monkey bars and slides. As she swayed, she watched the two men who were across the park seemingly walking toward her. With long hair, full beards, and denim robes that zipped up the front, they definitely stood out. As they came nearer, she had to decide whether to sit and wait or get up and hurry away.

She stayed, and watched, and waited.

They approached her slowly but deliberately and asked, almost apologetically, "Do you have a minute to talk about the Savior?" Their voices would rise slightly at the end as if they hadn't meant to intrude, and it was only a suggestion—it was the exact opposite, of course.

She nodded, maybe more out of curiosity than anything else, adding shyly, "I like your coats."

They smiled. "Thank you. But these aren't coats. They're robes, and we wear them for modesty because the Almighty teaches us to cover our nakedness to be pure and holy in his sight. Do you know anything about the Almighty?" When my mom looked confused, they continued, "He's real. And he's calling on all mankind to repent and be baptized, washed of our sins."

"All of our sins?" My mom asked hopefully. Having been raised Catholic, she understood the concept of absolution.

"Yes," they promised, "for all of us have sinned before God (this was before they knew the name YHWH), but he is forgiving and long-suffering, and he will set you free from your sin if you give your life to him."

I imagine my mom continuing to sway silently, thinking, measuring them up, and even though I wasn't there, I know the pitch so well that I can hear it even now as I sit here writing. Their voices would have been gentle, soft, and non-judgmental—the judgment didn't start until after baptism—they would've smiled slyly, knowingly, as if they possessed some mysterious knowledge that she would only understand by listening and following.

They'd probably be sitting or squatting on the ground in front of her, looking up—faces solemn but inviting, oozing sincerity. "We're all searching for something more, something to fill the void. God alone, he's the only one who can fill our emptiness." They would rock back and forth slightly, shake their heads in agreement with themselves and push forward, "he can wash away all your pain, give you hope and give you purpose because when you live for him, nothing else matters. True happiness is surrendering to his will."

They would wait patiently while she thought, rolled their words around in her mind, and then ask, "Do you want to know more?"

She did. She was drinking them in like a tall glass of water to an unquenchable thirst. She had questions, they had answers, all the right answers. They belonged to a group of people who were worshiping and working together, striving to support and love each other and live lives acceptable to God. A family far from her own who would always be there for her, to guide her, teach her and comfort her.

They talked for hours, and when she got up to leave, she told them, "Come to our home and talk to my husband. He needs to hear what you have to say."

My dad's face clouded with worry and contempt (how could she be so stupid) when he heard she invited two strange men home. Despite my mom's insistence that they were *really nice* people, my dad loaded his shotgun and placed it strategically behind the front door.

But when the robed men came, he didn't shoot them, he warily let them in, and then he listened with guarded interest to the same promises they'd made to my mom—salvation, purpose, brothers and sisters, purity of mind and body. He didn't leap to the call as quickly as my mom. For weeks, she attended church services alone, being driven there and back by one of the sisters Laycher had assigned to live with them until my dad "saw the light." Eventually, he relented. He, too, had a gnawing void that he needed to fill, a longing to belong to something that felt like it mattered.

A short time later, they were baptized into the church and were giving up their old life for their new one. My dad traded his army fatigues for a long robe and let his hair and beard grow. My mom traded her t-shirts and shorts for full-length dresses and a veil to cover her hair. She also stopped cutting her hair and shaving. Every bit of her body except her face, hands, and feet would remain hidden from everyone except my dad. After spending a few days in jail, my dad was awarded a dishonorable discharge from the army for refusing to show up for duty.

My parents rejoiced in that persecution because their new friends assured them that it was a part of being called out and would strengthen their faith. They moved from Colorado Springs to Pueblo to join the small group and devote themselves to learning about their new path. They had a blowout battle with my grandparents, my dad's parents, who were simultaneously desperately worried and livid when they heard what had happened. Concerned because, well, a strange church group had brainwashed their kids, and livid because, for my father's family, a military family (my Grandpa was a World War II veteran), being dishonorably discharged was a travesty, a stain not just on him, but on the whole family.

I try to imagine now what I would do if one of my kids ran off and joined a cult, and I know the worry would be debilitating, and my desire to stop them would be frantic. However, those reactions in my grandparents confirmed for my parents the gravity of their decision to give their lives to God. They took their troubles to Laycher, who comforted them in the choice that they'd made. "It's not easy," he told them, "To choose righteousness and to walk away from the world." And he counseled them with a stern warning, "Remember, scripture tells us that the only way to be truly free is to cut all ties with the world, including our unrighteous relations. If you've truly given yourselves to God, your old family is dead to you, and the saints are your only family now."

My parents tried to heed his advice, but in the end, weakened by the sorcery of family ties, they left the church and returned to their parents in less than a year. While they were there, my older brother, Joseph, was born. It was a happy time—I've seen the smiling photos of my parents and grandparents holding my big brother. And yet, they felt empty and adrift and longed for their other family, their family in the faith. By the time my mom was pregnant with me, they were on their way back to the church. Their church family greeted them like the prodigal son, they were welcomed back, but they forever wore the stain of *backsliders*. We never outgrew that stain, no matter how much my dad tried to demand respect or how meek and obedient my mom was. It was while they had been gone that Laycher picked up the hitchhiker, and the church started using the name YHWH—that was when the great re-baptizing happened, the one where the angels were singing—and when my parents returned, they had to be re-baptized as well. I was born just months after they returned.

It's hard to remember those early years. It's the ghosts of feelings, mostly, that have stuck with me, muddled forms, wisps, and mirages. I replay a blur of cold nights, driving to church, being carried to and from the truck by my dad, and especially having always to have a blanket thrown over my head during the winter, despite my protests. I remember shockingly clear nights, with full moons, looking up at the moon and asking my dad to "get me that ball."

"Oh, I can't get you that ball," he'd say, "it's YHWH's ball, and since he put it in the sky, it has to stay there." I remember confusing east with yeast, standing on a chair watching my mom make bread while looking out the window facing the eastern sky. I thought the 'east' used to raise the bread must've come from the 'east' I saw gazing out of the kitchen window.

"No, not east, yeast," she would explain. "Look at my mouth, ya-ya-ya-yeast."

"Ya-ya-ya-east!" I'd triumphantly repeat.

I remember that, for a while, one of the single brothers lived with us. His name was Nathaniel. He easily became a part of our family, and he was like an uncle to us for years afterward. We, kids, adored him. He knew how to wind us up like toys and let us shoot across the room. He would tickle us until we were breathless, and then he'd run out the door and leave for work with my dad. My mom, exasperated, would scold, "*Stop winding them up. You get them crazy and then walk out and leave me with a bunch of rowdy kids.*"

"Oh, we're just having a little fun," Nathaniel would dismiss her protest, laughing while he maneuvered a sharp turn one way and then the other, staying just out of reach of our tiny hands.

"But then you go to work, and I'm the one who has to deal with them." My mom didn't think it was funny.

Sometimes he and my dad would team up and tease us to tears like the time my grandparents sent us balloons. We seldom had balloons, so we were bursting with excitement, but we couldn't blow them up by ourselves. So, they helped us to blow them up and then, one by one, rubbed them on our heads to create a static charge and stuck them to the ceiling far out of our reach. We couldn't get them back, no matter how much we jumped or stretched. "Those are our balloons. Give them *baaack*," we whined.

"That's not how you get what you want—what do you say?" They continued to tease.

"Please, can I have my balloon back?" we asked meekly. I didn't think that made sense. Why make us say please for something they'd taken away from us in the first place?

I remember a short while later when one of the single sisters, Delia, lived with us for a few months. I heard the grown-ups talk about her as a wild woman with hair so short she looked like a boy. She was in her early twenties and had just joined the church. With a hot temper and mouth-wide-opened laugh, she embarrassed the grown-ups. They shunned her, so we did, too. When she was baptized, she ripped the rings off her hand and threw them into the river shouting, "*I'm free*" throwing her hands into the air and then falling backward, back into the water. That provoked a ripple of uneasy laughs in the crowd on the shore that day as she pushed her way through the swirling, muddy water back to us, her dress dragging heavily behind her. It was no way for a sister to behave. But when she moved in with us, we kids grew attached. Every night she'd put us to sleep with a soft song that she'd taught us to sing in Spanish. We would sing with her until our eyelids grew heavy, and we drifted off.

"Buenas noches, YHWH
Buenas noches, YHWH
Buenas noches, YHWH
Te amamos."

She had been a teacher before joining the church and was one of the few people in our church who had a college degree and spoke Spanish fluently. When I was in fourth grade, she was my teacher for a semester, and for the first time, I learned how to diagram sentences and I ended up loving a task I had previously despised—I think that's when my love of language, words, and how they fit together to form thoughts, was born. But by the next semester, they'd made her quit because Laycher's grandchildren said she gave them too much work and was mean.

But I am getting ahead of myself.

When I was five, I learned how to mourn the state of the world. It was Sabbath Day, and the single brothers were at our house for lunch. They were our favorite visitors. They would tickle us, throw us into the air, chase us around the yard—or, more often, make us chase them, *which was an exasperating game because we could never catch them*—but we drank in those moments all the same. Of course, we weren't supposed to play on the Sabbath, but sometimes we stretched that rule a little. After lunch, one of the brothers picked up his guitar and told us he had written a new song. My parents shushed us, and we gathered around, closed our eyes, and somberly prepared to let the spirit move as he sang:

"The winds of change are blowing,
It's growing mighty cold.
Prepare yourselves, my brothers,

For dark tales shall soon unfold.
The time has gone beyond return,
For this old ship called Earth.
And satan shall soon be struck down,
In the midst of his great mirth."

The song was in the minor keys, crying all on its own, trailing poetry of impending doom, the end of it all, the world, the evil in the world, a day of reckoning, the day of judgment. It built passionately into a crescendo inside my little chest until, abruptly, I was weeping, heavy sobs that shook my whole body. It was late afternoon, and the sunlight slanted into the living room, revealing dust worms that danced effortlessly in the air. The room glowed eerily like a message directly from YHWH. I turned away. I knew I should rejoice in YHWH's presence, but instead, I wanted to run from it. Antonio, one of the newest converts, barely twenty-two years old, noticed my upset and followed me into the dining room. He stooped down to my height and gazed his bright, blue eyes directly into mine, which also made me want to run. The only time my parents ever said, "Look me in the eyes," was when I was in trouble, but his eyes were gentle and compassionate.

"What's wrong little one, are you hurt?"

I shook my head.

"Okay then, are you afraid?"

I was very afraid—terrified of the world that the song painted and the horrors it promised, but that's not why I was crying.

"I'm worried about all the people in the world," I whispered. "I don't want them to burn, and I don't know how to help them."

That was my actual moment of birth. The moment that I began to comprehend what it meant to be me in that world. It was the moment that the weight of the salvation of the world descended onto my tiny shoulders and attached itself permanently. That memory is so crystal clear; it could have happened yesterday.

Antonio smiled, and his eyes turned misty, "We just have to do our best, Sweetie, to reach them all," and then, taking my tiny hand in his, "That's why we're here, here on this earth, to be examples of what it means to be righteous. To show the world what is expected of us by living a clean and holy life. We're like lights that shine in the darkness and guide people when they're lost, guide them to the true path." I admired Antonio and trusted him. He was fun, bouncy, always smiling, and cherished us kids. He always gave us his undivided attention, which was rare for a grown-up. He was the one who taught me how to tie my shoes, and to this day, I still loop them backward just like he does. I knew he was right and that we had a lot of work to do, and I also knew that he was very proud to see a girl who, at the age of five, was feeling moved to tears out of concern for the world. But I didn't want to feel it. It was suffocating.
    I knew that the people in the world were all going to the lake of fire if they didn't repent and join our church. The lake of fire, the one from Revelations, was a frightful place filled with wretched smells and flames that never burned out. First, YHWH would take anyone who wasn't in our church and give them bodies that wouldn't die. Then he would put them in the fire where they would feel the pain of being burned forever.
    There will be weeping and gnashing of teeth.
    I had burned myself on our wood stove before and couldn't imagine being burned forever. I didn't want anyone else to get burned, either.
    I wiped my tears and promised Antonio that I would try to be that good example, that shining light, then took the hand he offered and followed him back into the living room. But I didn't understand exactly what I was supposed to do. We were supposed to be good, and then when the people in the world saw us being good, they would want to do it, too. But how would they see us being an example if we were never around them? There weren't very many of us, no more than a hundred and thirty at our largest, and during

lean times, less than sixty. I knew that the brothers went on hitchhiking road trips to spread YHWH's word and warn people of their sinful ways, but even at that young age, living in isolation, I somehow had a sense that the world was a very big place. That would be a lot of walking to do, plus I knew there was no way to walk across the ocean—YHWHHOSHUA was the only one who could walk on water—and there were lots of people on the other side. I wondered how we could ever get to every place on earth and ensure everyone knew they had to join our church if they didn't want to burn. I knew that we didn't have much time.

Every day the grown-ups talked about the signs and how they were all around us, and Laycher reminded us from the pulpit. *"It is like it was in the days of Noah—giants in the land. When I was young, basketball players were 6 feet. Now they're 7 feet and more. You can eat or drink almost anywhere. There is violence everywhere. They are building everywhere. Marrying and divorcing and marrying again. Men are lovers of men, and they have gotten the plague of AIDS."*

The evil in the world had taken over. It was like an incurable illness. At any moment, YHWH could return to find the chosen few, take us to heaven, and burn the rest. First, he would send large, flaming stones down from the sky, hailstones of fire, to destroy the earth because he was so angry about what people had become. Because of all the sin, the world had to be cleansed. Then he would make a new earth, a perfect earth, where we would live. He would take everyone else and throw them into the lake of fire. My parents couldn't wait for him to return.

I could.

With each year that passed, I grew more convinced that I was not perfect and would not be one of the chosen few. In fact, it seemed that the older I got, the harder it was. I dreaded the day of his return. The fear of it was anchored so deep and so consumed me that it made me physically ill, and every time Laycher preached about it, I'd lie in bed and have waking nightmares about what was going to happen to me. *It could be tonight. When he calls, if we are ready, we shall be taken unto him. If not, wrath is prepared for us. The books will be opened, and the judging will begin. All will know what we have done.*

Every time there was a big storm, especially with thunder and lightning, I would study the dark clouds, expecting to see the fiery stones sailing through. When it would hail, I would apprehensively inspect the ground to determine whether it was covered in ice or glowing coals. When smoke boiled up in the distance from a prairie fire or a tornado tore up the horizon, I would wait to hear YHWH's booming voice and see his angry face in the clouds staring right at me, telling me that it was too late; I hadn't been good enough. We knew that YHWH used nature in all kinds of ways to punish the world for its evil. Storms and fires and floods were his tools of wrath. I always breathed a massive sigh of relief when each storm passed, and I hadn't been struck down. Then I would try, even harder than before, to become worthy.

4 UNRIGHTEOUS RELATIONS

    Recreating the moments that happened so long ago that they're barely a whisper is often like sifting through the ashes of a fire in search of any remnant of recognition. I close my eyes and submerge myself beneath the layers of logic and analysis that have formed over them in order to relive those days that were long and tedious in the relentless sun, the sun that scorched the grass and tumbleweeds and turned our clay driveway into fun bits of dry puzzle pieces. Those same pieces that shattered to bits when we peeled them up and threw them or crumbled them gleefully, letting them rain down in a dusty mess. Sometimes we'd peel and stack them or collect them to use as money or as food and toys in our make-believe store.

    My mom passes in and out of those moments, a busy wisp, her long skirts swishing around her legs as she walked, an apron draped over her clothes—forming a silhouette that tantalizes my brain—baking bread, cooking beans and rice on the wood-fired cookstove or doing laundry in our wringer washer. I liked to help put the clothes through the two rolling spindles that squeezed the water out. It required a steady, focused hand to aim the tip of the clothes exactly right so they'd slide into the rollers and then a swift pull back so my fingers wouldn't follow. I was good at it, mostly. My mom was fast and deft at stopping and reversing the machine to get my hand out when I wasn't fast enough. That only happened once or twice; oddly, I don't remember it hurting too much. It was more like just having my hand squeezed hard enough that my knuckles crushed together, like a too-firm handshake.

My mom relished splitting firewood for the cookstove and carrying buckets of water from the cistern when the plumbing broke. She craved the feeling of strength and self-sufficiency those tasks provided and idealized the past when modern conveniences were few and far between. The cistern was in the front yard, a small, concrete mouth about eighteen inches square, raised a foot above the ground, opening into a deep, dark tank full of water. I would lie on my stomach and hoot into it, my voice reverberating back to me, my small face bouncing about on the surface. A carefully dropped stone would break the surface, and my reflection, into lots of tiny ripples, the hallow plunk instantly swallowed by the abyss. And, if my parents saw me drop it, they'd scold, "That's our drinking water, don't put dirt in it!"

"It wasn't dirt. It was a rock."

"But rocks are dirty."

"No, I wiped it off."

"Young lady, if you backtalk me one more time"—she didn't have to finish that sentence—I knew the ending and I hated the taste of Ivory soap, which was the default punishment for backtalk and lying, a symbolic washing of the filth from our mouths. My dad was particularly gleeful and skilled at scraping it hard against our teeth so the taste lingered and our mouths filled with suds when we tried to brush it away.

That was at the first house we lived in. It was right on the highway in Avondale, and the massive cottonwood near the road, the one that has now grown through the roof and into the living room, was the perfect place to sit and watch the cars speed by. I was too young to do much work, so I mostly played outside with my siblings. There were only three of us at the time who were old enough to go out and play. My big brother Joseph, always a child of mischief, I, willing to do anything he asked me to, and Ruth, my younger but stronger sister, who could wrestle both Joseph and me to the ground at the same time. Our baby sister, Sara, couldn't walk yet, so she had to stay inside.

    I'd watch ants build their homes, piling one little piece of pebble on top of another, scurrying in and out of the pinpoint hole in the middle of that mound of tiny stones. When I got too close and they bit me, my dad would ask which one bit me, and when I pointed tearfully, he would squash it with his steel-toed work boot. One of our favorite games was chasing grasshoppers. There were loads of them that were eating their way through our garden, so the more we could catch, the better. In the garden, the alkali and mustard weeds were taller than we were and outpaced the corn, green beans, tomatoes, and pumpkins, all struggling to keep up, and that was where the grasshoppers liked to hide. We had to move slowly and quietly, sneaking up on them and cupping our hands over them as they perched on the stems of alkali. We would hold them by their hoppers and put our finger by their mouths. They would try to bite our finger and spit black sticky stuff all over it while we shrieked and giggled. Then we figured the best way to get them to stop eating the garden was to pull their hoppers off. You had to pull them both off at once. Otherwise, the grasshopper could swing around and bite you if you only held on to one. We never stopped to consider that even without hoppers, they could still fly and walk their way through the garden, nor that pulling their hoppers off was cruel.

    We had a goat shed in the back corner of the yard; the chickens lived there, too. I hated checking for eggs without someone with me because the billy goat, Neptune, was super creepy. He was dirty and stinky and always had a big, long finger-thing hanging out of his belly. His beard was yellow because he peed on it all the time, and sometimes, I even saw him drink his pee. I convinced myself he was a demon because I knew drinking your pee must be very evil. I also knew that the devil could possess any living thing, and seeing as how that goat had chased my mom all the way across the yard to the house and then battered his horns against the porch door trying to get in, it was obvious he was possessed. Also, I knew the devil had horns.

We never had many toys so we invented them. We turned ordinary, everyday items into whatever we wanted to imagine they were. For example, a small piece of a two-by-four would be a bus with two rows of tiny pebbles for seats. Then we'd drive that two-by-four bus down the dirt highway we'd made by dragging our foot through the dust, vroom-vrooming with our mouths as we went. For inside play, my sisters and I would make dolls out of pillows wrapped in baby blankets, but we had to do it secretly if we didn't want to get into trouble. We weren't allowed to have dolls (they were the same thing as graven images, which broke the commandment: *Thou shalt not make unto thee any graven image*) or to pretend anything else was a doll because then we'd be *pretending* we were playing with a graven image which was just as bad. I knew exactly how to wrap the pillow babies because I'd watched my mom wrap the actual babies. First, you lay the blanket down on the floor. Next, you put the pillow baby in the middle at an angle. Then you fold the blanket around it like an envelope, the bottom up, the sides in, one at a time. You never closed the top over the pillow baby's head unless you were going out into the cold. We would nurse the pillows, change them, and rock them to sleep. Sometimes we would load them into our couch car to drive to King Supers to buy groceries. We held the pillow baby on our lap with one arm and drove the couch car with the other, just like my mom did in the truck. *Playing house* was one of our favorite games.

"*The people of old lived good and happy lives at home with no bikes or toys. These toys, cars, and bikes are all to pull their minds from YHWH. And before all these sports games, there was peace in the* land. Soon they *[sports]* came into the schools, too, and now they've become required. We should want to be like the savior and the prophets, not like these sports idols. Every year children in schools die of these sports. And they can control you by the TV. They flash things before you, and it enters your mind. Your children don't need these worldly games. The only game my children and I played was bible quiz, and we enjoyed it."

Just because we didn't have toys didn't mean there weren't people who would have loved to give us some. My grandparents longed to provide us with all the toys we could ever want, but they had to follow the rules, or the gifts they gave us would be returned. They were allowed to give us wooden building blocks, a red wagon, and sometimes tea sets or Lincoln logs. My grandma tried to buy us other things, like dolls, tiny purses, or sparkly shoes with mini heels to play dress-up, but that was a terrible idea because my parents didn't want us to learn how to be harlots. The giant cardboard boxes, so big that I could fit inside and close the top, were delivered by a brown UPS truck to our back porch. Whenever we spotted the UPS truck, we exploded with excitement. We knew it had to be gifts from our grandparents because they were the only ones who ever sent us packages. The anticipation ate us alive, as my mom insisted unequivocally that we wait until my dad came home from work to open the box. We'd stand on a chair in the only bedroom, where the window faced the highway, and watch as pairs of headlights approached us, trying to guess which ones would slow down and turn into our driveway. We also watched the headlights in the sky, wondering how those cars got up there. I knew flying like a bird was an abomination because if YHWH had meant for us to fly, he would have given us wings, but it didn't keep me from wondering what it would be like.

When a pair of lights finally turned into our drive, we would race to the door and prattle in unison, clamoring atop my dad, "Grandma and Grandpa sent a box. Mom said we couldn't open it until you came home. You're home now.

Can we open it—please, *pleeease?*"

My dad would shoot my mom a knowing look. They never seemed very excited about the boxes. Now I know that it was because they wondered what was in them and expected it to be things they'd have to send back. "Wait just a minute," my dad would say, "I just got home. Who wants to take my boots off?"

"Me, *meee!*" We'd race to untie and unlace his heavy work boots and then struggle to pull them off with our skinny arms.

"Socks, too," he'd tease. One of us on each foot, we'd grip the sock at the top and pull, rolling it down over his foot and turning it inside out in the process. It would come off suddenly, and we'd fall backward.

"Now clean between my toes..." he'd prolong the agony.

Finally, at long last, my dad would stand and walk over to the box, cut the tape with his pocketknife, and open the flaps to reveal stacks of underwear, t-shirts, socks, and, of course, always a little something that wasn't supposed to be in there. My mom would draw her lips into a determined line and shake her head disappointedly, "I told you to talk to your mother."

"I did," my dad would insist, exasperated, "I've told her—again and again, who knows how many times—she doesn't listen to me. You know my mother. She's a willful and stubborn woman."

"And you're not willing to put her in her place because she's your mother," my mom would retort. We would get quiet as they argued, and then my dad would relent and make the dreaded call to his mom and argue with her. I could hear her sharp, pitchy voice even though the phone wasn't on my ear.

While the grown-ups tried to figure it out, I would peer over the rim of the box and study the things I couldn't have. I didn't want anyone to know that I wished we could keep the dolls and the black patent leather shoes. Sometimes I daringly reached my hand in to see what they felt like. They were smooth and shiny, their surface almost reflective like a mirror. There were little triangles cut into a half-moon around the toes and a perfect buckle that would fasten around the ankle, with a chunky square for a heel. I didn't understand why we couldn't keep them because other church girls wore shoes like that. Some were even related to Laycher, and they didn't get into trouble for it. I didn't dare point that out.

We couldn't trust our grandparents because they weren't in the church, period. We had to assume that anyone not in the church was trying to lead us astray. Laycher preached about it all the time, imploring us to be aware. "If you want to stay here [in the church], stay away from your unholy parents, brothers, sisters, cousins, aunties, and uncles. If you want to visit them, have a strong brother with you. If you don't, then leave this assembly, or I will expel you myself. Through these visits, your children are being defiled, and you, too." His words always played in the recesses of my mind whenever my grandparents visited. Even before I was old enough to listen to and comprehend the sermons, I knew that being around them wasn't something I was supposed to look forward to.

Despite that, I cherished each time any of my grandparents showed up for a visit. Until my late twenties, I had four living grandparents, something I grew to appreciate immensely once I left home and could spend more time with them. We called them Grandma and Grandpa, whether they were my dad's parents or my mom's, but for the purposes of this story, my dad's parents will be Grandma Jean and Grandpa Gordon, and my mom's parents will be Grandma Jo and Grandpa Bill. I didn't quite understand how they fit into my family because I knew that the people in the church were my family and that my grandparents were unrighteous relations. They came to visit purely to tempt us and lead us astray, but when they showed up, we couldn't very well pretend they weren't in our driveway.

We never knew in advance that they were coming, although now, I assume that my parents did. They would show up in our driveway, and we would all race out to see who was there. They would beam at us and open their arms wide for hugs, and we would hide behind our parents and stare uncertainly—we didn't know them, but it was evident that they knew us. Then, it never took them long to scoop us up and squeeze us, covering our heads in kisses, exclaiming over how tall we had gotten or how pretty we were. Trapped in my Grandpa Gordon's thick arms, I would push back a bit before I could relax into the tickles and the tossing and twirling. My grandpas teased us mercilessly, and we always went back for more.

I seethe as I write those words, and I wonder—how could anyone think it was okay to take that away from us? I never know how deeply affected I have been by each little thing until I relive it. I remember what it felt like to want to love them, to feel like they were a part of my puzzle, but to be afraid to because I wasn't supposed to get attached.

"You must reprove sin, call it out to those who enter your home, or your car, or even your presence. You've got to show them that their ways are sin, with love and authority, so they might get a conviction and repent of their evil ways."

Other visits were very different. Those were the times when they would show up in pants and short sleeves. My parents would go out and meet them in the driveway and block them from coming inside. We would stand inside the screen door on the porch, all three of us crowded onto one tiny dining chair, elbowing for a better view, and watch. I would hear them yelling and crying. It happened with both sets of grandparents, but my most vivid memory is of the time when my mom's parents visited.

"We've told you what we expect of you if you are going to come to our home. So why do you keep pushing?" my mom demanded.

Exasperated, my Grandma Jo shook her head, "We

drove three days and thousands of miles, and you're not going to let us inside or allow us to see our grandchildren? Who does that? What kind of person thinks that's okay?"

"Well, how can you think it's okay to show up here after all our talks, all the times we've explained our rules to you, and not respect our wishes? You knew before you came that we have rules, and if you want to see us, if you want to enter our home, if you want to see your grandchildren, you have to abide by those rules," my dad piped in.

"So, you'll condemn and turn us away simply because we are not dressed like you? A woman in pants is not a sin. This is insane," my aunt, my mom's older sister, adding her two cents. "This is your mother, your father. *We are your family.* Don't you care how much you're hurting them?"

"Do you care how much you're hurting me," my mom retorted, tearful now, "don't you think it hurts me to see how much you all don't care and don't respect what I believe? It hurts me to see you lost and not worried about your souls. It hurts me that I have to give up my family because they refuse to see the truth."

"You don't have to give up your family—*we're right here.*" My aunt threw her hands in the air and turned her back to the group.

"My brothers and sisters in the faith are my family," my mom maintained firmly, "and my beliefs are more important to me than my worldly family. A woman in a man's clothing is an abomination before YHWH, and we won't have an abomination in our home or near our children. We are raising them to be undefiled by the world, and if you want to see them, you have to respect our wishes."

My mom's words had a sense of forlorn finality to them. I couldn't always hear the words, but I could tell by the hand gestures, the accusatory finger wagging and pointing that everybody was judging everyone else. They were all insisting on respect and compliance and refusing to give an inch. No one else's beliefs ever mattered. We were right, the whole world was wrong, and we were completely justified in our self-righteousness.

On other visits, it would be my dad's mom, with fire in her voice and daggers piercing the space around her, demanding respect from my dad, not disguising her extreme disgust for our life and the church.

"You're so high and mighty," she would say, "insisting I follow your rules. Well, you love the Bible so much; what about the commandment to honor your father and mother? Is this how you do that?" My Grandma Jean was no fool.

"I only have to honor my parents if they are righteous," my dad would reply, a little too smugly. Then Grandma Jean glared at him like she'd like to slap that smug look right off his face. I took a second to wonder if adult children could be smacked by their parents, too, just like little kids.

My grandfathers rarely joined in the arguments. They were both reserved and contemplative, men who would intervene only if they decided things were getting out of hand. I was shocked the time Grandpa Gordon said to Grandma Jean, "That's enough, Jean," and she went instantly quiet. Grandma Jean was never quiet, she was fierce and passionate, and he was the only one who could shut her down like that. I knew that in the church, a man could command his wife; I just hadn't known that it was true in their world, too.

I was never angry at my mom. I was angry at my grandparents for making her cry and for not doing what they were supposed to do. And I was sad that they were going to the lake of fire. They would get back into their car and return to their hotel, and everything would feel empty and off for a while. If we were lucky, we would meet them the next day on neutral ground, the mall maybe. They loved to take us shopping. They would buy us things we needed and then beg to be able to give us an action figure or dress-up set or any one of the monster trucks, race cars, or dolls that filled the shelves that we filed obediently past. Sometimes we would go to the park for a picnic, my mom having dutifully chosen the food we would eat, painstakingly walking my grandparents through the health food store, selecting only foods without artificial colors and flavors, whole grain sandwich bread, canned tuna, and natural potato chips. *"You can eat with your relatives if the food is good, not offered to idols, and if you leave the word of YHWH with them. You can't let these defiled foods into your home, especially if it is offered to idols."*

By "offered to idols", Laycher meant that only we could bless the food because if my grandparents were to bless it in the name of God instead of YHWH, it would be defiled and poison our minds and our bodies.

At the park, Grandpa Gordon would push us on the swings, catch us at the end of the slide, and sometimes he would lie on his back in the grass, hold his breath and tell us to stand on his stomach. I would hesitate and eye him suspiciously. Was he serious?

"Go ahead," he would urge, "it's pure muscle. You won't hurt me." I'd climb up cautiously, and Grandpa's face would turn red, but he'd never release his breath until I'd climbed back off again. Sometimes, I would fall over on top of him and bounce up and down with his belly as he laughed. Although he was retired from the army at that point, he had never stopped doing his morning pushups and sit-ups. His other party trick was doing one-armed pull-ups on the monkey bars.

Grandma Jean would sit in the grass with a fixed smile on her face, and when I snuggled into her lap, she would whisper, "You have such beautiful hair, Sweetie. I could braid it for you, put some pretty bows in it." And then, indignantly, "You're just a little girl. You shouldn't have to cover your hair up." I always had my hair covered by a half-moon-shaped muslin veil, a head-covering that fastened at the back of my neck with a safety pin and fell loosely down my back to my waist. It made me look like a little nun, although at that point, I'd never seen one. I would have loved bows in my hair, but I knew better than to encourage her. Sometimes she would mutter, "How could it hurt to just take one little picture? What do your parents think will happen? That the camera will steal your soul?"

"No, Grandma, that's silly. Cameras can't steal souls. Only Satan can do that. We just can't do it 'cuz the Bible says not to. It's like worshipping a graven image because pictures are images. They aren't real."

"Pictures are not graven images; they're paper and ink and harmless. I want to remember you as you are now because you'll grow up so fast." I'd see her watch my parents closely, waiting for an opening to pull out her camera on the sly. I wish she had. I have no pictures of me as a child.

I would revel in her warmth and study everything about her, storing it up for later. Her long fingers twinkled with rings that I would stroke and twirl. Her nails were perfectly shaped and painted, sometimes red, sometimes pink, or sometimes just clear and shiny. She would remove her rings or wristwatch, let me look at them, and try them on, but only if my parents weren't looking.

Then would come the part I hated, when they had to leave. I knew it would be a long time before I would see them again, usually a couple of years, at least. Grandpa Gordon would pick me up and rub his stubble on my cheek "Scratchy, ain't it."

None of the men in the church shaved, so I would ask him, "Grandpa, what happened to your beard?"

He would chuckle and say, "I cut it all off."

"But why do you want to cut it off?"

He'd smile, contemplating his answer for a second, "It's too hot, and it makes me look old."

"But you are old, Grandpa," I'd rub the stubble with my little fingers. "It feels like sandpaper," and giggle.

My grandma would kiss us and leave a smear of lipstick behind, which she would quickly wipe off with her thumb. "Now, you remember, be good. Remember, you always have us if you need us. Remember, if you ever need a place to—" She never quite finished that sentence, but I knew what she meant. If we ever wanted to leave, she would fight for us.

My grandmas were like characters in a storybook. I studied them closely, like observing an apparition that would fade quickly when they left. Both had very short hair. The women in the church never cut their hair and covered it with head coverings. *"Our hair cutting also is wrong. You talk of all these split ends and say if you cut it, it will grow better—that's right out of the pits of hell. Brothers and sisters both, you don't cut your hair at all."* They didn't wear makeup because it was vain and seductive, an abomination, like Jezebel.

Jezebel was the wife of King Ahab of Israel, a woman who worshiped Baal, a nature god, instead of the Hebrew God, YHWH. She was vilified, as the most powerful women in history often are, as a wanton woman, power-hungry and strong-minded, adept at controlling men, including King Ahab, with her beauty and charms, thus ruling Israel through him. Her punishment in the Bible for being a strong, intelligent, and powerful woman was to be thrown out a window to her death and eaten by dogs. *Jezebel* was the worst insult you could hurl at a woman in the church. Although my grandmothers wore makeup, they didn't seem like Jezebels to me. They fascinated me when they were around, but I never wished I could live like them. Instead, I wondered why they weren't worried about going to the lake of fire. When I asked them about it, they would dismiss my concern with a kiss, and tell me not to worry, that there was more than one way to be good, that they loved God and went to church, and that everything was going to be okay.

I didn't believe them.

5 LIVE IN THE WORLD BUT BE NOT OF THE WORLD

"We are called to live in the world but be not of the world."
Being separate from the world was tricky when it was right outside our door. We lived smack-dab in the middle of the most corrupt and wicked country on earth. Until I was older and required to learn a minimal amount of US history in school, I knew the United States only as Babylon. Everything I learned about the outside world filtered first through Laycher, and according to him, the US was not only the vilest country on earth, but it was also the source of all the evil that was seeping into the rest of the world.

Living in the world meant driving our old, clunky, rusted-up cars to shop at King Soopers when I was really young and, later, at Walmart—I remember when the first Walmart found its way to Pueblo sometime in the mid-1980s. As we parked in the lot outside the store, my mom would shut the engine off and then turn around to remind us that she expected us to *be-have* and to set a good example for the world. "Don't touch anything," she would say sternly, wagging her finger toward us. "Don't ask for anything. We are only getting what is on the list. *Stay with me at all times*—don't wander off. And cut it out with the fighting and bickering. People are watching us, and you don't want them to think that's how the people of YHWH behave."

Walking through the automatic sliding doors that opened on their own into the air-conditioned stores was like stepping into a parallel universe, a world that existed alongside the one I lived in, but although it was right next to me, nothing about it was familiar. The moment the doors slid open, I would shift into autopilot, the jostle of the shoppers, the fluorescent lights humming, the shopping cart's wheels whirring, and the constant beeping of the checkout counters all muted, as if I was moving through those moments in a bubble. It was unnerving, and I regarded everyone as someone who could corrupt me, and yet, it was also strangely exhilarating to watch that world pulsing around me. I was in awe of so many people just going about their lives, completely oblivious to the fact that they would burn in the lake of fire, people with their bodies exposed in tank tops and shorts, their hair uncovered, jewelry and make-up adorning their nakedness.

"This nail polish, it's for attracting the opposite sex. Lipstick is the mark of the beast. Clear or not, it's for the same thing. The potions and lotions were originally for witchcraft. And a man who goes around in these tight shirts and pants reminds me of elves, and they remind me of demons. He said he'll destroy the wearers of strange apparel. When you know nakedness is coming, turn your eyes. People have no shame today. They'll show anything, so turn and walk away. If you stay around it, you'll get swallowed up like Adam and Eve did. Out of nowhere, temptation will enter your mind."

I would try not to look because seeing someone else's nakedness would defile my mind, but it was impossible unless I looked at the floor the whole time. People would stare, and we would shrink behind my mom. Sometimes they would smile at us, but we would not smile back. I knew I should be holding my head high because I was a beacon, a shining light to lead sinners to truth, but I mostly looked at the floor.

While we were out grocery shopping, people sometimes thought that we were Muslim, and they would stop us to ask if we were. I'd see them walking towards us in the store and think, uh oh, here we go again. We, kids, would corral ourselves behind my mom and peek out shyly from the folds of her generous skirt. Like any kids, we were painfully embarrassed by our parents. "Why do you have to talk to everyone?" We would whine.

"When we get a chance to spread the gospel, we have to take it. The Bible tells us not to hide our light under a bushel. You never know when someone is searching, and their soul is ripe for saving," they'd scold. "You should be proud to be an example of the truth and not hide behind us all the time."

I still hid behind them instinctively until I was older and had learned to wear our strangeness with pride, not immune to our difference but justified in it. For most of my young life, I thought that people were asking if we were muslin, which I knew was a type of cloth, and I thought it was a bit strange to name a religion after a fabric. I knew that Muslin people covered their heads with veils too, and our veils were usually made from muslin, so I reasoned that that must have been why they were called Muslins, because of the muslin veils. Once people discovered we weren't Muslim, their next guess would be Catholic, some rare, super-conservative sect they'd never heard of. My parents would shake their heads once again and smile smugly. Definitely not Catholic—Laycher called the Catholic Church the Mother Harlot of all churches, I'm guessing because of the prominent role played by the Virgin Mary, a virtual goddess in the very church that tried to quash goddess worship.

The food rules were ever-shifting. From the pulpit, they were crystal clear, but in practice, not so much. Despite unpacking and examining their reasoning, I've still not made sense of them. We didn't eat food with artificial flavors and colors. We weren't supposed to use white sugar or white flour, but Maxine made her tortillas from white flour, and sometimes people used white sugar to make cake frosting. People other than my mom that is. My mom lived and breathed the rules to the letter, and it took her a long time to give in and use white sugar occasionally, and only after she talked to Laycher first, and he said he didn't see the harm in eating it in moderation (Laycher was famous for his sweet tooth). Pesticides and sprays defiled foods, but we still bought beans, onions, corn, and melons from our neighbor farmers, all of which were heavily sprayed. We didn't eat pork because it says not to in the Bible, but our dietary rules extended far beyond not eating pork, restricting a slew of other foods not mentioned in the Bible. For example, we couldn't drink alcohol of any kind because drunkenness and debauchery go hand in hand. Even though the Bible talked about people drinking wine, Laycher insisted that the people who translated the Bible had gotten it wrong and were actually writing about drinking grape juice. So, we weren't allowed to drink alcohol or use vinegar or prepared mustard because they were fermented and therefore contained alcohol, no matter how minuscule the amount. We could only use vanilla if we could find a brand without alcohol. But we were allowed to make pickles and sauerkraut, even though they also required fermentation.

    Since the aisles in the grocery store overflowed with things we could not have, like all the half-naked bodies around me, it was an assault on my senses. Sometimes when my mom was distracted, I would hang back, squat down and reach for the Wonder Bread on the bottom shelf. I would squeeze it quickly and marvel when it popped back to its original size. My mom rarely caught me doing it, but still, my face would get hot, my heart would pulse in my temples, and I would race to catch up with her. If she did catch me, she would say, "Don't do that. That's someone's food." Then I would think, but it's poison food, so why does it matter if I ruin it? My mom baked our bread at home, and it was not bouncy or squishy. The loaves were thick and heavy, with a crust that sounded hollow when you tapped it. Don't get me wrong, I loved her bread, especially when it was fresh out of the oven, the heel preferably, with lots of butter.

Because there was barely any food in the store that we could eat, my mom mainly bought basics like flour, oil, honey, and salt to make our food. Most of the food there was unclean and would defile our bodies and poison our spirits. *"Spirits and foods cause your sickness. A lot of evil thoughts come from this garbage food. We defile ourselves, and so we can't walk with him."*

Of the countless rules I grew up with, the ones concerning food choices are some of the only ones that are still a part of my life—they're common-sense choices. The difference is that now they are choices. Back then, they were the word of YHWH, mandated and unequivocal. The message wasn't: *better not to eat this because it's bad for your health*, rather, it was: *your body is a vessel that belongs to YHWH. If you defile it with these foods, you blaspheme against YHWH and will surely burn in the lake of fire—there will be weeping and gnashing of teeth.*

That logic extended to include the people who prepared the food. If the people preparing our food were sinners, then the food was contaminated by default. That fact eliminated the option of eating in restaurants or buying pre-made food, even if it was organic. I only remember going to a restaurant once when I was young—Long John Silvers. I was puzzled when my parents agreed to let Donald take us, but I knew he was one of the brothers who constantly broke the rules, and for some reason, nobody did anything about it. He was also one who always gave us groceries when we couldn't afford them. He was the richest person in the church because he owned his own contracting company.

Donald was the only single brother who lived alone in a house he owned. The rest of us, besides Laycher, mostly rented. He was the only one who lived in town (Pueblo) on Damson Street, far away from the rest of us, just one block from where Laycher had lived on Catalpa when he first started the church. I liked going to his house for dinner first of all because he lived in a neighborhood with lots of homes right next to each other, which was highly intriguing. We could see the neighbors drinking and smoking in their backyards and hear the noisy racket from their parties. There was a barren dirt hill behind his house called Sugarloaf that we would sled down in the winter and run down in the summer, gaining frightening momentum with the downward slope to propel us forward. I doubt it was over a hundred feet tall, but we thought it was giant. The neighborhood kids would be there too, and they would try to talk to us, but we would just stare at them, smile shyly, and then avoid them like the plague. Secondly, I liked going to his house because he always made spaghetti and meatballs, knowing it was our favorite. After we ate, we would go to the living room, where he would tell us stories, play his piano, or lie on the floor while we climbed all over him. He used to give us nickels to peel his lips. Gross, I know, and such a random memory.

Of course, we needed money to buy food, gas, shoes, and clothes. On the one hand, YHWH will provide, and yet, on the other hand, YHWH helps those who help themselves. So, in solemn sacrifice, our men ventured out into the big, evil world to work, knowing that every day they would be buffeted by temptation and need to dwell in prayer to not fall into the devil's snares. Being the weaker sex and more prone to yield to temptation—we were all the daughters of Eve, after all, the originally tempted and thereafter temptress—there was no circumstance in which women were allowed to work outside of the home.

The widows, divorced women with children, and the single women relied only on money from The Box. The Box was a rectangular wooden box that lived at the back of the church that anyone could put money into. We didn't pass a collection plate; it just sat at the back, but the expectation was abundantly clear: to give often and in secret, not flaunting the good deed but being content knowing we'd have our reward in heaven. I would watch the brothers try to walk casually by and drop cash into The Box without anyone noticing and smile slyly to myself as if I was in on a secret. Laycher would check The Box every few days and then distribute the money to the utilities for the church building and to the single women and families as needed. No one was forced to give, but when The Box was barren, Laycher would preach about self-sacrifice, humility, and not laying up treasures here on earth where moth and dust doth corrupt, and The Box would become fruitful again.

Women aspired to their highest calling within the safety of the walls of their homes, where they performed YHWH's work from moment to moment—washing diapers, scrubbing toilets, preparing meals, and, most importantly of all, teaching their children to pray. I remember learning early on how to rejoice in my daily chores from a poem that was in one of my Mennonite textbooks (we weren't Mennonite, nor did we agree with their religion in any way, we just used their textbooks because they were Bible-based). The poem went like this:

"Lord of all pots and pans and things
Since I've no time to be
A saint by doing lovely things
Or watching late with Thee
Or dreaming in the sweet dawn light
Or storming heaven's gates,
Make me a saint by getting meals
And washing up the plates."

I never knew the origins of that poem, I just remember learning it as a way to remind myself that even when I was folding mountains of diapers, I was still worshipping YHWH, so I should feel fulfilled. I had to practice that feeling because I didn't really feel it. I thought that the boys got the better deal. They got to be outside, go into town, see lots of other people and places, and earn money, but our work was the same every day, and it didn't seem to amount to anything. When you wash dishes, they simply get dirty again, same with the clothes and especially the house. Try tidying up an entire home when you're twelve, and within half an hour, watch your little brothers completely destroy it again. It was exasperating, but I somehow convinced myself that I liked it. I would sing while I worked or close my eyes and lift my face toward the sun, breathing deeply when the wind whipped my hair into my face as I hung laundry outside, and try not to grimace too much as I scrubbed the toilet. Sometimes, having my mom's gratitude was enough. She called me her angel because I did my chores without complaining, "I knew there was a reason I named you Angela," she'd smile and give me a quick hug or affectionately stroke my cheek. I would bathe in her appreciation and work even harder the next day.

"Lay up your treasure in heaven and not here on earth. Better to be poor in flesh and rich in spirit than to gain the world and lose our souls." To have nothing or nearly nothing, to suffer and still be happy and devoted, was the mark of a true saint. That didn't necessarily mean that the poorer we were, the holier we were because we were very poor, but we weren't that holy. Why weren't we that holy? I can't say for sure. I just always sensed that we weren't all that important in the scheme of things. If you were one of the holy families, you'd be chosen to do important things, like my best friend Yahanna, whose dad was an Elder. Laycher sent her family to Oregon to start another church. I knew that my dad would never be an Elder. I knew my parents always sought Laycher's counsel, trying to learn how to be more holy, but it didn't work. I assume now that most of the time they went to talk to him, it was because of marital squabbles or discipline issues with us. If I sink back into that murky past and try to focus in on my parents as a couple, I can't say that I even remember them that way. They were two separate people who sometimes collided in a hug or, once in a great while, a kiss, although my mom would usually say, "Bill, not in front of the kids."

My dad was never the boss at work. The few bosses were

mostly Elders, and all the other brothers worked for them. Manual labor jobs paid low wages, and not being the boss made those even lower. The work was mostly construction and remodeling work, although very rarely, there was ditch digging and fieldwork in a pinch. It didn't matter what profession you had before joining the church. If you were a man, you learned to hang drywall and to tape and spackle. None of the men were licensed to do the work, so they had to take jobs only from people who didn't care about that. Because the government was *the beast*, we couldn't follow its rules. I never entirely understood what the beast was. I always imagined some sort of huge furry lion crossed with a deformed vulture with numerous heads—my fabrications were limited to whatever images I could conjure up from the book of Revelations. Sometimes I added horns, drool, and scary teeth. But that made no sense either because somehow the beast would mark people on their right hands and foreheads with the number 666. I knew that beasts don't read or write, so I wasn't quite sure how the mark would happen, but I did know that if they got to me, I would definitely go to the lake of fire because once you've been marked, you can't get unmarked. That didn't seem fair to me. What if they held you down and marked you, and you had no choice?

 I wasn't sure about what the government was either, but I did know that it had something to do with licenses, birth certificates, courtrooms, the police, and all the other scary things that lived out there. Breaking the rules was just what we had to do to be saints, and so when the government decided to persecute us, we needed to be ready to endure it with faith. Although I was registered with the State of Colorado when I was born, I had no Social Security number, just in case those numbers were the mark of the beast. We never really knew precisely which thing was the mark of the beast, so we preemptively rejected it all. One thing we couldn't avoid was bar codes on our food. *"I preached 20 years ago about the mark, and it came to pass. None of us used to buy it, but now it's almost on everything."* At the store, I figured the beast lived inside the checkout where the red light was that was talking to the black lines on the food. How can a red light talk to black lines anyway? There had to be something very evil at work there, sorcery, as Laycher would have said. I always tried to stay far away from the red light because I didn't know if it could stamp those black lines on my forehead if I stood too close.

No one had a driver's license or insurance. I never even thought to ask why we didn't buy insurance. Was it because we couldn't afford it? Did we believe that the government could keep tabs on us through it? Would it be interpreted as putting our faith in something other than YHWH? Or did we reject it as man's law and not YHWH's? The Bible didn't say anything about insurance, but it did implore us not to put our faith in man, so perhaps that was the reason. Also, we refused to pay taxes of any kind, and we kids didn't go to school. Homeschooling was illegal where we lived, but that didn't matter because the only laws we had to follow were YHWH's laws—we trusted that he would reveal them to Laycher. Eventually, the freedom of religion defense granted us the right to run our church school and, after many court hearings, get driver's licenses without pictures.

Working without contractor's licenses, for people willing to pay under the table, sometimes meant that the brothers weren't paid. Those people knew that because the brothers were doing the work illegally, they would never go to court over it. When a job ended in a battle for payment, it was a nail-biting suspense as our supplies dwindled.

The worst of those times was the time we drove for three consecutive days, as a family, to the job site, trying to meet with the boss (this was a boss who was not in our church, which was a rare occurrence) to get my dad's pay. We were down to only a small bag of cornmeal at home, and my dad had convinced himself that if he took his whole family, the man would feel pity and pay him, but it didn't work. We would fast all day, lying in the hot van waiting, and then drive home with nothing. My stomach ached, growled, and dry-heaved, and when my mom served us cornmeal mush without salt or honey for dinner, I was so grateful. She didn't eat herself, just served it to us, but my dad did eat because he needed his strength to take care of the family. That didn't happen often, but we frequently came close. My parents hated handouts but knew better than to refuse them. So, when bags of groceries would show up on our front porch unexpectedly, they would marvel gratefully at how YHWH always provided. As I got older, I knew that it meant my mom had talked to Laycher, and Laycher had bought the groceries or told someone else to do it. It was disappointing because I was always waiting for a miracle. I thought that YHWH providing meant turning water into wine, multiplying loaves and fishes, and making food appear out of thin air. But that never happened, just other people giving us things. I learned quickly, especially when I was little, to prattle loudly around people I knew had more money than us about how we had run out of flour or were down to a bag of beans or potatoes. I would guiltily try to cover up my blatant plea, "But we're not worried because we know YHWH's gonna provide." Usually, within the next day or so, several bags of groceries would show up.

6 DOING THE RIGHT THING

While navigating the tides of the past, I'm hijacked all over again by a singular objective—to not make waves—follow every rule, don't question anything. As a child, I couldn't wait to be grown-up. I knew it was the only way to be good, good enough for my parents, good enough for Laycher, and for YHWH. I knew that when I was grown up, I would *just be* everything I was supposed to be, and most importantly, I wouldn't get spanked anymore.

Grown-ups never got spanked, so I concluded that it was because they weren't bad. I'd imagine myself standing at the stove like my mom, surrounded by little ones, breezing in and out of my daily tasks, singing as I went, my husband off somewhere in town, hammering nails, and plastering ceilings. Alternatively, sometimes I'd imagine he would be home instead, out in a field growing our food or in a barn caring for our animals. We would succeed where the grown-ups before us had failed and would indeed be free of the world. We would live without electricity, a telephone, or anything that made us rely on the world. That was the ideal, after all, to be separate. Just because no one had made it happen yet, didn't mean I couldn't. My eighteenth birthday, when I could finally be married, if it was YHWH's will, was so far in the future—the waiting was eternal.

We were born evil and destined to spend our lives trying to overcome that affliction and/or have it beaten out of us. It was all because of the Garden of Eden and Eve, although I could never quite figure out what exactly happened in the garden that was so bad. The Bible said that Eve ate an apple, which YHWH told her not to do, and somehow that made the whole world evil. Laycher's favorite joke was, "It wasn't an apple. It was a pair."

"The sin in the garden was a pair—Eve and Satan. It ruined a happy life in the garden. Satan will hit you when you are alone. We must work by the sweat of our brow; the woman must bear children in pain to remind us of all these things. It starts with these little boyfriends and girlfriends. Soon there are children and no father. Let YHWH be in you and not the mind of a carnal man or woman."

I had no idea, at the time, what he was talking about, nor did I understand why Adam and Eve were naked before eating the apple, and then afterward, they suddenly wanted to wear clothes. And because Eve was weak and tasted the apple, we all had to wear clothes covering all of our nakedness, and women had to suffer pain when they had babies as punishment for that weakness. I wondered why we had to suffer even though we weren't Eve and why the guys didn't have to suffer. All the grown-ups would laugh at Laycher's joke, and I would think, "So now apples *and* pears make us sin?"

It wasn't just any old sin, either. It was the worst sin, one that made YHWH really angry. For some reason, we still ate apples and pears. (For those of you who don't know the Bible story about Adam and Eve, the forbidden fruit of knowledge that they tasted varies in explanation depending on who is preaching, but according to Laycher, it was sex, hence the pair joke).

From the moment we were born, it was a frantic race against Satan to save our souls. Being born with the stain of that original sin meant it was in our nature to be bad, period.

Being baptized granted us a semblance of protection, like a caution sign for Satan that we had already been promised to YHWH, so he'd better steer clear. But the rest was up to us—and the rod. We were expected to make the right choices; when we didn't, the rod would remind us of that expectation.

Spare the rod and spoil the child.

The grown-ups really seemed to love the rod. *"If they don't want to listen to you, get the belt and give them a good one. Let it sting. If they say they're gonna go to the police, give them another one. If they say it again, take them there."*

My dad relished telling us the story of how I got my first spanking when I was three months old. He'd square his shoulders and stand tall, his chest puffed up with pride and a self-congratulatory grin on his face, "you just wouldn't stop screaming," he'd recount, as if he were still baffled by the idea of a baby who cried a lot. "And we'd tried everything, walking with you, rocking you, changing your diaper, feeding you. Nothing worked. So, I took down your diaper and smacked your bare little bottom just once. That's all it took was one little smack, and after that, you quieted right down." It was a tale whose purpose was to remind us that hitting us was often the only way to teach us, even as babies. I believed him until I gave my first spanking, then I quickly changed my mind.

My littlest brother, Samuel, had started throwing massive tantrums as a toddler. I was fifteen, and my mom left me in charge while she went shopping and told me I could spank him if I had to. As I wrestled with that feral four-year-old, who was scratching and kicking at me as I tried to calm him down, I remembered there was one surefire option at my disposal. I took him to the bedroom as my parents had so often done to me, closed the door, and held the leather belt in my hand. It was nearly impossible to hit him with it as he wriggled and screamed, but I managed to swing twice before I froze.

I had not expected to feel like a monster.

My baby brother cowered in fear and shock, his tears changed from rage to pain, and he crumpled on the floor in heartbreaking defeat. I stared at him lying there, so tiny, so confused, and so resigned to whatever I was going to dish out. I threw the belt at the wall and sank down next to him. I held him tight, and we both cried, and I promised him I would never, ever do that again.

After that, whenever he would throw a fit, I would hurry to intervene so my mom would have no excuse to reach for the belt. I would wrap my legs around his legs and my arms around his arms and hold him tightly so he couldn't hurt anyone. I would speak to him softly and steadily for as long as it took, reminding him that I loved him and that we had made a deal. He would have to calm down for me if he didn't want Mom to spank him. After my first and only attempt at spanking, I was confident that there had to be a better way and surprisingly convinced my mom to let me try it my way in the future before she spanked him. She agreed that if he calmed down for me, she would let me handle it.

"Be perfect as YHWH, your father in heaven is perfect. You can't live like the devil and expect to get into heaven." Being perfect was the only way to avoid the lake of fire. If I was going to learn how to be a virtuous young woman, I had to follow the examples around me. That's what everyone told me to do. The grown women may not have been perfect, but they already had an advantage because they were not children. So, I would choose a woman, one of the single women, for example—most likely whichever was being nice to me at the time—to follow around, observe her closely, and imitate her meticulously. I would mimic her down to her exact movements and intonations. I would hold my head the way she did when she prayed, move my body like her when she walked, strum the guitar like her and change my favorite color to hers.

Then, when I had literally become a little version of her, Maxine would call me to her with a wave and whisper behind her hand that she had something to talk to me about.

Rolling her eyes, not masking her extreme disgust, she would give me a once over and then, "What's wrong with you? Stop bugging the sisters, leave them alone, and go play with the kids. You think they want you following them around all the time, copying them and stuff?"

Reminding me that I was just a kid meant *you are nothing, now disappear.* She'd beckon my parents and command them to keep a better eye on me because I was bothering the sisters, harassing and suffocating them. I can still plant my feet firmly in the very spot where these moments unfolded, at Church, back by her special pew, the only bench with padded seats, where she would sit and watch us, a queen surveying her subjects, her pointy nose in the air, gleaning gossip and storing it up for blackmail. I say I can plant my feet because they were rooted. I wanted to run, but I couldn't. She had a piercing glare and a commanding presence that dared you to move. I'd wait until she'd flick her hand and turn away, indicating I was dismissed. It was worse than being spanked because she was so gleeful in her ability to crush me and so satisfied with herself when I slunk away. I would wait until someone else told me who the most virtuous sister was and slowly start the cycle again.

Being an honorable woman was grueling—girded in humility, submission, meekness, and a bottomless fount of caring for everyone and everything before yourself—but attaining it was like being an angel, untouchable, and above reproach. I longed to be an angel—Maxine despised me so much because I was actually very good at it.

Like any kid, I learned swiftly and instinctively what pleased or displeased the adults around me. My mom called me her angel when I helped with the housework and the younger kids or when I asked if we could kneel and pray. She called me her angel when I did my homework all by myself. My teachers called me an angel when I studied silently and got straight A's. But mostly, they told me what a helpful girl I was when I tattled on the other kids. The grown-ups liked that and insisted they didn't know what they would do without me because I was the good girl, and they needed me to help them with the kids who weren't good. I responded by becoming the source of a constant stream of details about the transgressions of my peers happening in the quiet places—the corners at Church, huddled groups on the playground, the van ride to and from school. They would have much preferred to keep a constant eye on us, but that wasn't always possible, so having me as an extra pair of eyes inducted me into a sort of honorary grown-up club. I basked in their praise and felt a sense of purpose and safety—so long as they needed me, maybe they would be less likely to turn on me. I craved the validation that accompanied the honorary club, but it was more complicated than I thought, and sometimes I dared to wonder if it was worth it. Because no matter how much I aspired to be grown-up, I still wasn't, so I ended up someplace all alone, where I garnered little respect in the adult world but pure venom from the kids.

I surveilled the other kids with a sharp sense of longing and a palpable tinge of regret. They didn't want me around because they knew that I'd tell on them. I wanted to not care about being good, to be able to try just one bad thing now and then, but I was so petrified of getting into trouble and going to the lake of fire that I could barely breathe.

No matter what I longed for, there was only one right choice.

To be good, period.

And so I did, with enthusiasm and dedication. I tried to do the right thing every day, every hour, every moment. Mostly though, my best still wasn't good enough. Every time one of my parents spanked me for fighting with my siblings or washed my mouth out with soap because I lied about something trivial, like saying I'd brushed my teeth when I hadn't or sent me to bed without dinner for talking back (read: having an opinion about anything at all), I knew that my best was not good enough. It wasn't the severity of the transgression that mattered. It was the transgression itself. For example, not brushing your teeth isn't such a big deal—it was the lie that was so egregious. Lying is bearing false witness, breaking one of the Ten Commandments.

Similarly, talking back to my parents broke the commandment to honor your father and mother. The sin was the disobedience, not so much the talking. I knew that when YHWH, my parents, or the grown-ups were angry with me, it was because they loved me. I knew it because they told me so, I didn't understand, but I learned to accept that love equaled hurt.

I didn't just have to be careful about what I did—I had to be watchful of my thoughts. YHWH could see everyone's thoughts all the time—he was writing down those thoughts and deeds in a giant book; I used to imagine he was writing with his finger because it was doubtful that the creator of everything would need a pen—he would read them aloud to the whole world on Judgement Day unless I could figure out how to be perfect. I wondered how he had the time and hoped that when I had bad thoughts, he would be otherwise occupied with someone else's bad thoughts at that exact second and miss mine, but I knew better. He was all-knowing and all-seeing, and I wasn't supposed to be able to make sense of it. I was glad my parents couldn't see my thoughts because I knew I'd be getting spanked a lot more. I wasn't so sure about Laycher. As a prophet, I assumed there was a chance he could see my thoughts too, so I tried to be extra good in my head when I was around him.

It was so hard to control my thoughts.

Bad thoughts would just pop up, even when I didn't want them to, and when I told them to go away, they wouldn't listen. My bad thoughts were trivial, but brains will chatter, especially creative ones, whether you're in a cult or not. Mine would wonder about chewing gum—how bad would trying a piece be? It would linger too long on a girl my age wearing shorts and wonder what I would look like in shorts. It would crumple up its forehead and clench its fists when I was being spanked and imagine hitting right back, a slap across the face, or a punch to the gut. It would imagine that a boy was holding my hand, that maybe having a boyfriend wasn't a sin. I was trying so hard to be good, yet still, I was bad. I was bad whether I was actually bad or not. I was bad because the grown-ups said I was bad, and grown-ups don't lie. If I disputed the facts when an adult said I was bad because I actually wasn't bad, then I was even worse.

YHWH was a gigantic man in the sky who spent most of his time being angry with us and chastising us. Sometimes I could see his face, an old man with a big, puffy, white beard, in the shapes of the clouds, and my blood would run cold. Every time I was sick, I knew it was because I'd done something wrong; I was always sick. Every stomach flu, head cold, chest cold, and ear infection that circulated through the group, hit me with a vengeance. I would lie on the couch, burning up with fever, wheezing, coughing, or being perfectly still because if I moved, little swords would slice into my eardrums. Laycher would come over and lay hands on me after putting a dab of olive oil on my forehead to pray for me, but I wouldn't get better. I knew it was my fault. *"We don't get healed right away because we don't have enough faith and haven't repented fully."*

The prophets in the Bible would lay hands on people, and they would get better instantly. Laycher was a prophet, but I never got better when he laid his hands on me. I thought it was because he wasn't as good a prophet as they were, but I buried that thought deep. It was one of the bad ones, probably blasphemous. When I'd ask him why I never got better, he would say it was because I didn't believe. The next time I would believe so hard that I thought I would pass out, but it never worked. As I grew older and never experienced a miracle, I figured I would never know how to be good enough to have a miracle. I never saw anyone else have a miracle either, but it wasn't Laycher's fault. It was just that the Church *was full of doubting Thomases.* (Thomas was the disciple in the Bible story about Jesus' resurrection who didn't believe until he saw for himself. He was the cautionary tale of lack of faith.)

But I so wanted to see a miracle. Laycher would preach about miracles, the ones in the Bible and those that happened in the Church before I was born. *"I've had broken bones, arthritis, diabetes, cirrhosis of the liver, water in the lungs. You name it; I had it. But when I came to YHWH, he healed me of them all. By his stripes, we are healed, but I had to repent. If you go willingly to doctors for healing, it's blaspheme. It's the same if you go to the health food store looking for herbs. You shouldn't require of any other than YHWH, his ministers, and his elders. If you have faith, come to your pastor, and if you need food or an herb, YHWH will show him. He said he'd chastise us if he loves us and that the prayer of faith will save the sick. If you don't believe, he can't heal you, and if you have no faith, you are damned."*

He would ramble on and on with examples of how faith had healed people he knew who had terrible diseases. One of his favorite stories was how he brought a boy back to life once in City Park in Pueblo. The boy had fallen into the lake and drowned. The paramedics had done CPR on him, and it didn't work. Then Laycher laid hands on him, and he came back to life. Miracles only seemed to have happened in the Church before I was born. Laycher said it was because we had grown lazy—we were backsliding, losing the faith.

My parents had their own stories of miracles. When my big brother Joseph was a toddler, he had a bad case of croup. No matter how much they prayed or had Laycher lay hands on him, he only got worse until the night when he was barely breathing, and they thought he would surely die. My mom said she left him with my dad, went into the bedroom, closed the door, and cried. My dad prayed for him and then went to bed. In the morning, when they woke up, he was up, sitting on the floor playing with his blocks, wholly recovered.

But—back to being good. I knew the grown-ups were the ones who had the final say when they thought I'd done wrong, but sometimes, I'd dig in and insist that they were wrong or had made a mistake. I reasoned they would believe me since I was telling the truth. I was a kid, a kid who hated being spanked, so I sometimes lied about trivial things that might still get me into trouble, like saying I wasn't the one who'd left the door open and let the cat in, or it wasn't me who spilled the water on the floor. Still, I didn't lie often, so they really had no reason not to trust me. When I was four or five was the first time I remember trying to stand my ground. My parents were constantly fighting. I was far too young to have any idea what the fighting was about or to remember the fights in detail, but I imagine they were probably fighting about the usual things: money, time, exhaustion (they'd had four kids in rapid succession) and if you add to that the pressure of being in the church and wrestling with inadequacies, the fighting makes sense.

The reason I remember it so profoundly is because the whole situation was highly unusual. Laycher told them that it would be good for them to get away for a night and leave their kids with him, that they probably just needed a break. He told them to spend the night in a hotel up in Colorado Springs—to kinda take a mini vacation. He said that we kids could stay with him.

We'd never slept over anywhere before and were never away from my parents, and not very thrilled about the idea. They drilled into us incessantly how important it was to *behave* during their absence, or they would tan our hides when they returned. I begged them not to leave or to take us with them, not only because I'd never spent a night without them, but because Laycher's house was scary and creepy with lots of dark rooms and strange smells, odd sounds coming from the basement—voices, probably a radio, and flickering lights, most likely from a TV—but at the time I had no idea what those things were because we weren't allowed to have them. It was old, like all of our houses, but it felt even more ancient. It was a rambling house with too many floors, porches, and closed doors. The sofas were brushed polyester, that discount-store-mass-produced polyester fabric that was both soft and scratchy at the same time, flowered in dark yellow and brown, and all the floors were covered in drab, shag carpeting. It was the fanciest of the houses in the church. No matter where I went in that house, the one place always on my mind was the basement. Any time we visited, we were never allowed into, or even near, the basement. Sometimes, when the door was cracked, I would take a peek, only to jump at the sound of Maxine's voice, "You think you want to sneak around, young lady? Did you forget about the boogie man?" Her voice would take on a steady monotone—her eyes, unblinking, would peer through me as if I was translucent. I didn't know what a boogie man was, but I figured it was some sort of demon. The only people I ever glimpsed in the basement were her teenage sons in their jeans and t-shirts. Our unrighteous relations couldn't enter our homes in those clothes, but everyone knew and accepted the fact that all kinds of things happened at Laycher and Maxine's house that couldn't happen anywhere else. I'd guessed it was just because they were the holiest and better at not yielding to temptation.

Joseph, Ruth, and I arrived for our sleepover and said goodbye to our parents, a clingy, tearful goodbye. As soon as they'd left, Maxine gathered us and commanded us to sit on the couch and listen carefully. "Do you remember the boogie man that lives in the basement?" We shook our heads solemnly. Yes, we definitely remembered.

"Well, if you aren't perfect little kids tonight, I'll send you down there, and he really doesn't like kids who don't listen. Do you understand?" Our eyes, wide and freshly dried from our goodbyes, stared at her in terror, and we went through the motions of the evening silently and meticulously. I made sure that every single thing I said and did was perfect. I ate all of my dinner of beans and rice and tortillas. And at the table, I held my tongue even though I wanted to ask why the tortillas were made from white flour (it was one of the poison foods). Children were to be seen and not heard and to only speak when spoken to. I wasn't always so good at that when I was at home, but I knew that on that night, it was crucial. So when they told us to wait quietly in the living room, I did. When it was time to pray, I prayed. When it was time for bed, I went into the bathroom to change into my nightgown. I came out and handed my dress to Laycher.

"Are you still wearing your bloomers?" (Bloomers: big, puffy pants with elastic waist and ankles, always worn beneath our clothes lest an unexpected breeze dared to lift our dresses and reveal our nakedness).

"Yes, sir."

"Do you always wear your bloomers to bed?"

"Yes, sir."

"Are you sure? Is that what your mom said to do?"

"No, sir, I just do."

"Are you lying to me?"

"No, sir."

"Go to bed. Your parents will hear about this tomorrow."

I went to bed, not sure what my parents would hear about tomorrow or why I would sleep without my bloomers here when I always wore them at home. I lay awake for a long time, watching the door, waiting for the boogie man.

The next day, Laycher told my parents I'd lied to him. My stomach sank. He'd said he would, but I figured he'd forget or realize that I hadn't lied after all once he'd slept on it. My dad gave me *the look,* and I knew what was coming when we got home.

At home, I tried tearfully to explain that Laycher just didn't understand my answer to his question and that I really hadn't lied about anything.

"Why would he say you had lied if you hadn't?"

I had no idea. "He's the one who is lying," I whispered.

The prophet of YHWH does not lie.

That time it was a pants-down spanking. I was baffled. If I was going to get spanked even when I told the truth, the only option left was to agree with the grown-ups no matter

what, even if they were wrong.
And to grow up as fast as I possibly could.

7 SCHOOL

We were living in the third tiny farmhouse in Avondale in six years. It was squat, perfectly square, and painted aqua, with corn fields all around—the closest neighbor not even half a mile away. During one of my recent visits to Colorado, I went back there, and aside from being abandoned, it was exactly the same as when we lived there. It was even tinier than I remembered and not twenty feet from the corn fields. I wanted to go inside but thought better of it, seeing as I was alone and there was a padlock on the door. The windows were boarded over, but one was broken, and I could have easily slipped through the opening. I squatted down to push some stones around with a stick and decide what I was going to do, and I swear, even the ant piles were the same, right in the middle of the driveway—they were marching along like they owned the place—they did now.

The weedy yard was shriveled in the July heat, and the irrigation ditch was dry. I glanced again at the boarded-up windows and the lock on the rickety door. I'd wanted just one look inside, but instead, with a slight shiver at the thought, I climbed back into my rental car and drove away. I had been peeking into dilapidated houses and driving the old routes of my youth all day, looking for a thing that I couldn't name, that thing that would click into place and push my story forward with effortless momentum, but I found that I had only more questions. Questions about the helplessness that had crept back in, the desperation that had, not ten minutes earlier, when I pulled over to take pictures of the McHarg Road/Wheeler Lane crossroad, brought me to my knees on the abandoned gravel road. I had become momentarily transfixed by the water rushing into the culvert of the irrigation ditch when grief rampaged so fiercely through me that it pulled me to the ground, and for a moment, I wanted to stay there, willing that deserted, arid earth to speak to me. I sat there in the middle of the road, alone and gutted, but still not sure why I was there. Something just wasn't clicking into place like it needed to. I felt like I was beating my head against a wall, one that, if I broke through, would help me make sense of the rollercoaster.

But it was just an old house, just a gravel road, just a muddy irrigation ditch, all of which were pulling my strings like puppet masters. I know now that I didn't take that peek inside out of pure dread. I could have. There really was no one around for miles. I was alone, and that's what made it so hard. No buffer, just me and whatever images and memories would flood my brain. I wasn't altogether sure I was ready for them.

Moments like those happen repeatedly when I return to Colorado, and for some reason, I keep going back, keep driving the roads, keep going into those old houses, searching—grasping. But it wasn't until my latest trip there that I finally put my finger on it. I've been looking for something that isn't there. The houses are abandoned or have been bulldozed, the church building is boarded up, and the church—is gone.

My history has been erased like it never happened.

The only place it exists is in my memories, faded to a faint echo, reverberating and fragmenting, stranger than fiction, fiction brought to life only through the reviving magic of my pen. The power to kill that past or to enshrine it for the future is a power that has been laid deliciously at my feet, and I've chosen to preserve the story because some stories shouldn't be allowed to fade into the oblivion of whitewashed lore.

In that house, we'd had a basement for the first time, which was simultaneously exciting and unnerving. Did that basement have a boogie man, too? I didn't know, but I wasn't planning to find out. I determined instantly never to go down there alone and most certainly not without the light on. When I did go down with the rest of my family, I examined every corner and closet to assure myself that Maxine's boogie man couldn't travel or materialize. Still, when I nearly succeeded in convincing myself, I reasoned that perhaps the boogie man was invisible—most demons were. In any case, the best bet was never to go down alone unless I had to hide from a tornado. We, kids, *did* play in the basement. It was an excellent place to be loud and rowdy without getting in my mom's way. Of course, Joseph thought it was deliciously clever and hysterical to run up the stairs, shut off the light, and slam the door closed. My two little sisters and I would scurry up as fast as we could in the dark and pound frantically on the door while he held it closed from the other side. He was gleeful in his strength until Mom yelled for him to "open that door *immediately* and let your sisters out." His next prank was to coax me inside the barrel where we kept the old baby clothes, put the lid on and latch it. I didn't fall for that trick twice, but it could help explain why I am so claustrophobic.

The house had two bedrooms, one for my parents and the other with bunk beds for me, Ruth, and my other little sister, Sara. Joseph slept on the couch in the living room. Someone gave us a swing set with two rubber-seated swings and a small slide that we set up in the tiny yard. I'd only ever played on swing sets in the park, so having one at my house made me feel like the richest kid alive.

But the best part about that house was that my best friend, Yahanna, who was a year younger than I and, to this day, is my most fervent cheerleader and fiercest friend, lived less than a mile down the road. That meant we got to play together every week, a rarity before that, either at her house or mine. We would swing for hours, seeing who could go the highest, laughing and screeching when the chain went slack because we'd gone too high, and then, letting go while in mid-air, flying forward and landing with our feet planted firmly in the dirt. Took me a while to learn that maneuver, but once I did, it was my favorite—the higher the swing and the further the leap—the better. I thought it was the closest thing to flying I'd ever experience.

We played hide and seek in the corn or *went swimming* in the muddy irrigation ditch. I never actually learned to swim until I left home, so I was mostly petrified of water, but the ditch was shallow enough to stand in, so I managed okay. We would lie in the water on our bellies and kick our legs to swim, although we were really just pulling ourselves forward with our arms while making giant splashes with our feet. We would dare each other to crawl through the thirty-inch culvert while the water was flowing. It's a miracle none of us drown, and *I don't even want to think about the amount of pesticide in that water.* Later, after nap time, we would have sewing contests or bake bread and cookies. Before that, I hardly ever spent time with kids who weren't my siblings except at church. Which is why I was also counting down the days until I could go to school.

I was six, and I loved school, or rather, I loved my idea of school. I would watch with envy as Joseph left early each morning to attend the church school or study him quizzically as he sat in front of the window, staring out, wishing he could be outside playing instead of doing homework. He didn't know how good he had it. I would have traded places with him in a heartbeat. As my seventh birthday approached, the anticipation was eating me alive. I had been calculating the months, weeks, and days until my birthday. We weren't allowed to go to school until we were seven. That's because the state of Colorado required kids to be in school once they turned seven. Without that rule, I would have had to wait even longer, I presume. My mom would never have let us go if she didn't have to. I couldn't wait to learn to read and write, but I cherished, even more, the idea of leaving home every day, going somewhere on my own, anywhere without my parents.

My mom was pregnant with her fifth child, my brother Nathan, but none of us knew until the morning Maxine came to deliver the baby. As her belly grew bigger and she more fatigued, my dad insisted that I was *a big girl now* and that it was time I learned to help around the house. I remember vividly the first time I picked up the broom that was taller than I was and learned how to gather the dirt from the corners of the kitchen and sweep it carefully across the bumpy linoleum into a little pile in the center of the room. But no matter how much I practiced, I couldn't seem to get that pile successfully into the dustpan without leaving a little trail behind. Although I took my new responsibilities in stride, I didn't love sweeping the floor and knew that going to school meant maybe I wouldn't have to do it as much.

As my birthday approached, I was shattered by the news that Yahanna and her family were moving away to start a church in Oregon, where she would end up living until I was fifteen. We had waited so long to live near each other and to go to school together that we concluded the grown-ups were sending her away on purpose because we'd been playing together too much and *grown-ups were stupid like that*. Yahanna didn't mind saying *stupid*, and although I giggled when she did, I never would have said it myself. It was a bad word in our house, one that would get me an ivory soap rinse. I don't even remember saying goodbye. We ended up seeing each other no more than once a year after that. We didn't keep in touch very well. Phone calls were expensive, and letter writing could be tedious, and when we did write, our parents screened our correspondence. Regardless, ours was one of those rare friendships that picked up where it left off without missing a beat, one that I cherish beyond words.

After Yahanna left, going to school became my only bright spot, but my birthday came and went, and still, I didn't go. No one had bothered to tell me that because I turned seven in March, in the middle of the school year, I would have to wait until the fall to start. *I thought I would die from the constant postponement.* My mom didn't share my anticipation. She didn't want any of us to go to school; she wanted to teach us herself. Her battle was not with the state. It was with Laycher. He changed his mind constantly about homeschooling. My mom cried when he told her that Joseph had to go to the church school. This was after he had already told her she could teach him at home. It was a habit of his to resend his position on a decision he'd already made, and my mom was frequently on the receiving end. I think he liked to watch how she would bend until she nearly broke to follow him, then he would whiplash her in the other direction and question her loyalty if she fought back. He told her that if he started to make exceptions, people would be challenging his rules all the time—there would be no end to it all. How would he keep a congregation under control if he let everyone do what they wanted and never put his foot down.

He reminded her that she wasn't any holier than anyone else, and if it was good enough for them, it was good enough for her. I was in the living room with Joseph when I heard her muffled weeping in the kitchen as she relayed the conversation to my dad. I didn't know how to feel bad for her. I was thrilled because if Joseph had to go to school, then it meant that I would have to go, too. I buzzed around him like an annoying little fly while he did his homework and tried to mimic his lessons. I loved to "read" his workbooks. We didn't have little cardboard books in our home, those pre-K stories with big photographs and a few easy words. My parents read to us from the Bible or from

Mennonite books with Bible-based stories.

When fall arrived, all my waiting had been in vain. My mom had managed to convince Laycher that it was absolutely necessary that she pull Joseph out of school and teach us both herself. I didn't find out until shortly before the school year began.

That morning I found my mom in the kitchen at the stove, stirring the oatmeal, "What day do we start school, Mom?"

"Next Monday," she replied, not looking up.

"I can't wait!" I did a little dance and clapped my hands against my cheeks.

"Me either, because I get to be your teacher," she turned to smile at me.

My arms dropped to my sides, and I moved closer to her. "What? No—remember? Brother Laycher said we all have to go to the church school. I heard him preaching it."

Mom turned to take the bowls out of the cabinet, "Not anymore. I had a talk with him, and he agreed that it isn't a good place for you and your brother, my precious little ones; there are too many bad influences milling around there."

She smiled again, pleased and satisfied with herself.

I was furious, as furious as a little seven-year-old could be. Why did she always have to have a talk with him? Why couldn't she just leave it the way it was? Why was she smiling? How could she do this to me? She knew how much I'd wanted to go, and from my perspective, she relished the power she had to rip that away from me.

"Why would you do that?" I tried to blink back the water gathering in my eyes. "You know how much I wanted to go to school."

"You will be going to school—right here at home with me and Joseph. You'll see, it will be just as good."

"No, *it won't*," I stomped my foot. "There won't be any other kids here, and that's not school. That's just like every other day, and *it's not fun at all.*"

"It's special because you're a big girl, and you get to

learn how to read and write and do math, just like they do at school. You do get to go to school with your brother," she insisted cheerfully as if that was something special. At that exact moment, I hated my brother more than just a little "No," I was pushing harder than normal, "It's not *going* anywhere. It's right here, same as every other day." I turned to leave the kitchen. *"It's not fair."* Then, mumbling under my breath, "Joseph always gets to do *everything* and ruins it because he's bad, and when it's my turn, I don't get to do anything. I would be good at school, you know I would. *Not fair...*"

In the church, there was a hierarchy. At the top were the holiest families, Elders and their wives and children—my friend Yahanna belonged to one of those families. At the bottom were the families who did whatever they wanted, even if that meant breaking the rules, yet still came to church. They were all related to Laycher. That didn't keep him from rebuking them from the pulpit, but it didn't seem to faze them. Sometimes he threatened to throw them out, but he never actually did. In the middle were the soldiers who followed orders without question, who understood, and humbly accepted their place. We fell into that category. Laycher knew he could count on us to march to whatever tune he decided to play. I knew my mom wanted to keep us far away from the influence of the families on the bottom so their sinful ways would not defile us. And after Joseph's first two years in school, she had all the proof that she needed to insist that she had to protect us from them. His two best friends were from those families. Thanks to their influence, his downward spiral had begun. The three of them got into all sorts of trouble, and although he was not the ringleader, he was the one who always got caught and punished. And when he was spanked at school, he was spanked again when he got home. I wanted to defend him because I knew it wasn't fair, but knowing that I could take his side and lose my parents' trust or betray him and remain their angel, I chose to keep my mouth shut. I stood by and watched him get beaten down, called lazy and a liar, and be constantly compared to me. It is one of my most brutal regrets. I had no way of knowing at the time that being an angel was a cowardly choice.

My first day of school was no longer a milestone. We had ordered all of our books from the Mennonite publisher, and they arrived just in time. They were just the basics—including Math, Penmanship, Reading, Phonics, and Bible Studies. We stocked up on school supplies—some of which my grandparents happily sent—pens, pencils, erasers, crayons, and construction paper. The sight of it all made me giddy. And although my mom was a great teacher—patient, enthusiastic, kind, and dedicated, and I could see that it was her favorite part of the day—it didn't matter because it was just another day in my house with my siblings and my mom, but with schoolbooks.

I made believe it was still special by pretending that the little corner of the living room where my desk sat, next to my brother's, sunlight streaming in and pouring onto the bulky dotted lines of my penmanship page, was a world away from the chaos of the little kids. I was highly dedicated to my work. My lessons came naturally to me. I sat down enthusiastically early in the morning and worked steadily for a few hours, finishing all of my work with time to spare. I was a determined little perfectionist, and when I struggled, I crumpled into a ball of tearful frustration. My consolation prize was that because Joseph spent most of his time gazing out the window or getting distracted by our younger siblings, my parents scolded him and told him he should follow my example.

They thought it was very clever, *go to the Ang, thou sluggard, consider her ways and be wise*—a parody of the Bible verse, *go to the ant, though sluggard, consider her ways and be wise*. I'm sure it made him hate me.

8 ANGEL OR DEVIL

Throughout those years, we moved a lot. Each new house was only temporary until we found something better. Most of those temporary stays lasted more than a year, often two or three. When I was eight, the farmer who rented us the tiny aqua house decided he needed it for farmhands, and so we were forced to find a new place. It was okay. We'd outgrown it anyway. This time our search led us beyond the borders of Avondale, the tiny town where I was born, and we ended up in a house that was actually closer to Pueblo than to the church in Boone, which made Laycher furious. Eavesdropping on my parents as I often did, I heard my mom relaying to my dad, "He said he's really worried about us this time, that moving further away means we're moving away from our faith."

"That's ridiculous," my dad retorted, "it's just a house. Does he know how hard it is to find a house we can afford with five kids?"

"Don't get mad," my mom shot back, "I'm just telling you what he said. His exact words were more like 'may as well have one foot out the door already.' I'm afraid. What if he's right?" (Laycher said stuff like that all the time when he wanted to be dramatic. He'd throw his hands up in the air, shake his head and declare, "may as well have one foot out the door already," but he'd only ever said it about the weak families. I'd never heard him say it about us, so it grabbed my attention.)

"Like I said, it's just a house," my dad insisted, "it doesn't *symbolize* anything." I can imagine the effect that Laycher's words had on my mom, though, once the seed of doubt was planted and her pastor and her husband were at odds. She was always loyal, faithful, sincere, and eager to prove that she was worthy of respect and trust, and if she had to choose between the two, I wasn't sure she would choose my dad.

I agreed with my dad.

It was just a house. But I was curiously exhilarated. What if Laycher was serious? Even at eight, I wanted to rebel just a little, and if I'm perfectly honest with myself now, I think I was hoping that he would throw us out because then my parents wouldn't have had a choice. They would've had to go. I never admitted that to myself then, not even in the deepest recesses of my mind. I knew I would go to the lake of fire for simply wishing it, but I do remember letting the thought linger, just for a second, so there must have already been a war raging in my subconscious that I was detached from, a war that would grow stronger and louder over the next decade and lead me to this moment, to these words on these pages.

The new house was huge—extravagant by our standards. It had four bedrooms upstairs and another one downstairs. It had an *upstairs*! We were going to live in a concrete mansion with a winding wooden staircase, the handrail worn smooth over the years of fingers and palms whisking up and down. Within minutes, we had our rooms picked out and our hide-and-seek spots locked down. There was a barn and a chicken coop behind the house, a root cellar out front, fruit trees lining the shriveled lawn, and plenty of room for a vegetable garden. It seemed too good to be true, and I waited for my parents to hem and haw and list all of the reasons why it wouldn't work. I held my breath and, with it, my hope and excitement until I saw them hand over the eighty-five dollars for the first month's rent. I knew that even we could afford that.

As I've mentioned before, we were poor, even by Church standards. My dad worked as much as the other dads, but for some reason, we never had much money. I knew that being poor was nothing to be ashamed of because the poorer we were on earth, the richer we would be in heaven. So I held the shame close and wished for more silently. I'd dream of cheese for sandwiches to take to school instead of bean burritos, packed perfectly in little plastic sandwich baggies, with an apple, both settled nicely in another perfect paper lunch bag (we could rarely afford cheese, much less plastic sandwich bags and paper lunch bags). I'd wish for spaghetti and meatballs for dinner, hot dogs, and sloppy joes. We only ate those foods once in a while when an occasion warranted it. Our birthdays, for example. We never had a birthday party. My mom would just ask us what special dinner we wanted. We almost always asked for spaghetti, which, if she couldn't afford, she would make painstakingly from scratch with whole wheat flour, eggs, and water, rolled out by hand and cut into thick strips with a knife. She would cook down the watery canned tomatoes until they turned into a thick, flavorful sauce with a little dried basil and oregano. We didn't like that pasta as much as the store-bought, but we still devoured it. Now, of course, I know how much love went into those dense, coarse noodles.

Fifty-pound bags of beans and flour were more practical, and we had honey and oil in five-gallon buckets stacked next to the stove. We also purchased our rice and potatoes in bulk whenever possible, and we ate them every day. It was nice when we could have a garden or when it was harvest time at the surrounding farms, and we could buy bushels of tomatoes and green beans to can. I loved gleaning in the strawberry fields or going to pick peaches and apricots. I would gorge myself on the fruit and smile happily through my stomachache. My mom always warned us to take it slow, but I never listened. Eating all of that fruit right off of the tree when the rest of the year was a fruit desert, was blissful.

I finally got to go to school.

Since we'd moved anyway in spite of his warning, Laycher was eager to punish my mom and remind her who was in charge, so he declared victoriously from the pulpit one Saturday that if the church school was good enough for some, it was good enough for all and anyone who wanted to challenge that could go ahead and leave. "No more of this special treatment for anyone. Your kids aren't better than anyone else's, and if we don't have unity in this church, it'll never stand." He didn't call my mom out by name, but I knew he was talking to her. She suffered through the sermon and, when it was over, went directly up to the front of the church, to the bench where he always sat after the service, waiting for people who wanted to go talk to him. I knew exactly why she'd gone and wondered if she'd get her way again. There was a lot of gesturing and finger-wagging, but when my mom walked away from him, wiping her eyes, I knew he'd won.

My mom was devastated, but I wanted to screech in delight and jump up and down with excitement. I was so glad that there was someone who could boss her around, but at the same time, I felt really bad for being glad. I knew her well enough to know that she had pleaded with him and reminded him about the bad things that had happened last time with my brother, begging him not to force her to defile her little girl, her little angel—me. Later in the car, she told my dad, "I've never seen him like this. He usually understands and makes exceptions for special situations like this, *but he was mad*—he told me to leave, for real. He said that if the kids aren't on the bus on the first day of school, then it's over." She seemed flabbergasted, convinced that he meant it and would follow through. It was a showdown. Would my mom test his resolve? For a split second, I wondered again if we might actually leave the Church over it, but I should have known better. Laycher would win. He always did.

I'm also certain that he never would have actually kicked her out. He needed her just as badly as she needed him. In fact, probably more. My mom was a special kind of follower, one that, to this day, will still play the devil's advocate for him. She understands to a point, why I left, maybe even why the church crumbled, but she still defends him. What good is a dictator with no loyal subjects? In fact, there were few people who were allowed to push back quite as much as my mom and still be given more chances. I never stopped to wonder why, but after I left home and after Maxine died, Laycher asked my mom to marry him—maybe that had something to do with it. He would rebuke her, punish her, and belittle her, but he never kicked her out. And she would take it, not only take it but believe that she deserved it. I was flooded with relief the day that she turned her back on him and finally said, "I don't deserve this, and I'm not going to take it anymore." It had been a long time coming.

My mom was silently tearful as she packed our lunches and sent us off to the waiting van. I was at the same time bursting with anticipation and bloated with guilt that I could be so happy when she was so sad. No one had stood up for her, not my dad, not me, but that feeling of turmoil was quickly extinguished by a churning of excitement and nerves as the door closed behind me. The van was our school bus, and the driver was our teacher, Quinn. Our schoolhouse was an old garage next to Laycher's house. It had two rooms. One large room with old oil stains on the concrete floor and windows too high in the walls for me to see out, and a much smaller room that used to be the workshop with no windows at all. We had three teachers, all women. First grade was taught by Delia in the small room behind a closed door—there were about five kids in first grade. Second grade, my grade, was taught by Lenette, Laycher's daughter-in-law. She was one of the kindest, sweetest people I'd ever met and, in my eight-year-old opinion, a perfect teacher. Our grade shared the large room, our four desks facing Lenette's in a single file line right next to the front door. The third teacher, Quinn, taught all of the other grades, about nine kids, desks facing the opposite side of the room from ours. Somehow that was supposed to delineate between the two "classes". It didn't really matter that we were all in one room because our teachers demanded complete silence unless it was lunchtime or recess. If we needed help, we raised our hand and waited patiently to be called on, even if it took a few minutes.

I relished the quiet. No crying baby, no siblings running around and vying for my mom's attention, no hustle and bustle of a large household. I loved the way it felt to sit at my desk. The little groove for my pencil, the smooth formica top, and the cubby underneath where my books and notebooks were impeccably stacked. I loved the clean, white pages of my workbooks with big black letters and dotted lines for me to write on. I kept my pencil perfectly sharpened and my penmanship flawless because I didn't want to mess up the perfection. I was the picture of well-behaved. I wasn't going to give anyone an excuse to revoke my right to go to school. I knew that the only way that my mom would eventually be okay with me going to school was if she saw that it didn't affect me, that I could resist the bad influence of the other kids, and that I wouldn't turn bad.

After a few months, my resolve began to weaken. I continued to be the good girl and a spy for the grown-ups but ached with curiosity and an urge to be with the other kids. I was jealous of the fact that some of the girls had purses, and in those purses, they had delicate bottles of heavenly-smelling lotions, shiny hair bobbles, barrettes, and bubblegum-scented lip gloss. They would rub the lotion into the skin on the back of my hands, and I would marvel at the way it disappeared. The only thing we rubbed on our hands at home was lanolin, and it stayed greasy for a long time, and it smelled bad. Because of all the trouble kids were bound to get into, we weren't allowed to talk at all on the way to and from school. Plus, if we whispered, Quinn couldn't be sure we weren't plotting an evil plan, so one little peep would earn us a mark, and after three marks, we weren't allowed to go out at recess. Those fifteen minutes of recess would instead be spent writing *I will not talk on the bus to school*, fifty times on the chalkboard. Too often, Joseph was the one staying behind writing on the chalkboard. I always raced out the door with a stone in my stomach and pain in my heart, but our roles were clearly defined; I, the angel, he the devil, and the angel cannot waste her time defending the devil.

But not being able to talk on the bus didn't keep us from *getting up to no good*, and as I said, I was growing tired of my role, so I started to join in just a little. Being an angel doesn't secure friendships and I was lonely. Pink lip gloss was one of my first acts of backsliding.

The girl who offered the lip gloss, which I barely touched to my lips, was five years older, and I knew it was a test. Whose side was I on? She was an angel, too, and one of my allies in good behavior, but because she was so much older than me, she somehow managed to be an angel and still get away with pink lip-gloss. Once I'd tried it, I could tell I'd passed the test—Amelia smiled, but I was burning with guilt. It was almost like lipstick. It was even shaped the same—only Jezebels wore lipstick. My hand trembled as I handed it back, and I could feel myself slipping quickly away from angel-dom to an angel on the outside but a devil on the inside. At the core, I was bad. Little did I know that the nail buffer would be next, and I'd get caught for that one. Kinda hard to hide super shiny nails from your mom.

I knew those girls were the bad influence that my mom was worried about, and I should be keeping my distance, but they were glamourous and daring and I couldn't resist when they opened their circle to me. I loved the way they pushed their head coverings back just enough to show off their perfect middle part or flopped their hair forward from underneath their head coverings where it lay uncovered down their front—tantalizing. I mimicked them and felt deliciously daring, and defiled, and exposed, all at the same time. My mom would catch me once in a while and snap, "Fix your head covering" or "Go tie your hair back, young lady." I wondered why she was so much stricter than the other moms. There was no wiggle room. And the more I wanted to be like the other girls, the more often I got into trouble. So, I tried to do both. I experimented in the *back of the bus*, literally the last seat in the three-row van, masking my worry and uncertainty and putting on a brave face when they teased me for not knowing what they were talking about. I was very clearly the outsider, though I worked tirelessly to convince myself that that was not the case. I told myself I belonged even though I knew I would never have a shiny purse or a tiny tube of lip gloss. Then, I would dutifully wipe it off of my mouth and tuck my hair deep back into my head covering as the van pulled into our driveway at the end of the day.

We were the last stop, and my teacher would turn off the engine and sit in the driveway. I would sit in the van with her or sometimes stand outside the door talking to her through the rolled-down window until she got her full debrief from me about every little thing that had happened on the drive. I didn't know I was betraying my friends; I only knew that I had to keep her happy, keep her in my corner so she would never suspect that I was also one of the bad ones. If she did and she told my parents, I knew there would be no more school. It worked for a while, and I was content. I'd made some new friends, the wrong friends, but friends nonetheless. We hardly ever had people over to our house or went to visit at someone else's house, and after Yahanna's family moved away, my parents didn't really have any close friends. The family who lived nearest to us in our new house was an Elder family, and I had the sense, although I'm not sure why, that my parents didn't feel as comfortable being around them. Elder families were, by nature of their standing in the Church, holier than the rest of us, so maybe my parents didn't feel worthy. Who knows? Near the end of my second-grade year, I lost my friends. Laycher had been battling the IRS in court after they'd come after him for back taxes. He insisted that he was protected by the religious exemption. Taxes were used to fund things that went against our beliefs, like war and abortion, so he concluded we would simply claim a higher authority and not pay them.

"Anyone paying income tax is going to miss out on that kingdom. The money goes to feed The Beast. There is nothing good that it is used for. YHWH said to feed our enemies, not shoot them. Billions of dollars goes to space probes. All of it for vanity. Some of it goes to higher education, which teaches faithlessness and vain knowledge. The making and study of books is the weariness of the heart and mind. These books have departed man from YHWH. They look into the secret parts of man; it is an abomination. If you need healing, you need only to look to YHWH in faith. The money goes to abortions—murder. Much goes to medicine and Medicare. We were told to care for our aged, not send them to old folks' homes.

YHWH dealt with me first about social security, then income tax. I quit paying it. Social security used to be voluntary in the thirties, then it became required. I took my stand and got tried out. They came and looked over everything I owned. Then they said they were taking my home. So I prayed and looked to YHWH. So I wrote them a letter and sent it off, and YHWH made a way. They let us free of it. Then YHWH laid income tax on my heart, so I quit paying it. They sent me a letter and said I had to pay my taxes. So now they are going to take the property again. I told them they can only do what YHWH will let them do. I had a dream I went to prison for three years. If I do, I'm looking forward to it—preaching to the prisoners. To pay taxes, you have to have a social security number. Those numbers are leading to the mark of the beast."

Maybe he thought that because we'd won the court case to have driver's licenses without photos, that we could also win the taxes case, but the IRS is a formidable enemy.

We, kids, were never left unsupervised by an adult, but

for one of those court hearings, Laycher wanted as many people as possible in the courtroom to support him, so every adult who could possibly go was compelled to. After much deliberation, the teachers decided that a few hours alone at school would have to be okay, and they chose the two eldest kids, one girl and one boy, both fifteen years old, to oversee the rest of us. Our strict instructions were that we were to be diligent with our lessons just like always and do everything that Penny and Lucas said, or there would be hell to pay, although no one used the word *hell*. I glanced anxiously at the wooden paddle that hung behind Quinn's desk. Even though I'd never known her to use it, the thought made me shudder. Remus, one of the single brothers, had made it. Even though he didn't have any kids, he relished the idea of spanking them. He'd made the paddle without being asked to, and I'd overheard him explaining to Quinn and some of the parents the great lengths he'd gone to in order to make the most effective paddle, one that would hurt more but not leave any marks behind. It was flat, with rounded edges and holes drilled through. It was sanded smooth and finished with a fine wood finish and had a handle shaped for a comfortable hand feel and easy leverage. Remus was a gifted woodworker. He could build anything, it seemed, from fine cabinetry to musical instruments, including guitars, violins, and dulcimers—pretty much anything a person asked him to make, he figured out how to make. Remus was incredibly smart but generally grouchy and a bit mean, especially with us kids. He was a formidable six feet six inches tall, bony, and gangly, with thick, straight, red hair that grazed his shoulder blades. His nose was long and protruding, and his face was small compared to the rest of his body. He had beady green eyes that didn't seem to blink when he looked intensely at me while explaining that "no, the guitar isn't soft, it's smooth—your cheek," moving his hand to my face, "your cheek is soft—see?" He moved his hand back and forth, first stroking the guitar and then my cheek, "smooth and soft, smooth and soft."

The paddle was his gift to the school, and I felt a sense of shock when the teachers thanked him for it. I didn't like Remus. He was always telling people with kids that they needed to be even stricter and spank us more. I didn't know why he thought that, and I resented the fact that someone with no kids thought he had the right to tell grown-ups to be even meaner to us. I hoped they wouldn't listen. I didn't know why he hated us so much, maybe because he was mad that he wasn't a dad.

Within minutes after the teachers left for court, everything began to unravel. The boys who had defiled my brother started to whisper, pass notes, and snicker. Penny and Lucas stood resolutely in front of the chalkboard, hands behind their backs, snapping warnings and threatening spankings. The boys defied them. They knew that even though Penny and Lucas were in charge, they didn't have permission to spank us. Penny commanded the boys to put their heads on their desks as firmly as she could muster, and instead, they jumped out of their desks and raced to the chalkboard to write Penny and Lucas with hearts all around the names in pink chalk. It may seem like a ridiculously small thing, but for us, it was a huge deal. Not only was it embarrassing for Penny and Lucas, but it was also against the rules. We weren't allowed to have boyfriends and girlfriends, or to date, or draw hearts, or profess our love unless we were going to be married. We weren't allowed to flirt, or pass notes, or hold hands with the opposite sex. If we were caught doing any of those things, we were spanked, kept home from school, or banned from talking together; grown-ups would be rebuked in church. The lust of the flesh was a powerful force, perhaps the most powerful of all, and it was one of the worst temptations to give in to.

The more Penny and Lucas scolded them, the more the boys rebelled and continued their chalkboard coup. In no time at all, the room was mayhem and mutiny. I covered my ears and tried desperately to focus on my work. I was terrified by the ruckus and haunted by what I knew would happen when the teachers returned. There was no way I was going to be a part of it. Not only did the threat of that paddle flash in my head like a strobe light, but I also had, up until that point, maintained a spotless record in the eyes of my teachers and parents. Unable to regain control and restore order, Penny and Lucas sent everyone outside to play kickball. I didn't want to go out because I thought that when the teachers came home, they would think that I had been bad, too, but Penny insisted I had to go out or she couldn't keep an eye on me. I liked Penny. She had always been especially kind to me, protected me from the mean kids, and chose me for her team during games when no one else wanted me on theirs.

When the teachers returned, the room was solemn and dead silent. Penny and Lucas relayed the day's adventures and returned to their seats. I knew I wouldn't be swept up with the troublemakers because I had been painstakingly good, so I rested quietly with my head on my desk. The teachers spoke to kids one at a time in the back classroom to get a better picture of what happened. They mainly relied on the good kids for an accurate account. Amelia, who had kept to herself like me, went first to tell her story. When she came back, it was my turn. I trembled a little but steadied myself knowing I had nothing to worry about. I told the teachers what I'd seen and heard and promised them that I wasn't lying—*They'd had the nerve to ask*—*it seemed to be every grown-up's favorite follow-up,* "*Are you lying to me, young lady?*" And then, I went back to the classroom to sit with my head on my desk with the rest of the kids. Days passed while the teachers convened with Laycher and our parents to decide what our punishment should be. I knew Penny had stuck up for me, so I continued to work hard and try not to think about it much. Imagine my shock when, a few days afterward—all of us gathered together in the large classroom—a room that was heavy with silence and the dread of what was to come, when Quinn, unable to look at us, announced, "You all know that what happened the other day was real bad. We tried to trust you, we asked for respect and obedience, and every one of you disappointed us. We've learned all we need to learn about what happened and have decided that all of you, except Penny, Lucas, and Amelia, need a good whipping."

I hadn't heard my name. That had to be a mistake. *Why didn't she say my name?* I was too petrified to ask. I looked over at Amelia, my eyes already filling with tears, wondering what lie she'd told about me. She smiled smugly and turned back to the book she was reading. She was Laycher's niece, and for the rest of our time in school, she was my arch-rival, my competitor for being the best and the best-loved. She always won, but she was an imposter. After all, she was the one in the *back of the bus* who had given me lip gloss.

Quinn walked out to the outhouse with the wooden paddle. Then we each had to go out to her when our name was called. Lennette had the unfortunate job of calling our names. I could tell she hated it, the disgust was clearly written on her face, but she couldn't stick up for me. The decision was not her's to make, and she had her marching orders. My heart was racing, and my stomach was in knots as I waited to be called. They'd started at the other side of the room, so I was one of the last. I had time to try to formulate a plan. I knew I could change Quinn's mind once we were alone. When Lennette called my name, I stood robotically and walked out the door, but I still couldn't believe it was happening. The sun glared, beating down on the black gravel in the driveway, but the only sound was that of my feet dragging as I walked. I opened the door to the outhouse, and there was Quinn, looking frazzled and desperate and like she just wished the whole thing was over. She didn't look at me, eyes fixed instead on the dusty floor. Inside, the outhouse was dark, not night-time dark, but dark like a room with the curtains drawn. The toilet lid was closed.

I stood there. "Bend over the lid," she said.

I hesitated.

"You know I wouldn't disobey you," I blurted out. "Whatever they said about me, you know it isn't true. I've always done exactly what you've asked. I've always told you what you've wanted to know. I haven't lied to you once. Why don't you believe me?"

"I do believe you," she said, "but I wasn't here to see it myself, and I didn't make this decision. I can't play favorites (Except with Amelia, I thought). I won't hit you that hard, I promise."

"Please—no—this isn't fair." I was crying already. "You know I'm not lying." I wanted to keep pleading, but when she just sat there, silent, looking at the floor, I almost felt sorry for her, and I decided to just get it over with and bent over the closed toilet lid and let her hit me. After all, that's what I usually did at home; I'd had plenty of practice.

The humiliation was always worse than the pain, the pain would subside over time, and she really didn't hit me very hard. But I was mortified. No one besides my parents had ever spanked me, and I had worked so hard to keep it that way. As I walked back to the school, deflated and wanting to crawl into a dark hole, I knew that Maxine would be looking out her kitchen window (everyone knew what was going down at the school that day), feeling gleeful, watching me go by, and when I opened the door to the classroom, everyone would look up and see my red face, and they would know—they would all know. I had promised myself that I would never get into trouble at school so that my mom would never have an excuse to make me stop going. This was the first strike against me. How many would it take? I could hear her voice in my head. If even her angel had been brought this low, she would have no choice, and she would have no problem convincing Laycher. And I was right. The next year, in third grade, we were homeschooled again, but only for that year—Laycher changed his mind as per usual, and the rest of my education took place at the church school.

9 YOU'RE TOO YOUNG TO KNOW ABOUT IT YET

I was nine, and unbeknownst to me, my mom was pregnant again. She was taking lots of naps and racing to the bathroom at inopportune moments (I would hear her retching, but never really stopped to wonder why) and eating the boxed macaroni and cheese—we never got to eat boxed macaroni and cheese—that my dad had ordered specially from the health food store for her. Occasionally, she would cook a box for us or give us a bite of hers, but mostly, it was all she could eat, so she ate it on her own. Women in the church concealed their pregnancies for as long as possible in tent-like dresses that draped loosely over their bodies from the small buttoned-up yokes at the top. When their round bellies pushed stubbornly against all that fabric and declared their state to the world, they shrunk behind the command of—be fruitful and multiply—blushing demurely as if they'd been caught doing something they shouldn't. And they were never *pregnant*; they were *with child*. I didn't learn the word pregnant until I was fifteen and snooping around the books piled in the bathroom tub at the school, and I found one on midwifery.

I never knew my mom was pregnant until the baby was born. My parents never told me because it was something I was *just too young to know about*, but that time would be different. I was happily oblivious of my mom's state until, against her wishes, just moments after I'd heard muffled arguing from the kitchen, my dad appeared and said they had something they wanted to talk to me about, motioning for me to sit on the stairs with them. A familiar nervous flutter started in my stomach, and I stared at them, wondering what I had done wrong and how scared I should be. My mom reached out her hand and took mine, "It's okay, you're not in trouble," but she didn't look thrilled either.

My dad, on the other hand, looked like he would burst with giddiness. "We've decided that it was time we told you why your mom has been so sick lately—you're going to have another brother or sister in a few months." He glanced at my mom, who was looking at the floor; I could tell by the way her lips were set in a fine, white line when he said *we*, he meant *he*. Why did my mom never want me to know anything?

"You're turning into a big girl," he smiled too broadly, "a big girl who is going to have to start helping your mom out more. It's hard for her when she's feeling this sick. She shouldn't have to do everything on her own." I wondered why having a baby made her sick, but I knew better than to ask questions. The fluttering in my belly calmed to a whisper. I was relieved that I wasn't in trouble, but as my dad continued to ramble, insisting that, because I was the oldest girl, I needed to help my mom out as much as I could, that she needed to be able to rely on me, I glanced nervously at her, hoping for some kind of sign, some inkling that this was what she wanted, too, that I, her oldest daughter was grown up enough to have her confidence, but that assurance never came. She just kept looking down, her face reflecting the fact that she had been forced into trusting me. As my dad finished his speech, my mom touched my cheek briefly and gave me a weak smile. Then she stood up and went back to the kitchen. My dad put his arm around me and squeezed my shoulders, "Look at you, my big girl. I knew I could count on you." I was glad that he trusted me and knew that I could handle it, even if my mom did not. Every time my mom would go into the bathroom to throw up, I'd smile to myself in grandiose self-importance, knowing that I was the only one who knew. I was growing up and was glad they finally noticed.

My dad had definitely noticed because a few weeks earlier, when sore lumps appeared beneath the skin on my chest without warning, it was him that I called to from the bathroom in a terrified screech to ask what kind of awful disease I had. I'd surmised that it would be him and not my mom who would give me a straight answer. Instead of telling me what kind of sickness I had and calling Laycher to come to lay hands on me, he smiled until his eyes narrowed to slits and squared his shoulders, beaming with pride as if he'd just won a parenting trophy. He found my mom at the cookstove, stirring our breakfast of cornmeal mush, and whispered in her ear, "Our little girl is becoming a young woman. She's beginning to *develop*." I heard it because it was a loud whisper, and I was standing right behind them, wondering what *beginning to develop* meant, waiting for my mom to turn and beam at me, too. I knew she was probably hurt and a little sad that I had told him and not her, but he liked me better. He trusted me with grown-up things, while she insisted that I was still a child. He told me all the time that I was his special girl and that he and Mom didn't know what they would do without me.

My mom didn't look at me. Instead, she glared at my dad and snapped sharply, "She's still a little girl." I didn't know whether to be excited or scared. My dad thought it was a good thing—my mom seemed to think it was a bad thing. I looked forward to having breasts (I assumed that's what *develop* meant), although I had no idea what they were called. Once in a while, we'd catch a glimpse of my mom's when she was feeding the baby, and I remembered how the meter-lady's (the woman who came to read the electric meter every month) burst out of the top of her unbuttoned shirt. She was most definitely a harlot, showing them off like that, but I still thought they were magical because they belonged to grown women. I knew that when I was a grown woman, I would be good, I would be magical, and I would not have to worry about being spanked anymore.

Not long after that, my dad started giving me *lessons* in how to be a woman. In the middle of the night, when everyone was asleep, he would tip-toe into the bedroom I shared with my two sisters, careful not to rouse them from their slumber across the room. He would climb into my single bed, shaking me gently awake, and cover us carefully with the heavy quilt that my grandmother had made for me. He started by explaining to me how the baby got into my mom's stomach—slowly, delicately, in whispers. "Now that you know that your mom is with child, I'm sure you have a lot of questions." I didn't actually have any questions, but I sleepily let him blather on, wondering why he had to talk to me in the middle of the night. "Every woman has a special spot in her body where babies grow and live until they are big enough to be born." His fingers traced lightly against my stomach to the round spot that was my womb, the two long tubes on the sides where the pre-made babies live, and finally down—to where the babies came out. "The father has special seeds that he puts inside here," he demonstrated by slipping his finger inside the place where the baby was to come out.

That woke me up.

"The seeds travel," I held my breath, wondering what on earth was going on—he pulled it out and traced back onto my stomach, "on the inside up to the womb where the mother's egg is waiting. Together, they make the new baby. Someday," he assured me, "you will have a husband who will put a baby in your belly, too. I know that it is your mom who should be telling you this, but she thinks you're too young, and so it's up to me." I really wished my mom would stop doubting me, but I was glad that my dad trusted me and believed that I was ready to be a woman. What he told me made my head spin, and I wasn't sure I believed it. First of all, I thought that babies had to come out of bellybuttons because why else would you have a hole in the middle of the exact place where babies lived? Secondly, we all knew that YHWH was the one who blessed people with babies when he thought it was time. Thirdly, how did fathers get seeds to come out of their fingers, and how did seeds make babies— I knew seeds turned into plants, but humans? Also, I wasn't looking forward to having a husband who would stick his finger into the place that even I wasn't supposed to touch. None of it made sense, but I listened because he said it was an important secret, and I wanted to prove to him that I could be both important and keep secrets.

It wasn't at all strange to have my dad in my bed. Because my mom was usually breastfeeding or caring for a toddler most of my life, when we were afraid (which was often), or sick, or couldn't reach the light switch to go to the bathroom, he was the one we called for.

I didn't expect that I would need more than one lesson, but it turned out that I did. My dad in my bed became almost a nightly occurrence even though I already knew everything I needed to know about having a baby. But my dad decided that I wasn't quite ready to fulfill my duties as a wife—it was important to practice. For a while, his focus was on *getting me used to* what it would mean to be married. This involved a lot of fingers slipping inside of me and hands and lips caressing my budding breasts. Then he added monologues about being a good wife, "Never refuse your husband," he whispered while breathing heavily into my hair, "when he wants to touch you or wants you to touch him—you need to learn how to touch your husband to keep him happy. It will be the most important thing you can do for your marriage. It will keep you from having fights like me and your mom do." I hated when they fought, which they seemed to do all the time, and I was relieved that there was a way around it. Up until that point, he had only touched me, but it was the night we spent together on the roof of the chicken coop, both of us in the same sleeping bag, a loaded shotgun by his side, that he decided it was time I learned how to do the touching. Naturally, he'd chosen me, his special girl, for his camp-out companion. Something had been killing the chickens, probably a fox, and my dad decided that he should spend the night on the roof to kill the thief. It would be like camping under the stars. Excited by the idea of adventure, my younger siblings jumped about, hanging on his hands, "Pick me, pick me," but he insisted that it had to be someone who could be very quiet and not scare the animal away. I knew he'd choose me, but I wished he'd chosen my big brother instead. Seemed like more of a man's job to me. Not long after we climbed into the sleeping bag, another lesson began, the most important one, he said. I curled up on my side to indicate that I didn't want any more lessons, but he took my hand anyway and guided it down to his part that no one was supposed to touch. He told me to squeeze it, and I did as I was told. It felt like a pickle. After a few minutes, he jerked away from me and said, "Whoa, that was close. I almost lost some seed. That would be a sin. The Bible says not to spill your seed on the ground."

"So that's where the *seed* comes from," I thought, "that's disgusting." I wanted to wash my hands, but we were on the roof of the chicken coop, and there was no water. I wanted to go back to the house, but it was dark, and I knew he wouldn't take me. I was too terrified to go by myself, especially with a wild animal killing the chickens. I wanted to climb out of the sleeping bag, but it was cold, and there wasn't another one. I curled up into as tiny of a ball as I could and went to sleep. The cold settled at the center of me, turned dark, and began to spread. After that, sleep became my coping mechanism. Any time I was scared, confused, or uncomfortable, I would go to sleep and know that when I woke up, it would be over.

The chicken coop wasn't the end—far from it. I started to wet the bed, which I'd never done before. It was a mortifying experience for a ten-year-old. Wetting the bed was what babies and little kids did. When I'd call my dad in, petrified and ashamed, he'd help me clean up and then take the opportunity to climb into my bed afterward to comfort me, even though I didn't want to be comforted. I would try to wiggle away or roll over to show him that I'd had enough practice and just wanted to sleep, but he would pull me firmly back, whispering, "I'm sorry, Honey, but you need to learn, and I'm the only one who can teach you." Often, right before he climbed back out again, he would sigh and say, "You are growing into such a beautiful young woman, but I need to remember that you don't belong to me. Your beauty isn't for me; it's for your husband. You need to help me remember that." I hoped he would learn to remember on his own. I started to think of those nights as any other lesson that my parents said I needed to learn, something I hated but tolerated, like learning to wash dishes or fold diapers because I had to do it; all the while, I imagined the other girls in all the other families were doing the same, muttering under their breath and rolling their eyes when no one was looking. I thought specifically about my best friend Yahanna, wondering if she hated it as much as I did. I wished she was still in Colorado so I could ask her. It didn't seem like the kind of thing I could write in a letter.

At first, I was happy to be my dad's special girl. It came with privileges. I was glad that he was depending on me and trusting me to be a secret member of a world that the other grown-ups thought I was too young to know about. I was so sick of closed doors, hushed conversations, and being told that it was none of my business because I was a child. The grown-ups seemed gleeful in their exclusion of me, and my dad was the only one who could see that they were wrong. He tried not to spank me so much, or when he had to, he'd pretend to hit me and tell me to pretend to cry. He took my side during arguments with my mom and always chose me to go with him for a quick trip to the grocery or hardware store. Once, when we pulled into Chet's parking lot, the small grocery store that was fifteen minutes from our house in Vineland, he shut off the ignition and then turned to me slyly. "If you want," he said, "you can go in without your head-covering—you know, just to see what it's like." I studied his face to see if he was serious. He was grinning again, that grin that turned his eyes to slits, while at the same time lifting his finger to his lips. "Shhh," meaning, again, our little secret. A waterfall of questions cascaded through my head. *What did that mean? Was he rewarding me for letting him teach me? How was this a reward? What would Mom think? Could I go to the lake of fire for doing something that my dad said was okay? Did this mean we were leaving the church?* My heart leaped at the thought, as much from fear as from possibility. If my dad said we were leaving, he was the boss, and my mom would have had no choice but to do what he said. I did wonder what being in the world was like, but I also knew that we would burn in the lake of fire. Curiosity got the best of me, and I left my head covering in the truck and followed him inside. It was unfamiliar to feel the sun on my waist-long hair, its beams radiating off the black pavement of the parking lot. The parking lot was mostly empty, but I glanced anxiously around anyway to see if anyone was looking at me. Once we were in the store, pushing the rickety cart down the aisle, my heart started to pound in my temples and pulse up into my throat. Everyone was looking at me! At least, it's what I assumed. I felt so naked and so ashamed that I climbed onto the bottom rungs of the cart, that spot reserved for bags of dog food or paper towels, and curled up, my knees hugged to my chest until we were back outside. Neither of us said a word as I quickly put my head-covering back on and released my pent-up fear in a sigh of relief. On the silent drive home, my dad would glance over at me and smile now and again, but he didn't say anything. I knew I was supposed to like him more because he had let me do something that my mom would never have, but the truth was, I wasn't sure I had wanted to do it, and although I didn't know it at the time, buried in the cascade of guilt and fear that was coursing through my insides was a bit of anger—and resentment, two feelings that I wouldn't be able to name for many years to come. I didn't want to have secrets from my mom, but I was already in way over my head, and in the grand scheme of our family, my dad was the one with the power, so it was better to have him on my side than my mom.

When it came time for my mom to have the baby, I just knew it somehow. It was a feeling I had deep inside, one that I tried to push away from, but that was overwhelming, nonetheless. I woke up that morning to a permeating, noxious smell in the house, and my stomach lurched. My dad had lit the coal stove even though it was the end of May, so the room would be nice and warm for the baby. The smell of the burning dust that had collected on the top over weeks of not being used made me feel sick. I came downstairs and peeked into the living room. My mom sat with her eyes closed, rocking methodically in the rocking chair, breathing rhythmically, and grimacing. She opened them briefly to look at me, "Good morning, angel." But she closed them again quickly, her forehead furrowing as she again focused her breath. The lights were low, and it was too quiet. I walked back into the dining room and ran into my dad. He was beaming as he said, "Today's the day. Soon you will have a new brother or sister! I've already called Maxine. She's on her way here." I ran outside to the outhouse and threw up. I didn't feel excited. I felt repulsed. Like I was somewhere I shouldn't be, like I knew something I shouldn't know. I wanted to get as far away as I could, as far away from him as I could. I was done being a secret grown-up. I may have been in on a secret, but it had begun to feel like a dirty secret, one that I should be ashamed of.

I returned from the outhouse with the vile taste of vomit in my mouth. My dad was in the kitchen telling Joseph, who was twelve, to walk over to the neighbor's house with the three little ones—Ruth, who was seven, Sara, who was five, and Nathan, who was three. I didn't give him a chance to make me stay, although I was certain he would try, and instead hurried out the door with my siblings and down the dusty road through the field. The neighbors were a church family, David, and Karen, and they had two children who were the ages of Sara and Nathan. David was one of the Elders, and they were a good family to have close to us. Karen loved having her house full of kids, and by the time we arrived, she already had an itinerary planned. We spent the day playing hide and seek, coloring and pasting, running around outside, eating cookies and milk, and singing bouncy kid songs like, *if you're happy and you know it, clap your hands.* Karen seemed to relish every moment, to sparkle with the magic of it all. I felt like a kid again, far away from the grown-up things that were happening at my house, and I was surprised to have enjoyed myself.

But too soon, the telephone rang with the call that told us that we had a new little brother, Enoch and that it was safe to go home again. We retraced our steps back through the field and entered our yard just in time to pass my dad, who was carrying something bloody in a bucket. I wanted to vomit again. I knew all about animal guts since I had watched goats, chickens, and sheep be butchered lots of times, but I couldn't imagine what bloody guts had to do with having a baby, and I wanted to disappear before he could take me aside to tell me. I took Nathan's hand and hurried past him and up the steps into the kitchen. As it was, I already knew more than I was supposed to know about too many things. Only, none of the grown-ups knew that I knew, so when they'd say, "You're too young to know about it yet," I'd think, *That's what you think.*

Yahanna was right; grown-ups could be pretty stupid sometimes.

10 AND THE PRAYER OF FAITH SHALL SAVE THE SICK

Our fascination with that giant concrete house had not yet worn thin. It had hallways and staircases to enhance our games, more rooms than we'd ever had in any house, and countless closets and nooks in which to play hide and seek. There was a long crawl space connecting my and Joseph's bedrooms upstairs that was about twenty feet in length. It was dark and spooky. We would dare each other to run along from one end to the other, bent over, dodging the bits of insulation and spiderwebs that hung down from the rafters. I ran like a rabbit being chased by a coyote every time I answered that dare because I *just knew* there was a demon living in there that was ready to tear me to bits.

Laycher constantly told stories about demons, and they were never far from my mind. Demons tempting him, demons poking him in the back and then flying out the window. Demons that looked like birds, demons that looked like cats. Then the other grown-ups would chime in with their demon stories, mostly always seen in cemeteries, but sometimes in houses and cars, and always at night. On those evenings, I would lie in my bed petrified, eyes fixed on the curtain that hung in front of the crawl space, waiting to see two glowing eyes, and when a slight breeze would make it sway, I would hold my breath and wonder if that demon would make it impossible for me to scream. If we saw a demon, we were supposed to say I rebuke you in the name of YHWH, over and over again until it disappeared or burst into flames or something. The name of YHWH was so sacred and so holy that something as vile as a demon would not be able to withstand hearing it. But I always worried that I wouldn't be able to say it loud enough or with enough authority to make it work. If you said I rebuke you in the name of YHWH, but you were still scared and didn't really believe it would work, then that demon would just laugh in your face. I didn't know how to not be scared. What if I opened my mouth, but no sound came out, the same as it was in my dreams when I couldn't scream or run?

During our second year living in that house, I had my own room for the first time in my short life. Jenna, the single sister who had been living with us, had moved out. I begged to move into her room—having my own room made me feel like I was actually as grown up as my dad insisted I was—so once I was there, I didn't want to admit that I was scared. I would wrap up tightly in my blanket and always, always, sleep on my back. I knew that if I slept on my side or stomach, I wouldn't see that back-poking demon coming and wouldn't be able to protect myself. It came into my dreams often, faceless, those dreams where I would scream and scream for help, but no sound would come out. It would shock me awake, and I would feel its evil presence just beyond the curtain, and I would sit and wait patiently for the sun to come up while my heart thumped so hard it felt like it would jump right out of my chest.

Although I was being tortured by nightmares and by my dad at night, daytime was pretty average. Joseph and I were learning how to shoot a bow and arrow. We would practice on hay bales behind the barn. The first time I tried to shoot, both of my arms quivered as I pulled back on the string. Then, when I released the arrow, the string pinched my cheek. But I kept practicing until I was steady enough to hit the bullseye we'd pinned to the hay bale, a white plastic trash bag with black and red circles drawn on it in magic marker. When we decided we were good enough to hunt, we planned to shoot a grouse. My dad had gone hunting a few times. Because he had been in the army, he knew how to shoot a gun and promised us that he'd have no problem getting a deer. We fantasized about what it would be like to have meat in the freezer all year long—but he never got one. We figured we'd try. A grouse was by no means a deer, but it was something. We knew we'd have to go far away from the house and be very, very quiet. We crept low to the ground on that dusty road between the cornfields, our bows slung over our shoulders, arrows in hand. The dirt was loose and powdery, with tire tracks that ran on either side of the sunburnt grass that grew in the middle. We thought that the birds could be hiding in that grass. The fact that we never saw one didn't shake that theory.

We spent a lot of time playing around in the chicken coop after collecting the eggs. The roof of the coop was so low that we could easily climb up onto it with a short ladder. We found it thrilling because rooftops were generally places where we weren't allowed to play. Sometimes when my dad or one of the brothers had to climb onto a roof to fix a leak, they would let us climb up there with them as long as we were very careful and stayed close to them. Those roofs were steeply slanted, like a triangle; walking on them was tricky, and maybe that's why it was exhilarating. But this roof was flat, so it was safe, and we loved to climb up there simply because we could. After a while though, we grew bored with just climbing up there and running around. We wanted to do something on the roof. So Joseph and I were sitting there, our legs dangling over the edge, swinging them absentmindedly, trying to decide what that thing to do would be. Just below our feet, there was a woodpile dumped willy-nilly up against the side of the chicken coop. "What if we moved all that wood up here," Joseph suggested, "we could stack it nice and neat. Pa and Ma would like it if it was all stacked by winter." We didn't stop to wonder if our parents would enjoy climbing a ladder every time they needed firewood, we were kids, and our brains didn't consider anything past the point that it would be fun to stack and it would be nice and neat—both positives on the face of it.

"Good idea" I hopped up to climb down the ladder.

"No, you stay up here. I'm stronger, so I'll climb down and throw the logs up."

Joseph turned and scurried down to the ground. The first logs flew neatly into my hands and from there to the pile that was beginning to grow on the roof. Then, he picked up his pace, and I missed one. The log launched past my hands and into my face. We both froze for a second. I was eerily calm, considering what had just happened, and all I remember thinking was that I needed to get to the house and that I didn't want Joseph to feel bad. He was always getting into trouble for hurting me, even though it was usually an accident.

I stepped gingerly onto the ladder and climbed down with one hand, the other pressed firmly against my left eye. Joseph tried to pull my hand away to assess the damage. "I'm sorry," he said frantically, "I didn't mean to. Are you okay? Let me see. You're okay, right? You're not going to tell Mom, are you?" I knew he was worried about me, and at the same time, worried about being in trouble. I hurried toward the house with him on my heels. The harder I pushed, the less it hurt. We burst through the door into the kitchen where my mom was cooking dinner, and I blurted, "I got hit with a log." I released my hand from my face, and my mom gasped. I hadn't felt all the blood before, but once I'd taken the pressure off, it ran freely, sticky and warm, down the side of my face.

Abruptly aware of the blood, and the pain, I bawled and screamed while my mom tried to clean my eye with a wet washcloth and seal the gash with two bandaids placed vertically over it. I could feel my face swelling up, and the ends of the bandaids were stiff and scratchy against my lower eyelid.

We didn't go to the ER. No matter how bad the cut, or bruise, or break, or flu, or fever, we never would. We would pray, and wait, and know that whatever happened was solely in YHWH's control. I had watched people accept YHWH's will over the years. One man cut clean to the bone of his leg with a chainsaw. I overheard Maxine recounting the tale for a small group of women gathered in her kitchen—I wasn't supposed to overhear, but I overheard a lot of things I wasn't supposed to—of how she had to cut his clothes off of him in the bathtub because he was bleeding so much, and how he drifted in and out of consciousness as she painstakingly picked out the bits of cloth and wood. After she'd cleaned the wound, she bound it as tightly as she could, put him in a makeshift splint made of slats of wood from the porch, and, aside from changing the bandage regularly, leaving the wound to heal as it would. He didn't die, and he did walk again. I listened intently, imagining the blood seeping out of the long gash steadily, filling the space around his body in the bathtub, red and sticky against his dark blue denim robe, Maxine bent over him, the man moaning and groaning, confused and in desperate pain, (I had a very vivid imagination) and it dawned on me that Maxine was the only one allowed to see other men besides her husband naked. Puzzled by that thought, I eventually made sense of it because, obviously, as Laycher's wife, she must've reached a state of perfection that set her above and beyond temptation.

As far as I know, only one person died for lack of medical care. It happened when I was about six. Timothy had diabetes and had to stop taking his medication when he joined the church and put his faith in YHWH. After he slipped into a coma, the elders prayed for him around the clock for days before he finally died. We, kids, weren't allowed to see him. There was no funeral, just men digging a grave behind the church building on Laycher's land to bury him while the women surrounded his wife inside, comforting and consoling her as she wept. I felt sad for his family, but I also wondered how he had sinned; what had he done to be struck down like that? I knew that sickness was YHWH's way of punishing us or getting our attention to tell us to change. The worse the sickness, the worse the sin. "He said he would chastise us if he loves us. You can't pray for just anyone. I prayed for Brother Timothy when he cut his wrists, brought him out of the hospital. Why is he gone now? His cistern leaked, and he never fixed it."

Timothy was a tale of warning. I never knew until this very moment, reading through the old notes from Laycher's sermons, that he had tried to commit suicide. That, of course, was the sin that he died for. I had no memory of him, only the memory of the solemn tone of any conversation about him. The only other body in the church cemetery was a man who had been electrocuted while on a ladder trying to disentangle his child's kite from the power line. He should have known better than to let his kids fly kites. They flew like birds in the sky, breaking the commandment to not make any graven images. So, I knew that his death was the wrath of YHWH, too.

I remember one other man from when I was little, about four or five years old, who stopped taking his medication but didn't die. He did end up back in the State Hospital, though. Roosevelt was a big man with an even bigger laugh, giant hands, and an infectious smile. We used to sit on his lap and play Paddy Cake. In fact, his favorite thing of all was to play with us kids, and the feeling was mutual; we looked forward to his visits.

We didn't know much else about him except that he wasn't like the rest of us. There was something wrong with him, but Laycher was praying for him, and YHWH was going to deliver him. One day after church, after most people had gone home, Laycher and a few brothers who were left were praying and talking in hushed tones, and for some reason, I was there with my dad. My mom and siblings may have been there, too, but I don't remember them. Roosevelt was sitting alone, agitated, rocking back and forth. Because I loved him, I wanted to know what was happening, but the brothers just kept sending me away every time I tried to get to him. They'd say, "No, go stand in the back of the church. He isn't safe to be around right now." I was tiny, frightened, and worried. I heard whispers about demons and fighting their voices in his head. They said when he opened his mouth, they could see the demon's eyes in the back of his throat. I didn't understand how someone who was so loving could be possessed by demons. They tried late into the night to cast the demons out, praying fervently, the hands of not only Laycher but two other elders laid on his head, his shoulders, his back. They spoke in tongues, eyes closed, brows furrowed, faces raised heavenward, and shook his body with the intensity of their prayer, but his rambling got worse, and he started to push back and to yell at them to stop touching him. They reached for him again, and he swung at them. He tried to stand up, and they pushed him back onto the pew.

I watched and listened silently as small children do, and I heard them say that they were getting worried he would hurt someone. Laycher shook his head in disappointment, "we have no choice. We have to send him back."

"Back where?" I asked my dad timidly.

"He's not getting better," my dad explained, "so we have to send him back to the State Hospital." I didn't know what the State Hospital was, but it sounded ominous.

Roosevelt's reaction to the plan confirmed my assumption. He cried and pleaded, "No, please don't send me back there; I can't go back. You don't understand. I want to be here; I like it here; I can do it, I promise. Just let me try again."

He reached out to no one in particular, his big hands opened wide, but then he turned to me, begging me not to be afraid, "Come on, Honey. Don't you wanna play paddy cake? Come on, like we always do. You're not afraid of me, are you? You were just sitting in my lap this morning. Tell them you're not afraid, Honey. Please tell them you're not afraid of me." I stood motionless next to my dad, his hand resting protectively on my shoulder. Roosevelt's arms dropped to his side, and water seeped from his eyes and ran down his cheeks. I had never seen anyone look so defeated and alone, and it made me so sad, but I was afraid, I was very afraid, not of him but of seeing the demons in his throat. I didn't go to him. I didn't tell them that I wasn't afraid. I didn't help. I just stood there motionless and mute. I remember the darkness of the night and the blue and red lights of the ambulance strobing round and round. I had never seen an ambulance up close before, only flying by on the highway. The men who drove the ambulance wore uniforms that looked like the police—I was afraid of the police. They loaded Roosevelt into the back; he had surrendered without a fight and was strapped down to a bed with handles on the sides that the men could pick up and move. They closed the doors to the back of the ambulance and locked them, and then they drove away. I watched it grow smaller and watched the lights flash further and further away until it was gone. It was one of the most heartbreaking things I'd ever seen. I held my dad's hand and cried and wondered why it was YHWH's will not to save him, why Laycher hadn't been able to cast out the demons and make him happy again even though he kept saying, I rebuke you in the name of YHWH?

Months later, as we walked along the edge of the park, I looked up at a brick building with bars on the windows. "What's that building?" I asked no one in particular.

"Oh, that's the State Hospital," someone replied. "That's where Roosevelt lives now."

I wondered why they put him in jail.

I turned to look again, craning my neck while being pulled along by my hand, feet tripping over themselves, the way we do when we're tiny and at the mercy of the bigger person who is hurrying along, even though we may want to stop and look.

11 THE SINS OF THE FATHER

The Colorado Department of Social Services kept a close eye on us. They hadn't found a reason to take custody of the children in the church yet, but they wanted one, or at least, that's what the grown-ups wanted us to believe. Years before we moved to the concrete house when I was seven and Yahanna still lived right down the road from me, one of Laycher's relatives had gotten a divorce. Even though divorce was a sin, in that case, we made an exception. Her husband, Eddie, had left the church and was telling all kinds of lies about Laycher and everyone else because he was mad and wanted to get back at her. He even attacked Laycher and beat him up so badly that he broke his ribs. I assumed that because Laycher was a prophet, he would definitely get a miracle, and so when he didn't, I was supremely disappointed and not a little perplexed. He was in bed for weeks and could barely breathe or walk. I asked him about it when we went to visit. He had a bandage wrapped tightly around his chest, and his arm was in a sling. He was sitting up in a hospital bed in the living room. The curtains were opened to let in the sunlight, the slanted rays landing somewhere near his feet. I stood next to his bed, timid at first, not sure if it was a question that I should ask, but I eventually garnered the courage. "Grandpa, why didn't YHWH heal you? Why didn't you get a miracle?"

"Well, Jita," he assured me, "It's not our place to

question his wisdom. He has his reasons that are beyond our understanding. Sometimes YHWH doesn't give us miracles because he's testing our faith to see how much we can bear and still believe in him." I wondered to myself if maybe it had to do with the fact that because no one else was a prophet, and Laycher couldn't lay hands on himself, there was no way to perform a miracle even though the rest of us were praying for him.

Eddie had reported the church to Social Services as a place that was neglectful of children, and they started to drop in at people's houses unannounced to check on the kids. They popped in at my friend Yahanna's house, and she hid in the shower while they argued with her mom. After a while, her mom was forced to bring her out and show that, yes, she did have severe, untreated eczema on her hands and legs, just like Eddie had told them. I don't know what the social workers did or said when they saw it, but they didn't take her away.

After that, we had Social Service drills the same way most people have fire drills. What do you do if they show up at the house? Well, in the concrete house, you run upstairs to the dark demon closet and stay utterly silent until someone comes to tell you that it's safe to come out. Every car that drove too slowly past our house could be them. They drove regular cars just like everyone else, not marked like the police, so you never knew. We would stop what we were doing and wait, poised for the sprint into the house. When the danger had passed and the car had driven by without even a glance in our direction, we would resume our spot in the plum trees, where we were getting a quick education about green plums and stomach aches. Our perch in the trees was a perfect place for a lookout and could be, we figured, a backup hiding spot in a pinch.

One perfect summer afternoon, we froze as a long, black Lincoln Continental turned on its blinker and floated slowly into our driveway. We held our breath in unison. There was no time to run, nowhere to hide—and we were all outside, even my mom. We scurried like mice, all five of us, to hide behind my mom, who was holding Enoch. We stretched out her skirt from either side, forming a curtain between us and whoever was going to get out of that car. I couldn't see what was happening, and I didn't dare peek. I heard my mom say, "Can I help you?" And then, after a few seconds, a full-throated laugh of relief as she recognized the man who was walking toward her.

"Don't worry, you can come out," she coaxed, looking back at us over her shoulder, moving first to one side and then to the other to extricate us from the folds of her skirt. "It's just your great Uncle Billy." We peeked out, first one little head, then two, Joseph bravely stepping into the open and then one by one, each of us following, eying the stranger suspiciously.

Uncle Billy, my grandma's brother on my mom's side, had just been passing through and decided to stop by. My mom hadn't seen him since she was a kid. He lived in California and had never been to visit her at the church. He was wearing shorts, so he couldn't come inside. Instead, we stood and chatted with him in the driveway. He made jokes, pinched our cheeks, and patted the tops of our heads while we smiled shyly but didn't say much. He kept saying, "I can dig it," which made us cover our mouths with our hands and giggle, *dig what?*

"So, this is where you live." He was looking up at the tall, white-washed wall with two windows upstairs and two downstairs facing the road.

"Yeah, we've been here for about a year and a half now, you know, with the family growing, we needed more space."

"I can dig it."

"And you dress—different—do you always wear that?" Gesturing to, well, the whole of us. "And the kids, too?"

"We do." My mom replied a little too enthusiastically. "The Almighty teaches us to be modest. It says in the Bible that we are to cover our bodies and our hair."

"I can dig it."

"And look at all these rascals," Uncle Billy squatted down to poke our stomachs and tickle us.

"All of them blessings from YHWH," my mom smiled.

"I can dig it."

The conversation went on like that for about an hour, and then, just as strangely as he had appeared, he floated back down the driveway and was gone. My mom was uncharacteristically happy.

It made me miss my grandparents.

Soon after, our time in the big house came to an end. The fire that forced us out ignited while my dad was away for a month. He was being publicly chastised for something he did, something that we kids were not allowed to know. All we knew is that Laycher showed up one day with one of the elders, David (the one who was our neighbor, whose house we went to when Enoch was born), and they, my parents, and Jenna (the single sister who had been living with us, the one whose bedroom I took), all had a very long meeting in the living room with the door closed.

We didn't like Jenna, and we didn't try to hide that fact from her. She was cranky and mean and constantly taunted us with the fact that she was the adult and we had to obey her, and when we told her we didn't have to obey her because she wasn't our mom, she told my parents we backtalked and stuck our tongues out at her, and we all got our mouths washed out with soap. I don't remember the tongue part, but we probably did it. She was a miserable person, in hindsight, probably depressed, maybe even something more, but we didn't know that then.

Before the grown-ups disappeared into the living room, I overheard David telling Laycher, 'She was walking down thirty-sixth lane crying, and she didn't have her head covering on." I knew thirty-sixth lane was about a forty-five-minute walk from where we were. "I stopped to see what was wrong," he continued, "and she wouldn't even look at me. She refused to get into the truck and said she was leaving [the church]. I asked her why she was leaving, and she said she didn't deserve to be here, that she was weak and a sinner. I finally talked her into taking a ride, and that's when she told me."

Told him what? I wondered, but that was all I would ever know until I asked my mom about it once I started writing this book. Jenna and my dad had been having an affair or had tried to, or it had almost happened or only happened once. My mom still isn't clear on the details; she told me that she hadn't wanted to know.

When the meeting was over, everyone left, and my mom cried and cried and cried. Then my dad cried, and then we cried because they were crying even though we didn't know why we were all crying. My dad went upstairs into my room and snatched up my set of Little House books. They had been a gift from my grandparents that he had reluctantly allowed me to keep, only because I'd begged, only because I was his special girl. We weren't supposed to read anything but the bible or stories that were based on the bible. He brought them down into the living room and one by one, threw them into the fire. He said that he had grown weak and let evil into the house, and evil grows when you let it. He said that things were going to have to change and that we needed to get holy again.

I cried harder as I sat and watched my books burn. I wanted to run upstairs and hide, but he made us all stay and watch. He wanted to teach us a lesson. I wondered what lesson we were supposed to be learning because he was obviously the one who was in trouble. He had done something wrong, almost wrong enough for Laycher to make us leave the church, but I was the one who was losing the only thing I had that was mine. When he finally let me, I raced up to my room and hid between my bed and the wall, curled into as tiny a ball as possible, and covered my head with a quilt. I couldn't really breathe in there, but I didn't care. I loved those books. I loved the stories, the black-and-white drawings, the whimsical covers. I wasn't supposed to love them—he told me so as they burned, that

I should be ashamed to be crying over something so worldly—but I did. Laura was rough-and-tumble and tough, a lot like Ruth, I thought, but Mary was my favorite. She was beautiful and fragile, and elegant. I wanted to be Mary. She was the oldest girl, like me. I would trace the drawings of her with my finger. The puffy dress cinched down tightly at the waist, her sculpted bosom rising above the tiny waist and meeting the delicate lace at her neck. I adored the books themselves, wrapped in soft covers all lined up neatly in their case. It was the nicest present anyone had ever given me, not that I'd received lots of presents, and I read them over and over again, my secret world that I retreated to as often as possible. And now, for some reason, because of them, or something else I didn't know about, my dad had been ordered to leave. I knew I should be sad about that, but I was sadder about my books.

Laycher gave my dad a choice—to leave the church immediately or to go live with Yahanna's family and *make himself right with YHWH*. Yahanna's dad, Jerry, was the pastor of our other church in Oregon. Her mom was my mom's best friend. My parents were shamed, and we were shamed. No other dad had ever been evicted from his own home and sent off to live apart from his family. My dad left on a Greyhound bus and called us two days later when he arrived. He was going to be there for a month. He would work with the brothers there and send home money every week. He would be monitored constantly and spend his time being circumspect, repentant, and in hours of prayer, becoming holy again. We settled into a comfortable routine without him. My mom seemed happier, more relaxed, lighter. She spent her time doing fun things with us that we didn't normally do, like playing kickball, softball, and tag. We took lots of walks, and she cooked us organic hotdogs for dinner and took us to the store to buy ice cream. It seemed like we had more money with my dad not there. I wondered why, but I didn't waste too much time trying to figure it out.

My dad was gone for the month of February, and in the dead of winter, the temperature often dropped suddenly. Brothers, single and married, stopped in periodically to check on us to make sure we had enough coal for the stove and to check on our food and household supplies. The water pipes kept freezing, and after days of painstakingly thawing them with a blowtorch, David decided to set up a kerosene heater (called a salamander; the brothers used them on their job sites in the winter) in the utility room pointed directly at the pipes. "Keep the door cracked," he told my mom, "we don't want the fumes to build up in that room." That night the water pipes didn't freeze, but the next morning, as we finished cleaning up from breakfast, Ruth ran naked and screaming out of the bathroom, where, from the tub, she'd seen flames leaping toward the window that was in between the bathroom and the utility room.

"Fire! Fire!" She panted.

My mom took a quick peek and then turned to Ruth, "Put some clothes on," she said, "you have time. Do it quickly." And then, despite having five panicking kids milling around her and holding Enoch in her arms, she calmly led us to the other side of the house, to the living room, and called the fire department while instructing us to collect our coats and walk outside. We were unnaturally giddy while we waited for the fire trucks. Sure, it was scary too, and I knew I should be worried about losing the house, but we'd only seen a fire truck up close once before. That time, the fire department had to come to our house, the same house, when my dad couldn't get the valve to close on the propane tank. He had jerry-rigged a hose from the two-hundred-gallon house tank to a smaller tank in the back of his truck because we didn't have money to fill the gas tank in the back of the truck, but we already had the propane in the big tank, so it made sense to use it. The truck could either run on propane or gasoline; it had some sort of converter or something. I could read the panic on his face and knew it was an extremely dangerous situation as we

130

watched him struggle with the valve that had turned icy white. We stood far away in case the whole thing blew up. When the firetruck came, the firemen were furious with my dad wondering aloud how he could be so stupid. "People doing stupid things waste our time and cause more dangerous situations than actual accidents." My dad reminded me of a scolded dog that day.

We waited for the sound of the sirens in the distance at our neighbor's house across the street. They'd seen the smoke, and all of us gathered in the cold out in the front yard and called to us to come over. My mom hesitated for a moment before ushering us across the street and through their door. We had never met them or been in their house because although they lived right there, they weren't in the church, so we weren't supposed to be friends with them. The TV was on in the living room, and I had a hard time turning away even though I knew I wasn't supposed to watch it. They were an older couple, probably the age of my grandparents, and they seemed excited to have kids in their house. They tried feeding us all kinds of goodies—cookies, candy, Coke, a sandwich—all of which my mom politely declined, explaining that it was against our religion. They shook their heads in bewilderment (how can food be against someone's religion?) but kindly let us stay until it was time to cross back over the road and assess the damage. The firemen said that most of the house only had smoke damage (it was a house built with solid, poured concrete walls, after all—even the interior walls), our things were okay, but the kitchen and porch, which were built of wood, were blackened skeletons. When we walked back in, it smelled like smoke. The cookstove was dripping with water, and anything that had not been in plastic was soggy and useless. The roof of the porch had holes burned into it; I looked through to the sky above. The rafters were black and gnarly—stark against the blue. The drops of water from the fireman's hoses glistened with small specks of sunlight. I shivered. Just like that, our house was gone.

A few days later, we moved to a house a couple of miles down the road. It was tiny, with only one bedroom, a living room, a kitchen, and a bathroom. We didn't care. We all slept on the floor of the living room with my mom. She liked it better that way, and so did we. When we were all together, I wasn't as afraid of the demons coming to poke me. I wasn't afraid of much at all until the cat died in the engine fan of our van. It had crawled up onto the engine to stay warm. When my mom started the van, the fan blades chopped the cat's head in half, and it fell onto the ground. Then Ruth had a nightmare about it, and after that, I couldn't even sleep with the whole family because I kept thinking about the dead cat and Ruth's nightmare about the ghost cat.

My dad came home early, not long after the fire. We didn't pick him up at the bus station; we met him at the church. He was sitting up front all by himself, and I thought he looked punished, but I couldn't tell if he was really holier or not. We ran to him, and he cried as he hugged us. My mom hugged him, too, but turned her head to the side, away from his face, away from his kiss. When we arrived home, he declared solemnly that we were all going to be stronger as a family and do everything we could to root out sin in our household. I knew that meant more spankings. Whenever my parents wanted to get holy, it always meant more spankings. He took me into the bathroom and closed the door to tell me he was sorry for asking me to help him when my mom was too tired to be a wife. "I promise, I'm all better now. I know I'll have the strength to resist temptation, but if I am tempted, if I come to you like I used to, I need you to remind me about what I'm saying now. Remind me that I almost lost my family, and I almost got kicked out of the church. I know that if you help me, I can do it." He smiled and reached out to me. I hugged him and turned to skip out of the bathroom. I was so glad that it was over, and I absolutely believed him when he said it was. I didn't like *filling in* for my mom. It felt like he thought I was his wife, too, but I knew I was supposed to be someone else's wife someday, and I really didn't want to be his wife. He kept his promise—for about a week when I sleepily felt him crawling back into my bed. "I'm sorry," he whispered, "your mom told me she would lay with me more, but she is still refusing. I just need you for a little longer until she stops being mad at me."

12 SECOND CHANCES

We knew that the one-bedroom house was too small. And even though it was fun to have giant sleepovers on the living room floor every night, it was time to move again. My mom wanted to move closer to the church; my dad wanted to leave the state. He was having meeting after meeting with Laycher, trying to convince him to let us move to Indiana to start another church. My dad assumed that since he went away and got holy in Oregon, his second chance should be that he would get to be an Elder. If Laycher would just believe in him, have faith in him, trust him more, then he wouldn't make mistakes. I had an instinct about it then, but now I know for sure that my dad would always blame his mistakes and falls on the fact that no one believed he could be any better. He was intensely wounded by the reality that he was one of the earliest members of the church, but it still hadn't earned him the title of Elder. It was a coveted position in the hierarchy, and I have no idea how Laycher decided who would be an elder, but he was most certainly never going to choose my dad.

Regardless, my dad thought he could force him to. First, he demanded, then he tried to reason, then he begged; my dad was good at whining and begging. "I hate Colorado with a passion," he moaned, "you can't grow anything here. It's dry, it's hot, the soil is so hard you can barely dig a garden bed, and if we do manage to grow anything, the bugs eat it before we can. We want to be self-sufficient, to grow all our own food, to use horses and buggies like the Amish. You know, to really *get back to the old ways*. We can't do that here. And my eyes, my eyes are so dry they hurt all the time." My dad had the perfect solution to all of his problems—the family farm in Indiana. His parents said they would give it to him as an inheritance (a bribe, really, to get him away from the church, a mission that my Grandma Jean was relentlessly committed to.) My dad saw it as a perfect opportunity to start fresh and prove himself. There was a wrenching, twisting feeling in the pit of my stomach at the thought of being that far away with just my family, shut off, not just from the world around us, but also from the world of the church, *completely alone*. I hated the idea; it terrified me. I think I somehow knew that if we were that far away, with no guilt hanging over his head from church, with no check-ins from Laycher, there would be no limit to what my dad could do. If he was the elder of a new church in Indiana, he could make whatever rules he wanted, and there would be no one to stop him. I was petrified that my dad would try to marry me (maybe in Indiana, they would let him), and then I would have to have babies like my mom, and he would make me his forever, and the thought made me want to wretch.

Laycher crushed the idea without even giving it a moment's consideration and said, under no circumstances, would he ever allow it, but my dad wouldn't give up. The more he pushed, the angrier Laycher got until he finally told him to *forget the idea or get out; I mean it this time*. Whenever Laycher wanted to be super threatening, he'd always say, get out, and people would crawl away from that command with their tails between their legs, so committedly did they believe that getting out was the worst possible option. My dad was furious and broken. My mom was hurt and desperate. My dad was dragging us down. We were cursed by his sin and she was drowning in the guilt of it. She wanted him to try harder to get closer to YHWH; he wanted her to stop judging him. My mom cried a lot. My dad consoled himself by crawling back into my bed.

Instead of giving us the family farm, my grandparents decided to sell the farm and give my dad a loan. The inheritance offer had been conditional—my Grandma Jean never gave anything without strings attached. If we weren't going to leave the church, there would be no inheritance, just a loan, and they would be co-owners of anything my parents bought. My mom *did not* like that idea, but my dad convinced her—did she want to live closer to the church or not? Laycher always preached against accepting gifts like that from unrighteous relations, but somehow it was all okay in the end. I didn't know or care how; I was just flooded with relief that we weren't moving to Indiana.

My dad used the loan to buy a mobile home and five acres of empty prairie a mile from the church, Laycher's house, and several other families who had moved to the same area within the preceding couple of years. A few square miles connected by dusty, gravel roads became the default home base for most of the people in the Colorado church. For the six years that I lived there, I could count on one hand the number of homes in that tiny area that weren't occupied by church families. With the land secured, we went as a family to look at mobile homes. After living our whole lives in one tired, old home after another, I couldn't comprehend the idea of a new home. I had developed a habit, which I continued to hone over the years, of not believing in anything good until it actually happened. I had deduced that my dad was a good talker, but it never really amounted to anything most of the time.

There were only a few trailers that fit within our budget, but that didn't dampen our enthusiasm. Of course, they were used, but to me, they looked brand new. Some of them were furnished—I liked those. One had bay windows in the kitchen with flouncy lace curtains around them. I thought about how lovely it would be to stand and do dishes looking out of those windows. It had a living room with light blue carpet, a brown sofa and lounge chair set, and a coffee table.

Both of the bedrooms had perfectly made beds, with light streaming in through more lace curtains. For a moment, I thought just maybe we could live in a place that beautiful.

The salesman led us into the next fourteen by seventy, a plain, empty tube with brown carpet everywhere but the kitchen, which had beige linoleum with brown and gray specks. He explained that as far as trailers go, this one was much sturdier and would not be as deadly in the case of fire, although, he admitted, a tornado would still completely demolish it. And it had three bedrooms instead of two, one for the girls, one for the boys and one for my parents. Predictably, my parents chose the plain, sensible one. I thought that someday I would choose the nice one, even if it wasn't sensible. One week later, a semi-truck towed it out to our patch of prairie grass and left it, the triangle tongue resting on a cinderblock, exposed and bare, as it would remain the whole time I lived there. It felt like an eternity before we could move in. We waited impatiently for the footers to be poured, and the hole for the septic tank to be dug, and the tank to be installed and buried.

Then we had to wait some more—for water. We would need to drill a well, but first, we'd have to find the right spot. My dad took two metal coat hangers, unwound them, and straightened them out. Then he bent them into an L shape. He explained that the best way to find water was to walk slowly and deliberately while holding the wires balanced on your hands, the long side of the L pointing directly forward, the short side folded over your hands, and pointing down. If you passed over a vein of water underground, the wires would swing to cross perpendicular to the vein. The stronger the swing, the bigger the vein. What we needed to do was to find a spot where two veins met at a crossroads of water, preferably not too far from the trailer, because plumbing was expensive and we were running out of money. We took turns looking for water. For the life of me, I couldn't figure out how the wires knew where the water was, but I'd had a lot of practice learning how to believe things that didn't make any rational sense. Every time I rested the cold metal against my hand and set off in a straight line, holding my breath, afraid it might upset the balance, I would watch again and again in disbelief as the wires, pointed straight ahead, would then swing suddenly and decisively to the side. We spent hours happily dowsing the entire five acres.

While we waited for the trailer to be ready, we lived in a house across the field. Unlike our trailer perched starkly on a bare patch of land, that house was nestled into a stand of old oak trees that shaded nearly every corner. There was a tractor graveyard in the back field with every rusty farm implement you could think of and an old garage full of hoarded junk. It was a gold mine of curiosities. We spent long, lazy afternoons out in the field *driving* the tractors and climbing around on the equipment looking for salamanders and snakes. We took turns climbing to the top of the old grain elevator with its leaning barrel and rickety ladder.

But my favorite pastime, by far, was rooting through the boxes of discarded books and clothes we found in the garage. The books were covered in mildew and mold and filled with lines of text that I was most definitely not supposed to read. They were romance novels, the steamy kind, with images of bodies and kisses and heartbreak saturating the pages, so real that they took my breath away and filled my stomach with shame. The clothes smelled like mothballs and rotten cardboard. They were ordinary clothes—jeans, shorts, dresses and t-shirts, silky satin nighties, and bras, but to me, they may as well have been exotic costumes, storybook costumes; they would never be real, just forbidden playthings. In spite of their degenerated state, they were treasure. Of course, I had seen people wear clothes like those, but they were *other*, far away, and all I could do was watch and wonder. There and then, I had nothing but time and no one turning my head the other way with their hand as I stared with curiosity. I was filled with a sort of tingly, shimmering daring, which helped to mask the guilt as I took them, one by one, out of the box and shook off the dust. I would study them.

I had never seen a bra before, and I didn't know what it was called, but it didn't take me long to figure out that the two cups were meant for breasts, breasts that I didn't have but wished I did. I glanced at the door, petrified that someone would discover me. It was barely ajar, illuminating my world just enough. I held my breath and listened for a bit until, satisfied that no one was coming, I held up the silky cream underthing by the straps and then carefully slid it over each of my shoulders. I pinched it tight in the back with one hand and looked down at the two cups protruding out from my chest and wondered if I would ever actually have a chest like that. I heard a door slam and jumped. My heart thumped in my ears as I ripped it off, tossed it back in the box, and raced out the door. I would go back to those boxes time and again to try things on over my own clothes and prance and twirl alone in the dusty dark, only a few beams of sunlight slanting in through the broken window. Then I would feel sick to my stomach because I knew I was committing so many sins—deception, envy, lust (for the ways of the world), and finally, disobedience—to YHWH because he told us to forsake the ways of the world and instead, I was trying them out. I would throw everything back into the boxes and race back out into the sunshine, trying to push the feeling far away, but it gnawed at me.

Eventually, my parents found the boxes and burned them.

13 DANIELLE

I was ten and had a new best friend who was eleven. It was the first time in three years that I'd had a friend my age, and I was ecstatic. I remember the first time I saw her at church, having just arrived from Oregon with her family. Her mom didn't have a husband, so they'd traveled with two of the single brothers whom they would also end up living with. That was weird because single moms were like single sisters who weren't supposed to be alone with single brothers—but like all of the other things that didn't make sense, I let it slip easily from my mind.

Danielle was dynamic. I didn't know the word dynamic when I was ten, but her larger-than-life presence that filled my world can be described in no other way. She breezed in on such a wave of confidence, serenity, and ease—I worshipped her instantly. I was shocked and in awe when she stood up with her siblings on the very first day, in front of the whole church, and sang songs that she'd learned at the Seventh Day Adventist church that they'd been saved from. She was new, and yet the transition from the world to the church didn't seem to faze her. I'd watched so many children join the church with their parents, and it was always traumatic, a transition punctuated with tears and hiding and running away—kicking and screaming when it was time to be baptized. Those kids never liked their new life better than their old one. They missed their old lives, talked about the way it used to be, and longed to go back. Not Danielle. She was perfect, embracing her new life like it was one she'd always known. I knew on that first day that I wanted to be her friend and was sick with agony at the thought that she may not want to be mine.

I'd worried needlessly. Danielle breezed into friendship just as easily and smoothly as she had into her new life. The grown-ups and the kids loved her just the same, and I took note because in my experience, I could either be liked by the grown-ups or the kids, but not both. She chose to spend her time with me, and I drank her in like a parched plant in the desert. I learned tons of new songs from her, and we all sang together in front of everyone at church, something I'd hated doing before, something that used to make my hands sweat, my heart race, and my stomach flip-flop. But it was so easy and natural when I was with her. And she was like me—she wanted to do the right thing—she wasn't like the other girls who were always doing things they weren't supposed to, and she didn't make fun of me for wanting to be good, we were good together.

It was always nearly impossible to get the moms in the church to let us hang out with each other as kids. They were afraid we'd *get up to no good*. Laycher would preach about kids being left alone and *getting up to no good*.

These children shouldn't be sleeping over at other houses [Read: sleepovers prohibited by the word of YHWH] *unless it is an emergency or if you're out of state. They start getting into things they ought not to do. You've got to watch them and guide them in the right way. If you want them to get to know each other, be with them. You should discourage the little ones from kissing the other little babies. We should greet one another with the right hand of fellowship. Satan starts working when they are young. Think of yourselves when you were young.*

Danielle's mom didn't seem to worry about that, so Danielle got to come over to our house a lot, although I never went to hers unless my mom was with me. My mom was much stricter about such things. She never thought anyone else would watch us as closely as she'd like them to.

She would chat with Danielle's mom in the kitchen, and we would go off to the barn and pet Bun Bun, the bunny, or walk down the road to see the neighbor's cows.

And, I suppose, we did *get up to no good* from their perspective. When Danielle came to my house, my mom would say, "Stay where I can see you," but she was always busy, so she couldn't watch us every single second. We'd sneak off to a quiet spot under one of those big oak trees, or sometimes, hide under the bunkbeds and talk for hours about everything and anything—including the bumps on our chests. I was profoundly embarrassed by the subject and could feel myself turning various shades of red, but it didn't seem to bother her.

"Did you get hard bumps on your chest yet?" she asked, surprisingly nonchalantly.

I wasn't sure what to say. I had never talked to anyone about them. "Yeah," I whispered, "they hurt. Do you know why they're there?" I pretended not to know, even though my dad had told me that it's what you get before you get your "woman bosoms".

"My mom says they're mammary glands." She said matter-of-factly.

"Mommy glands?" I asked, perplexed.

"No, mammary," she corrected.

"What's mamm-ar-y?" I had to sound it out, "And what's a gland?"

"I don't know; I'll ask my mom."

She would answer my questions when she knew the answers, and when she didn't, she'd just go ask her mom and then come back and tell me. She was brave to ask her mom. I never would have tried to talk to my mom about any of the things I talked to Danielle about. But that was Danielle, from my perspective, brave.

The trailer was finally ready, the dirt over the septic tank was freshly piled and tamped down, and the well sputtered water through the brand-new pipes as it struggled to keep up with the demand of a large household. Fully moved in, I felt strangely secure, knowing that because we owned this new home, we wouldn't have to move again. I settled into a routine of school (we were now so close we could walk to class), chores, and spending as much time as possible with Danielle. For a short while, I forgot about keeping the grown-ups happy; plus, since Danielle was older than me, they had started to depend on her for leadership, which was a welcomed reprieve. I no longer had to set the example for the younger kids—I could just follow hers—and follow I did. I turned back into a kid for a while, a very pious kid, following her example, but a kid nonetheless.

But alas, not a year passed before, just as suddenly as she had come into my life, she was gone; and I definitely didn't see it coming. It happened early one morning before school. She showed up to school with her whole family and a fully packed car, a trailer hitched to the back, and bags and boxes belted to the roof. She grabbed my hand and dragged me into the bathroom, "Quick, we don't have much time—I barely talked my mom into bringing me here." She closed the door and locked it behind us. Her face was puffy and red, and her eyes were damp. I knew that something really bad was about to happen. Tears started before I even knew why.

"Dani, what's going on? Why are we in here? Why are you crying?"

We were both sobbing and talking over each other. "I'm so sorry," she was saying, "it's not my choice; I don't want to go. She's making me go."

"No, you're not leaving, please, you can't. Not really, not for good, right? Why? What happened?"

"I don't know. It doesn't even make any sense. My mom says she's just lost her faith. She doesn't believe anymore; she can't do it. But I haven't, I do believe. I'm going to keep on believing."

"No, Dani. It doesn't work like that; you know it doesn't. If you leave, you're a backslider, and that's even worse than just being a sinner."

"No, I asked my mom. It does work. I'm not going to do anything differently. I'm still going to wear long dresses and head veils, and I'm still going to pray and obey the word. She said I can still worship even if I'm not here. Take this," she shoved a note into my hand, "and if you don't hear from me, remember what I've said; keep this so you'll know I'm serious."

Her mom was banging on the door. We clung to each other and made promises of staying the course and seeing each other again when she was old enough to leave her mom. She insisted she'd write if she could do it without her mom finding out.

I did keep the note, and I read it so many times that the pencil faded and it fell apart at the folds. And I believed her when she said she would keep the faith even though her mom was dragging her away. I hoped that because she was a kid and it wasn't her choice, YHWH would bend the rules a little, but deep down, I knew it would not be enough.

"*Consider Lot's wife, she didn't heed the word, and she died. The backsliders are the same way. You can keep on with them, but you shall surely die. The ones who left and cursed the church, they became sick and died.*" (In the Bible story about the fire that destroyed the cities of Sodom and Gomorrah, Lot was told to flee the city and not look back, but his wife didn't listen—she looked back and turned into a pillar of salt. In referencing people who died after leaving the church, Laycher was talking about a former brother who had gotten cancer after he left.)

I knew Danielle wouldn't curse the church, so she wouldn't die, at least not right away. But I also knew that no matter how many rules you followed, if you didn't follow them in the church, it didn't matter. You couldn't live outside the church and still be good. I didn't want my best friend to go to the lake of fire—I didn't want her to be struck down. I was inconsolable. I disappeared into myself while pretending to be okay—being an angel. There were two of me, the one that everyone loved and encouraged and the one that was slowly suffocating, panicked, terrified, and confused. I felt like I was falling into a dark vortex that I couldn't climb out of. I took over her role, took back my old role, expanded a little to carry on her legacy of leading the other kids in singing. I tried to be as brave as she always was, but I never felt that I quite measured up.

14 BLOOD AND BIRTH

It showed up without warning in the summer of my eleventh year, and as I sat and watched the blood dripping into the toilet, I had a dilemma. Of course, I already knew about *the time of the month* from my dad, but he wasn't supposed to tell me, and my mom didn't know that I knew, so I had to decide, rather immediately, what I was going to say. I called for my mom with as much panic in my voice as I could realistically fake. "Something is wrong with me," I whispered as she came to my side. I leaned to the side to show her the toilet bowl, "I think I'm dying, I'm afraid, Mom, am I dying?" (I may have overdone it slightly, but I was trying to sound exactly like I thought a girl would sound if she found herself suddenly bleeding).

Mom assured me I was not dying, "Oh, my little girl," she sighed resignedly, "I'd hoped this wouldn't happen for a long time." I wished she wouldn't call me *little girl*; I was far from it, especially now. Then she went to the cabinet under the sink where she kept the maxi-pads. I knew what they were because my dad had already shown me. She showed me how to use them and then sat on the tub to give me a very brief overview, with as little detail as possible, about how my womb was practicing to have babies. Then, she got up and left.

It was over. I was relieved, momentarily ecstatic—I was really a grown-up now—then horrified. The cramps were debilitating; the pads were messy and always leaking, and I now had to carry a purse with me everywhere I went. I had waited forever to be allowed to have a purse, but now, I hated it and the attention that came with it. Grown-ups eyed me suspiciously, and the little girls would follow me around, even to the bathroom. They would stand by the door and try to figure out what I was doing in there. I would tear open the packages as quietly as I could, but the sound practically screamed around me, and I was sure everyone could hear it. They would pepper me with questions—why did I get to have a purse and they didn't? Why did I have to take it to the bathroom with me? Why wouldn't I let them see what was inside? I wasn't allowed to tell anyone—they were too young to know about it yet—so I would dodge their questions and make my way back to the safety of the grown-ups where they all hated to be, but I wanted to hide from everyone. I was feeling Danielle's absence acutely—I knew I would have been able to talk to her about bleeding and maxi pads.

 I took refuge in school and in the books that I was allowed to read. The Mennonite publisher that supplied our schoolbooks also provided our storybooks. Although we weren't Mennonite and our doctrine was far more restrictive, they were the only ones who published books that were close enough to our doctrine that we could use them. They were Bible-based, and so were okay to read as long as Laycher wasn't on one of his rampages. Sometimes we had to burn all of our books on a giant bonfire in the backyard of the church, but then he'd change his mind again, and we'd slowly replace the ones we had burned. As I grew older, the stories told in those books were less about dogs and ducks and building snowmen and more about kids my age learning important lessons about lying, cheating, and rebelling against their parents. There was an obvious moral to every story. I was starving for anything pertaining to kids my age, so although the stories were prescribed and highly curated to present young men and women in godlike images, I devoured them anyway. I particularly enjoyed the stories about boys and girls together at a dance, boys and girls daring to hold hands in the dark, boys and girls blushing as they glanced at each other across the room. There was always a lesson in those ones, too, usually a reminder about how important it was to let God, parents, and church leaders guide your love life, but it still gave me a thrill to read them. However, if my mom found out about those parts of the book, she would glue a sheet of paper over the pages or use white out to cover them up. We didn't have dances, we didn't date, and we most certainly didn't allow adolescents to hold hands. We also had to white out all of the names of blasphemy (God, Lord, Jesus) and write YHWH in their place. Reading the names of blasphemy would defile our minds. Whiting out the offending words was a job that often fell to me, one that I found oddly grounding and pleasant.

I had a hard time reading the Bible—it never made much sense to me. The wording was odd, the verses repetitious, and the stories either boring or terror-inducing. The Pilgrim's Progress, a book written in 1678 by John Bunyan, was supposed to be about a metaphorical journey, I think, and although I did read the whole book more than once, I read it literally, with all the imagery my vivacious young mind could conjure. All I really remember of the storyline is: a man was on a journey to somewhere, up and down mountains—rivers of fire? Demons? Tests?

The Martyr's Mirror, a book first published in Holland in 1660, had pages that were littered with putrid, gruesome tales about the persecution of true believers by the Catholic church. There were no restrictions on my reading it, and at night I would fade off into an unsettled dreamland, my panicked brain riddled with scenes of limbs being torn from bodies by implements of torture. Bosoms branded with red-hot irons, men and women burning at the stake and being ripped to shreds by hungry lions. I knew that someday we would be persecuted, too. When it was time to march out of Babylon, we accepted the assumption that we would be asked to endure the same torments that were in that book. Learning about it was a way to prepare ourselves, to remember that no matter what we were suffering, we couldn't denounce our faith, or we would go to the lake of fire, which would be worse than any amount of torture and pain that the beast could inflict in this life. I wasn't sure I could do it, and I wondered if there was a way to practice being able to endure torture.

Sometimes my dad would make up stories about the great march out of Babylon (the US). I was never clear about where we would be marching *to*, but I assumed Israel, us being the lost tribe and all. I would also take a second to wonder how we would march across the ocean, but figured that YHWH would simply part it like he did the sea for Moses and his people—I hoped Laycher would get his miracle-working figured out by then. Seeing as how I had not yet witnessed a miracle, I worried that when he pointed his staff at the ocean and commanded it to part, nothing would happen, and then, of course, we would get caught and tortured.

They were our bedtime stories, lying around my dad on the living room floor, chins cradled in our hands in rapt attention, my mom sitting in the rocking chair nursing the baby, or knitting, the fire flickering intently in the wood stove. It was our together time, our family time. The stories usually began, "It was the middle of the night..." detailing the final calling—the persecutions, which were going to be our trials before the second coming—and the moment we were always waiting for, a physical march, fleeing our homes with only the clothes on our backs, running away from an enemy that had no form except that it was the beast, seeing the cities burning in the distance, being caught by the beast and having to endure horrific tests of faith. In those stories, he conjured up fantasies of ancient stone prisons, damp and cold, where we would be chained to the wall and left to hang, fed on moldy bread and dirty water, or sometimes not fed at all. I knew from our once-a-week fast (fasting—an essential exercise in denying the needs of the flesh), a practice that came and went with our *getting holy* phases, that I was really bad at it, and I wondered how I would be able to go for weeks without food and still not denounce YHWH. I would snap back to the present as my dad continued his tale. Relentlessly, the agents of the beast would drag us from our cells, burn us with hot irons, dunk us in cold tanks of water—I needed to learn how to hold my breath, I noted—slice us with knives and stretch us out on *the rack* (an instrument of torture I had no difficulty coaxing out of my pulsating imagination and with the help of imagery from The Martyrs Mirror—a rusty old contraption with lots of gears and wheels and a crank to tighten the four chains attached to our arms and legs), slowly pulling our limbs from our bodies trying to get us to let them stamp 666 on our foreheads. After all that, we would be chained back to the wall, slumped over, barely skeletons, all except my dad, who would have to be tortured more because he was the man. Predictably, a guard who'd been inspired by our commitment to our faith would decide to set us free, but he could only free the women and children. We would have to flee quickly and quietly through dark tunnels underground. As my family was escaping, I would turn back, wailing dramatically, "I'm not leaving without my Pa!" I would race back to the prison cell and let them chain me back up.

I hated those endings. I knew I'd be the first one out the door and not look back for a second. I also knew that meant that I was a very bad daughter.

I turned twelve, and my mom was pregnant again. That time, I knew the moment she started throwing up. I knew it was time to step up and take on as many chores as I could manage. I was at the point where I could clean the house on my own and even cook a simple dinner, with my mom overseeing my time at the stove from the couch or sitting at the kitchen table. I would start early in the morning, going through the motions that were so familiar to me—making beds, picking up laundry, hanging laundry, folding laundry, washing beans and putting them in the pot to soak for dinner, rolling out tortillas, peeling potatoes. Thirty-three years old and carrying her seventh child, my mom was exhausted, more so than during her previous pregnancies. She was barely sleeping at night, which would leave her in tears during the day, and I was happy to be her right-hand girl. I could sew and knit and was learning how to spin yarn. It was easy to fill my day, and I was glad. It kept me from feeling frantic and lost. Her belly grew, and once, when the wind blew her dress tight against it, I remember thinking it looked exactly like she had a kickball stuffed up there. It was right around then that my dad took me aside one morning, "I'm sure you've noticed that your mom's gotten really fat. That means she's going to have the baby soon, and I think that this time you should be there." My stomach twisted into a tight knot. "You've been a big help lately, and it would be good if you were around to help when she has the baby. I think your mom would be really grateful."

You'll be grateful, I thought. I was absolutely certain that my mom wouldn't want me anywhere near her when she had the baby. I thought about the things he whispered when he was teaching me about what it meant to be a woman. I was only six years away from when I could get married (Laycher's nieces were married at eighteen and nineteen, and one was already pregnant when she got married—a fact I learned after leaving the church), and because I was beautiful and virtuous, he said, the brothers would be lined up at his door. "Sadly," he'd mourn, "one of them will take you away, my little girl. It will break my heart, but I'll have to let you go." Next, he droned on about how it was time I learned what was in store for me as a wife and mother; it was time that I witnessed it first-hand. He tried to put his arm around me, but I ducked away. He was trying to make me into her again, his second her. He was trying to suck me into their world, to remind me that it was the three of us, not the two of them, at least until someone came to take me away. I told him that I didn't think my mom or Maxine would want me there.

"It's not up to them. I'm the head of the house. We may need you to grab a washcloth or a glass of water."

"Isn't that what Roksana does?" (Maxine's niece was training to be the next midwife)

"No, she needs to watch and practice if she's going to take over when her aunt gets too old."

"Well, then you can get the water."

"No." He was getting impatient with my impertinence. "I'll need to help hold your mom's legs or wipe her down or change the sheets when her water breaks."

Hold my mom's legs? Water breaking? What on earth was he talking about? My dad had taken it upon himself over the years to educate me about everything that happened *before* birth, but never anything *about* birth. I could see there was no getting out of it, and I spent the rest of her pregnancy dreading the end. When it was time for the baby to come, I could scarcely breathe. I waited for my dad to send my siblings away and make me stay. But, before he could do that, my mom called me back to her bedroom and asked gently, between measured breaths, if I would please walk the younger kids across the field to David and Karen's house. "Yes," I said, "Of course, anything you want"— *thank you, thank you*—I wanted to cry tears of relief. Instead, I quietly and quickly gathered up the kids. I felt my dad's eyes on me as I hurried out the door, but I knew he wouldn't dare stop me because he, too, knew that my mom would have been appalled that he'd wanted me there in the first place.

I loved my little brother, Samuel, from the instant I held him. I had never seen anything so consumingly adorable, and we all smothered him with kisses and hugs until my mom had to pull us off before we suffocated him. I was capable of doing everything but nursing him, and I did. I adored playing with him on the floor and making him smile.

I loved rocking him to sleep and then carefully laying him on the bed...slowly...slowly, a little at a time, his tiny body pressed to my chest—and then, after settling him on his back, backing quietly away, one tip-toe step after the other. I loved it when he started to roll over and tried to crawl. I loved carrying him around propped up on my hip, just like the grown women. Luckily, I didn't have to change his diaper because that was disgusting. Instead, I had to help potty train my other brother, Enoch, which was also disgusting, and help wash and fold all those diapers.

15 FASHION IN A FISHBOWL

How can one know, when writing about the past, what matters and what doesn't? I slog through some of these chapters, like plodding through sticking, sucking mud, one foot in front of the other, always the details I don't want to see vibrant and singing, while the ones I need, the ones that balance out the gloom, disappearing into a thick fog. It is into that fog that I wander now, with days and weeks in between that run together like a sentence with no punctuation. I want it to all fit neatly into *a paint-by-numbers*, but instead, it's a watercolor without form that won't stop bleeding at the edges, the colors blurring into each other, refusing to be trapped.

Memories weigh so much; they're tricky and contorted. They tease, with brief glimpses of clarity. And, of course, memories aren't linear, but my journey through them is. I can think of my life as a ruler with lines marking the days, months, and years, all marching along in some kind of perfectly ordered predictability. I'm moving into the twilight zone now, of my memories, and I say that in a literal sense because twilight is the time of day when nothing is quite as it seems, and your eyes and mind can play tricks on you, as can your memories. I am painfully aware of this as I pick through the rubble of those years. My teenage years are so much more muted than my early childhood; there are large spaces that are simply blank. So I jump from stone to stone of big events, and impactful moments, hoping to build a working storyline.

As I spend so much time focused on memory these days, it is literally the lifeblood of what I am doing here. I am constantly trying to understand how it works and why sometimes, it doesn't. I've been forced to retrace every stage of my existence to try to breathe life back into moments that have long passed. Those times when it feels like my memory was simply extinguished, purely blank, haunt me. Sometimes my childhood friends or one of my siblings will say, 'Remember that time you said this, or you did that, and then this happened?" And I will try, try to remember, try to let their images sink into my brain to resurrect that thing, but no, there's nothing. Usually, if someone brings up a memory that you've forgotten, you can find it again with their help because even if you've actively forgotten, it is still stored somewhere. For me, that isn't the case. There is simply nothing. I think I finally know why. It has to do with the tunnel that forms when you cease to live and begin to simply survive. Survival mode, or flight or fight mode as it is also called, created a world for me in which my vision of my life shrunk down to simply getting through whatever was taking place right in front of me. That tunnel didn't allow me to fully experience everything that was happening on my periphery or even more so, to register and retain it. And so, this wall that I feel like I've been beating my head against now makes sense, but it still shows no signs of crumbling.

Deep in those moments of tunnel vision was right around the time in my life that I met Gwen. Gwen showed up right before Samuel was born, and she taught me how to break rules. Not big rules, not the kind that would get me into trouble, just the little ones, the ones that annoy, the ones that I would learn were preferences rather than rules. Gwen was more than a decade older than I was, but I didn't mind. At twelve, I had already begun to insist that *age is just a number*, especially when people tried to use my age to put me in a box, or to exclude me, or paint me into a corner. Of course, I didn't know what I was pushing back against; I just knew that every time someone said I couldn't be, or do, or understand because I was only twelve, I felt like they weren't seeing me or believing me, or even trying to hear. I felt invisible and dismissed. Gwen was different. She was timid and reserved when she first arrived from Kansas City with two brothers who had been out there witnessing. She'd met them there and, in short order, had packed her things and driven back with them. And although her smile was a genuine, if not shaky, smile, she seemed terrified to me. It happened a lot. People would drop everything, uproot their lives, say good-bye to their families, or sometimes not say good-bye, and follow the brothers back to that wretched, little town of Boone; they would get baptized, then freak out and bolt, usually in the middle of the night or sometimes in the middle of a sermon. Gwen had dropped everything and come all the way from the Midwest, all of her things packed into her tiny Datsun. She had *that look*, and I knew if I didn't do something fast, she might run.

She needed a friend. After making and losing friends repeatedly, I'd become quite good at it. Since I'd lost Danielle, I'd tried and failed to be friends with some of the single sisters but always ended up on the outside again, a kid who didn't quite measure up, always caught by surprise when something I'd said to them would come back to me from in the form of scolding or admonition from my parents and Laycher, or mockery from Maxine. Those ladies *could not* keep secrets. I learned how to be cautious and guarded for a bit, but then I was also easily fooled into trusting them again. And so, the cycle repeated, often. I know now that I was simply a kid who always wanted to see the good in people. When they said they were sorry, I believed them and forgave them, and trusted they wouldn't do it again.

And then, there was Gwen, alone, scared, fresh, and impressionable, everyone wanting a piece of her, hovering, smothering. I knew I had to step up and help ease the onslaught. From the beginning, she treated me like nothing more or less than a friend, an equal, and in true form, I worshipped her and wanted to be her. We bared our souls to each other, talking for hours about everything and anything, from last night's sermon to our sewing projects to the way the sun looked shimmering down through the sparse leaves of the two young trees growing on the postage-stamp church lawn. We laughed together, sang together, baked, canned vegetables, and took long walks on the dusty tracks through the shriveled grass. We screamed like banshees in the middle of an empty field just because, for once, we wanted to feel what it was like to let it all out, to not be meek and quiet, to not control ourselves, to give our pain and frustrations a voice, a loud shrieking voice. I remember the first time we did it and come to think of it, it was probably the last time as well. I don't recall the exact conversation, only that I was swimming in that feeling you get when everything has simply gotten to be too much, when there's a giant lump in your throat, one that won't go away no matter how much you swallow, when you've reached a boiling point, but the lid is on tight.

"Why don't you just scream then?" Gwen suggested.

"What do you mean, scream?"

"Like right here, right now, in the middle of this field."

"I can't do that."

"Why not, who's going to know? Who's going to care?"

"I don't know…I just…I never…I don't think my mom…"

"You're mom's not here. We're in the middle of any empty field. If you need to let it out, let it out."

"Really? You're serious."

"Come on, I'll do it with you. On the count of three— one, two, three."

I screamed from the deepest parts of me, screamed like my existence depended on it, like when the sound ripped through my abdomen and chest, it would vanquish the turmoil. Then we flopped down in the scratchy grass and laughed until we cried.

We may have been in the middle of a big, empty field on the prairie, but it was a field that was surrounded on every side by people we knew. Every church trailer on the block heard our bloodcurdling cries, and when we arrived at Karen's house ten minutes later, she exclaimed, "Good gracious! What on earth was that all about?"

Gwen smiled amusingly, "We were just letting off some steam."

"Well, find another way," Karen admonished, "Sisters shouldn't walk around screaming in fields, and plus, I thought something was wrong, that you'd been bitten by a rattlesnake or something. Please don't do that again!"

I *really* wanted to do it again, I wanted to do it every day, but I didn't because they told me not to, and even though Gwen didn't see the harm in a little cleansing howl now and again, she complied.

I told Gwen my secrets, and unlike with the other sisters, they never came back to me from someone else's mouth. And yes, she showed me that some rules were meant to be questioned, bent, and sometimes broken—like sewing rules. My mom had taught me to mark every mark, pin every seam, stitch on the line—follow the pattern. Gwen insisted that sewing was a creative process, one in which you could really do whatever you wanted; however you wanted. You could even make anything you wanted without a pattern. It drove my mom crazy and made me feel deliciously daring. The other ladies were annoyed, jealous, and hurt because they wanted me to tell them everything like I used to, but I ignored them instead. Because what I couldn't tell them was that they could never be Gwen. She built me up; they tore me down.

Gwen had a best friend, Patrick, who she had left behind in Kansas City. He was madly in love with her, and a few months after she'd settled in with us at the church, he appeared on her doorstep, ready to commit, determined to be baptized. Immediately, Laycher sent him to live in Oregon. It didn't matter how much he loved her; they weren't allowed to marry, *"and the rule still stands that no one shall marry who has not been here at least one year to clean their minds and bodies."* Laycher didn't like it when people fell in love on their own. Then they would be tempted to sin, so sending one of them away was the standard practice.

I knew Patrick would be lonely and heartbroken, and might start having doubts about his conversion, so I acted quickly and decisively by sending him a letter. My mom read it before I sent it like she did all of the letters I wrote to men or boys. I wrote in pencil just in case there was something she wanted me to change. Patrick wrote back instantly and became my most reliable pen pal. On Sabbath Days after church, I would race to the mailbox, giddy and breathless, hoping for a letter, and deflate with disappointment when it was vacant. His letters were always three or four pages long, full of passion and zeal for his new faith, or sometimes riddled with minute details of his gardening adventures, the bloated slugs that slid across the stones by the river, or about being chased by giant insects in the night while everyone laughed at him. I loved the way he wrote them on unlined paper, and halfway down the page, his sentences would begin to slant down to the right until, by the end, they were almost sideways. I wrote my letters on notebook paper, sentences marching in a straight line, letters perfectly formed, just like I'd learned in school—I had never imagined doing it any other way.

I hadn't known Patrick well before he moved, but because of our correspondence, he was quickly becoming one of the most important people in my life. I adored the fact that he loved Gwen, and I hoped that someday my two best friends would be together. If Gwen taught me how to rebel in little ways, Patrick taught me how to be a revolutionary, to rebel in bigger ways, to embrace questions and demand answers. But that would be a long time coming.

Head coverings were a great way to test out rule bending.

Head coverings could be irrationally infuriating. They were always too tight or too loose, always slipping back and twisting. I was constantly fiddling with my head covering, pulling it forward and backward, trying to get it to stay put. I ended up with a matted bit on top of my head that was excruciating to detangle at the end of the day. I tried lots of things to fix it. High ponytails made my head covering stick out in the back, and low ponies didn't catch that short hair on the top that always turned into a knot. Finally, at one point, I learned to French braid, and that seemed like the perfect solution until Laycher decided that braids were an adornment, like jewelry, and commanded that we stop using them. That rule came and went depending on his moods and who he was letting whisper in his ear at the time. So, I'd stop braiding my hair and wait for him to change his mind back and then braid it again.

I never cut my hair. We, women and girls, weren't allowed to cut our hair under any circumstances, not even bangs or a split ends trim. Men weren't supposed to cut their hair either, but Laycher changed that rule if their hair was *getting long like a woman's*. Being effeminate was an abomination. Guys had to have full beards, too, because it was a sin to have a face that was *soft like a woman's*. Anything that made a man *like a woman* was an abomination. I'd had my head covered ever since I was a baby. We had a barrel of old baby clothes that we carted around from house to house. Sometimes we would dig through it and ooh and aah at how tiny we used to be. In that barrel was my first head covering from when I was an infant. It was made of off-white muslin and covered my head and the top of my body, like a sack, with little holes for my arms and my face. We covered our heads to tell the world that we were pledged to, and sanctified by, YHWH. As we grew older, it was also to prevent us from seducing men with our hair. If they lusted after us because our hair was uncovered, it was our fault because we had tempted them. That's what Eve was, the original temptress, but not the only example in the Bible of how sly and wonton women could be. There was also Jezebel, that pagan princess I mentioned previously, who was married to Ahab, a king of Israel. The more power she sought, the more chaos ruled in the kingdom of Israel. A woman with power equals disaster every time. Our hair would give us power over men, and so if we willingly *flaunted our glory*, we were just as wicked as Eve or Jezebel.

Any time I left the house, I never went without my head covering. When I was at home, I wore it if I was praying, which we were supposed to do always. If a visitor showed up at our house unannounced and I didn't have it on, I raced to find it.

The quest for the perfect head covering was ongoing, and despite our isolation and the war against vanity, fashion, in some iteration, was alive, and trends abounded in our world. Whether it was the type of fabric we were using to make our clothes or the color and style of the clothes themselves, there was usually someone who would start a trend, and the rest would follow. Gwen was a trend starter, and since I was her mini-me, I repeated every single trend she started. My dresses grew wider and wider until they practically swallowed me whole, and my head coverings morphed into long pieces of cloth that I draped over my head, one side hanging short to my waist, the other reaching long down past my knees. I'd take the long end and throw it over the opposite shoulder, which created a tight wrap around my head and the dress that was swallowing me whole. I could barely move with my arms tied down by the wrap, but since Gwen did it, I learned to love it. And finally, right before I left home, I started my own trend by stuffing my hair into a large beanie hat. When the grown-ups gasped in shock and dismay and told me to put on a real head covering, I retorted drily, "The Bible says to cover our hair—my hair is covered."

But I'll get to that later.

So, the trends came and went, just like in the real world. They ebbed and flowed. The prairie dress obsession that is currently sweeping the fashion world makes me cringe because I wore mostly prairie dresses over the years—even bonnets—tragically. During my favorite stages, we would park ourselves at our sewing machines and stitch together dresses with more daring silhouettes; panel dresses or drop waist dresses instead of balloons, pastel colors instead of grey, blue, or brown, and maybe even a ruffle or two, and if we were feeling really audacious, a touch of lace. We'd all be feeling a bit lighter, a bit more bold, a bit like we could breathe easier and deeper. I remember those stages of lightness when the people around me seemed to glow with real happiness. The reason those moments are so vibrant in my memory is because they were rare. As children, we tend to remember best those things that were out of the ordinary. For the most part, the faces that flash through my memory are drawn, frowning, brows furrowed, shoulders slumped with the weight of shame and responsibility that we were all but required to carry around with us. Grown-ups snapped at me constantly, for no apparent reason, miserable and on edge. One summer afternoon, I asked one of the moms if her kids could walk with me to Laycher's house to see Maxine and cheer her up because she was sick. That mom glared at me piercingly, like my request was a colossal imposition. Just by nature of being children, we were always *up to no good*, and they constantly assumed the worst. She reluctantly agreed, but didn't smile, didn't say *what a good idea to go sing for the pastor's sick wife*. Instead, she turned to her son and barked, "Not until you go brush your hair; you look like a bum!"

I stepped forward quickly to shield him and offered, "I'll help him brush his hair before we go." I couldn't fathom why she was so angry. I assumed she was tired. Her kids were young, and she had no one to help her with them. That was the reason I was there, after all. My mom had asked me to take a couple of the kids for a walk to give her a break.

So, of course, I remember the lighter times. I relished them. But they never lasted. Laycher would preach a gloomy, accusatory sermon about backsliding and *losing the faith*, modesty, and sanctifying our bodies for YHWH, and the pendulum would swing severely in the opposite direction. Shapeless clothes in dark colors and head coverings that covered most of our bodies would become the new norm. I hated those phases. I wanted pink, and lace, and ruffles and gathered waists with buttons down the front, long fingernails, and pretty barrettes, but Gwen thought those things were silly, so I kept that longing to myself. Instead, I continued to climb into dresses that were five sizes too large and wrap myself in yards of cloth to sanctify myself for my spiritual bridegroom, YHWH.

16 FALLIG IN LOVE

I didn't fall in love until I was thirteen.

And yes, I did say thirteen. It wasn't such a strange thing in the church. After all, there was no one around who was my age, and spending my time submersed mostly in grown-up concerns made it seem perfectly logical to me. The only other two women who had been teenagers and grown into women in the church had both been married while teenagers to men who were ten and twelve years older than them and immediately proceeded to have oodles of kids.

Before I get into that, though, I want to dip into the slightly perverted simplicity of falling in love in the church. With so many restrictions on male/female relationships, all that was left was a very black-and-white interpretation of male/female interactions. Stark lines meant that there was no nuance, no simple friendships or basic connection; there was only a hard boundary, holy communication between brothers and sisters, or falling in love. With so few opportunities for finding love in such a small and isolated group, it wasn't unusual for couples to have a bit of an age gap. There was a notable lack of women in their twenties and men in their teens.

Therefore, it wasn't at all strange for the young brothers to have crushes on us when we were in our teens. We were sweet and innocent; we were way too mature; we comported ourselves like grown women. We were restricted by all the same rules as grown women—so why not be treated like them? Some of those young men were harmless. Others were like Tim, the mousy cowboy with a crooked nose and a tiny head perched atop a lumbering body, who had painstakingly underlined specifically chosen words throughout a letter from Patrick to me that I'd let him read. "There's a message in there for you," he said, as he handed the letter back to me. He shifted nervously from foot to foot, agitated and giddy at the same time, and his unsettled state overflowed onto me, rippling through my own limbs, causing my eyes to follow his as they darted around the room. A room that was full of other people, none of whom seemed to notice him when he looked at me, and his eyes softened, and his face smiled. Until that point, I'd liked him well enough, in a sort of little sister, big brother kind of way. He was boarding his horse, Pepper, at our house, and he let us ride her as much as we wanted. She was a retired barrel racer who was as gentle as she was lazy—white, with black speckles—hence the name.

So when Tim handed me the letter, I was slightly perplexed but not alarmed. I went to my room and closed the door to decipher the secret message. I sifted through the letter more than once because at first, I didn't want to believe what I was reading. The words he'd underlined were "Angie, I love you," and *not* in a little sister kind of way. He was twenty-eight; I was twelve.

Then there was the time that Frank, also in his late twenties, asked me if I'd *found it yet*. I didn't have a clue what *it* was and told him so. Frank was another one of the brothers that we tended to flock to as kids, probably because he *acted* like a kid. He was immature, playful, and creative. He went out of his way to spend most of his time with us; he loved to tell stories, and he was exceptionally skilled at building little houses out of matches and glue. The day he asked me if I'd found *it* yet, he was sitting in his car in our driveway with the windows rolled down, just chatting with us, the little boys swarming in and out of his car like ants. He motioned for me to come closer and then whispered in my ear, "Check your underwear drawer." If I had known how to swear, I would have thought, "Oh *shit*, not again." But I didn't know how to swear, so my stomach swore instead. It collapsed in on itself in a tight tangle of dread as I waited for him to leave. Not a moment after he drove away, I raced to look in my underwear drawer, baffled and afraid of what I might find, and there, folded intricately into a tiny square, nestled deep into one of my pairs of cotton panties, I found a handwritten note. I don't remember a word of what it said, but it was also a love note.

Not long after that, he left the church and returned a year later with a fifteen-year-old wife who was pregnant with his child and already had a one-year-old. He was so proud of his new family. He said he wanted me and his wife to be good friends. I wanted them to disappear, back into whatever twisted world had led them to meet and allowed them to get married. The thought of his child growing inside of a girl barely older than me made me want to vomit. I was floored by the fact that Laycher had even allowed them back into the church.

On that note, back to falling in love. Mateo was the opposite of those guys. He was a seeker; his deep yearning for light in the world, for community, and the chance to connect with people who were committed to continually trying to be better versions of themselves was what landed him in the church. I met him when I was twelve, but for more than a year, he was just another one of the brothers, the brothers who I couldn't be alone with, the ones I couldn't talk to without my parents or another married couple present, one of the people I couldn't be friends with, one of the people I had to always wear my head covering around, and I barely noticed that he was there and vice versa. We orbited in two very separate micro worlds, worlds that rarely overlapped, me at home and school, and him living with the single brothers, working, hitchhiking, witnessing, and being initiated into the very sacred role of being a male in the church, a high calling, one of authority and privilege. After I turned thirteen, the rules sharpened and grew more restrictive. I was a grownup when it came to the rules and a child when it was time to do as I was told. One of those rules was to comport myself with virtue and honor. Until I was married to a man, I was married to YHWH, subjected to him and in service to him, expected to reflect the purity and perfection that a union with God connotes.

Mateo was on the periphery of my day-to-day, appearing only in moments of overlap at church and fellowship. A road trip together changed all that. Just barely out of his teens himself, his youth made him relatable, and on that trip, I connected to his lighthearted nature. He was laid back and easy to talk to, which had not been my experience with many other grownups. In a group of about twenty people, two families and two single brothers, traveling far from the prying eyes of our little cluster of trailers in the sticks, it was easy to disappear into the background, to sing, talk, and laugh out loud, without someone disappointedly accusing me of trying to seduce him. Too often during that time in my life, I'd found myself on the receiving end of reprimands, not only from my parents, but from other grown-ups too, for giggling in the presence of the single brothers or even around boys my own age and, I never understood it. Were girls not supposed to laugh? Boys were funny and stupid sometimes, and I was thirteen, so I laughed, and when I laughed, they would laugh, and then the giggles would continue to ripple along *out of control*. Abruptly, some shadow of a person who was bigger and grumpier than us would loom and have not a word of admonition for the boy in question, but for me, a command, "Go find your mother; you're out of control." An *out-of-control girl*—what an ugly thing.

This particular road trip was to a three-day, Sacred Name convention at the Assembly of Yahweh, 7th Day Church in Texas. We were one of several fringe groups who were invited to come even though we had no affiliation with them, and the only thing we had in common was using the name YHWH. Even that wasn't the same; they spelled it with vowels—Yahweh. After some deliberation, Laycher decided that he would accept their invitation because, just maybe, we could save some of them. He wanted two families to go, along with one older brother (meaning older in the faith) and one younger brother (both in the faith and in age); that way, when we met people, we'd have all our basis covered, and they would hopefully be able to see themselves reflected in us—a variety of representation, so to speak.

The Assemblies were there to worship and to compare doctrine and teachings; we were there to show them the error of their ways. We only went into the church building a couple of times a day for the singing and when our brothers were scheduled to preach. We spent the rest of our time making certain they knew we were *separate* and there only to teach *them*. We camped out in the parking lot singing or went for walks, or played games, and cooked food on our camp stoves. I was thrilled to be there. Laycher never picked our family to go witness because, as we've established by now, we were insignificant in the holiness pecking order. The fact that he chose us had less to do with my dad and more to do with the fact that my brother Joseph and I were the only teenagers in our Colorado church at the time. There would be kids in Texas who were our age, and we would be living examples of what it meant to serve YHWH. I watched the girls from the Assembly of Yahweh come and go from the parking lot into the church building. Lots of them were my age, but I never tried to meet any of them. They all said they believed in the same things as us, but they wore makeup, styled their hair, didn't wear head coverings, and walked around in tight, acid-wash Wranglers and tank tops. I was desperate to talk to them, but I didn't dare. I longed for a day there would be that many girls in our church.

After the trip, I took every chance I could take, which

was really only at church, to find Mateo and talk. We'd play guitar together, play tag outside with the other kids and wax poetic about a loving god and about learning how to submit to his will for us. He'd come to our house with the other single brothers on Saturdays. My little brothers would climb all over him and make him say words in Spanish repeatedly because they thought it sounded so funny. In fact, he won us all over with his carefree nature and generous smile. He brought so much joy into our world. I'd never met someone who smiled so much; *even his eyes smiled*. It was like the simple act of breathing made him happy.

And then, abruptly, it seemed, everything changed. He stopped talking to me after church, barely came to our house anymore, and suddenly carried the weight of something on his countenance. I hadn't a clue why the sudden shift, but I had a strong sense that it had something to do with our trip to the mountains, which took place shortly after our trip to Texas.

Every August, we all packed up our cars with ice chests and cardboard boxes full of organic hot dogs, homemade chocolate chip cookies, watermelon, homemade marshmallows, and giant, used army tents that smelled of ancient oiled canvas and took hours and several grown men to set up, but easily slept a family of nine. Then we'd drive the two and a half hours to the Sangre De Cristo mountains for three days to camp. The trip was compulsory, but I couldn't think of a better thing to be forced to do. I cherished that wilderness, the icy river that we spent hours swimming in, fully clothed, our teeth chattering and our lips turning blue, the steep mountain directly behind our tents where we would sit on our butts and slide down the dusty trail. Some years we'd climb to the top, which was no small feat, it was steep and craggy, but I was a kid, and therefore half-monkey, and a climb like that didn't faze me. Every day the brothers would gather wood, not just sticks and small logs, but huge, downed trees that they'd use to build a giant bonfire in the middle of the campground after dark. We'd all sit around and roast our pork-free hot dogs and those homemade marshmallows that quickly caught fire and burned to a black crisp. That was just how I liked them. I would peel off the black part and eat it and then put the rest back into the fire to catch the flame again. Afterward, guitars, mandolins, and flutes would be lifted gently from their cases, and we'd sing and tell stories late into the night. I never wanted it to end.

But that summer of my thirteenth year, nothing seemed right. Laycher called a somber grownup meeting in his RV that included my dad and the other brothers who'd gone to Texas. Whatever they talked about in that meeting left my dad red with fury, my mom throwing up, and Mateo with strict instructions to stay away from our family. I wanted to know why, but the only thing they would tell me was that it didn't concern me.

After that—everything, all the time—made me cry. I was unsettled, and rattled, and frantic, and I just felt *bad*. I wondered what I had done wrong. I noticed that people were watching me talk to Mateo. I knew there was something wrong with me because I couldn't stop thinking about him. I couldn't stop wanting to be around him all the time. I didn't understand what I was feeling when I was with him, that warm, longing, thrilling sensation, followed by a strange sense of shame. The feelings were cloudy and just out of my reach, but not light, fluffy cloudy; those clouds were dark and stormy—churning tornado clouds. And I couldn't ask for help, couldn't tell anyone because I knew I would either be scolded, dismissed as silly, or rebuked publicly.

As if on cue, Patrick's year of purification was up, so he returned to Colorado and moved into the twelve-by-sixty mobile home where Mateo and two of the other single brothers lived. Patrick was unlike any other new recruit I'd met during my whole, short life. There wasn't a boundary he wouldn't test, a rule he wouldn't question, or a tradition he wouldn't challenge. Traditionally, only the single sisters had taught at the church school, but Patrick adored kids, and he loved teaching, and somehow, he convinced Laycher to let him be the first male teacher at our school. I was thrilled, and so were the other kids. He walked to and from school with all of us, so we spent more than just the school day with him, and because he was our teacher, there weren't so many rules. We flocked to him because he acknowledged us. He didn't dismiss us and boss us around like the other teachers. He was present and available, and genuinely interested. He'd walk along beside us, his bag with papers to grade bouncing against his back and his guitar slung around his shoulder bouncing against his front. He'd strum it absentmindedly, giving his full attention to us and our antics. And rather than frowning at our silliness, he'd laugh out loud and do a little dance. He was a welcome distraction for those nagging dark spots in my brain that I had no answers to.

We had grown comfortable with each other during our pen-pal days, and once I was spending every day with him, we grew closer than ever. He'd lit a fire in me that I never knew could exist. He taught me how to write poetry; he taught me how to write, period. I had never thought to write poetry; I'd never considered that just anyone could do it. Once I learned how; I couldn't stop. I'd sometimes write three or four poems a day, and he read them all. He wrote poems and read them to us in class. Some of them would take my breath away. I hadn't known that poetry could do that. He taught history from *A People's History of the United States* by Howard Zinn. History class up until that point had been mostly traditional, although slightly more focused on the Puritans and freedom of religion, a country founded on the right to worship as we pleased than anything else. Patrick taught us about the Holocaust, which I can't really remember learning about before that, except when Laycher preached about the six-day war and YHWH giving his chosen people back their homeland.

I was the only student in his literature class, a class that he made up. It was my favorite time of day. "I want to get you reading more books," he mused, talking as much to himself as he was to me. "Definitely more books about someone your own age," he tucked his hair behind his ears and tapped his pen against his lips. "And the classics," he continued, "there is so much great literature out there." Of course, any book that Patrick assigned would have a social justice angle. "Let's start with the Diary of Anne Frank, then I have a few others in mind; War and Peace, maybe, Leo Tolstoy is a literary icon, and for history—well, let's just start with those and then we'll see what comes next."

A few days later, he snuck The Diary of Anne Frank into my school bag. He had to sneak it to me because it was not on the acceptable reading list. It burned a hole in my bag until it was time to go back home. Once alone in my room with the door closed, I pulled it carefully out, listening for footsteps in the hall. I'd told my mom I had a headache and needed to lie down, so the chances of someone bursting into my room were slim, but not impossible as I had no lock on my door. It was a small book; I could hold it easily in one hand. The cover was worn and fragile, but from the moment I opened it, I devoured it. Ironically, the main point of the story, hiding from genocide, wasn't what immediately grabbed my attention. Instead, it was the moment-to-moment experience of a girl my age, locked away from the world, writing in her diary. She was hiding from the authorities just like we would hide from child protective services, and would one day hide from the beast. I hadn't learned about the Holocaust prior to that moment, so I didn't understand the magnitude of the story, nor had I ever heard the word *genocide*. I'm sure that Patrick's intention was to teach me about an important time in history from the point of view of a girl my age, but initially, all of that went right over my head. Instead, I disappeared into the moments. I felt them fully and poignantly. I could feel her butterflies as she watched Peter, mute, and from a distance and wrote furiously about it in her diary. They felt like mine as I watched Mateo in church, or from the corner of a living room on Saturdays, or waited for his car to pass by in the morning and evening on his way to work.

The Jungle, by Upton Sinclair, was the next book he assigned and I devoured for hours on end. It was a story about the exploitation of immigrants in the Chicago meatpacking plants. Again, I probably didn't glean exactly what Patrick intended. Instead, the teenage bride giving birth to a giant baby on the dirty floor of a shack in the freezing cold Chicago winter, was the thing that was burned into my brain. It was an abundance of new information all at once, most of the time, I wasn't even sure what I was reading, but my world was exploding; my brain was colliding with the wonder of it all against the backdrop of breaking the rules to experience that wonder. I had never actually learned so much at school, and I was starving for more. I would read what I could sneak after school and at night, and then we'd discuss it the next day at recess while the other kids played.

By the time he sent me home with Anna Karenina, by Leo Tolstoy, I was petrified that someone would find out. That book was downright scandalous. Still, I couldn't put it down. I couldn't forget the scenes when they stole moments alone together, the looks across a crowded room, the brushing of hands as they passed. The rest of the book barely registered with me, especially the names and the sex. I felt red-hot guilt reading those scenes. A lot of them I skipped simply because I couldn't bear it. I couldn't keep most of the characters, with all their difficult-to-pronounce names, straight, except the two most important ones, the two who couldn't live without each other. I spent every free moment I could steal reading it. It was tough to hide anything, my mom would always find me out, but somehow, I managed. I'd sneak it into my bag with the rest of my writing stuff and walk out into our field for *alone time* or *to pray* (I was never praying), and instead, I would read for hours at a time.

Reading about forbidden love did nothing to improve my state of mind. I was more confused than ever and more weighed down with guilt than ever. Whatever was wrong with me, I knew it was really bad. I couldn't even bear to be in the same room with Mateo anymore, and when he tried to talk to me, I'd hide behind Patrick, mute and embarrassed. Patrick was determined to get to the bottom of it. Although I was shy, he knew I wasn't *that* shy and that there must be something else going on. One spring day at school, while all the other kids were distracted with recess, playing kickball, tag, or Red Rover, Patrick motioned with a jerk of his head for me to come over to sit next to him on the concrete steps of the church building. "I want to go over some of your math problems with you," he said out loud to derail any suspicion from the other teachers. We both knew we weren't working on math because we both despised it. It was code for getting some alone time to talk. I sat next to him, and he tapped the blank page in his hand with his pen.

He wrote, "I know something is going on, and I think I know what it is." My stomach sank to my feet, and my hands grew clammy. He kept writing. "Do you have special feelings for someone, a certain young brother?"

I began to tremble, shivering like I was cold, only I wasn't. My cheeks and neck flushed, and I wanted to shrink until I disappeared. I knew that no one could know. The shame that had settled in the pit of my stomach extended long fingers through my body—fingers of physical pain. I stared at those words but didn't answer. Patrick didn't give up that easily. He whispered, "How about him?" He wrote *Mateo* on the page. It wasn't until I released my breath that I realized I'd been holding it. It felt like an eternity before I finally covered my face and nodded ever so slightly. He tried to pry my hands loose, but I couldn't bear to look at him. I knew he was going to be disappointed in me, or disgusted with me, or both. After an extended silence, I peeked through my fingers, and he was grinning. He let out one of his big chuckles, throwing his head back, his eyes twinkling.

What? He wasn't mad? He wasn't going to scold me? Was he going to tell Laycher or my parents?

"You can come out now," he teased. "It's okay. It's nothing to be ashamed of. He's nice, right?"

Perplexed and suspicious, I lowered my hands. He was still smiling, but I didn't trust it. I was waiting for the speech about how I needed to ask YHWH to deliver me from those foul feelings.

"It was bound to happen at some point," he said matter-of-factly. "Everyone has to have a first crush."

"A crush? What's a crush?"

"A crush is when you like someone a whole lot, and it feels more special than normal. When they make you feel warm and tingly and, you just want to be with them all the time. And you think they're cute."

"Cute? You mean like a baby?"

"No, cute, like *handsome*."

Weird, I thought. *Crush meant you liked someone, and when you liked someone, you could call them cute, like a baby, only it didn't mean cute, like a baby.* I had never heard of calling a grown-up cute because they just weren't, nor had I imagined how relieved I would feel to tell someone my secret. I was confident, however, that I didn't want anyone else to know. I trusted Patrick, but I knew instinctively that most grown-ups would not have been so supportive. "You really can't tell anyone," I looked intently into his eyes, "No one else will understand." Patrick promised he wouldn't, but I assumed he'd tell Mateo because they were best friends. Strangely, I didn't care. Somehow, having him know felt right. I went home and wrote Mateo a letter, imploring him to forgive me for being rude and for not being able to control the way I was feeling, I knew it was wrong, and I hoped he wasn't mad at me. The next day at school, I slipped it to Patrick. "Will you give this to Mateo, please? I want him to know why I've been hiding from him and that I'm not doing this on purpose."

Patrick hesitated, then said, "Okay, I guess it can't hurt,

but maybe you should just talk to him; he's really not that scary, and I know he'd understand."

"*No way*, I could never do that," I shuddered. "I can't even be in the same room with him or look at him."

The next day, during recess, while everyone was busy playing kickball, Patrick slipped me a folded piece of paper. I glanced at the other teachers, who were eyeing us suspiciously, and disappeared into the outhouse to read it. I saw the handwriting and knew immediately that it was from Mateo because he'd already written letters to my family when he'd been off on hitchhiking trips. My heart pulsed rhythmically in my ears; *he had taken the time to write back*, and the letters on the page blurred. He wrote that I had nothing to apologize for and that what I was going through was perfectly normal. He insisted that I didn't really know him or the turmoil in the deepest places of his soul, the darkness that had led him to seek light and that what I thought I liked was probably just *my idea of him*. He urged me to *just be a kid*, focus on having fun and doing the things I loved, and forget about him. As I read the letter, I was freshly embarrassed and felt dismissed, but I was also relieved. I was so glad he wasn't angry. I did need to clarify a few things for him, though, so I sat down to write again.

First of all, *I wasn't a kid*. I was practically grown up. Second, I knew I wasn't idealizing about him because I hadn't planned to feel the way I did; it just happened. And third, how exactly was I supposed to *just forget*? I didn't try to think about him; I just did. I didn't decide that I wanted to be with him every minute; I just did. I didn't ask for it; *it just happened*. How was I supposed to make it stop? How could I make it go away? *Please tell me how to forget about you*, I was pleading. I slipped the note to Patrick on the walk home from school.

Mateo's next letter wasn't as gentle as the first, and I twinged with guilt and felt a new surge of self-loathing. He reiterated that it was *just a stage and that it would pass*. He told me not to worry and to turn my attention to other things.

He ended by asserting firmly that he couldn't be my friend, that he couldn't help me through that process, and that I needed to stop writing to him. I wrote back again, apologizing profusely for what I was doing to him and thanking him for being so nice.

In the weeks that followed, I tried to do precisely what he told me to do. I tried playing with the kids at recess, but my heart wasn't in it. It tried not glancing at him during church and not thinking about him all the time. It wasn't working, and I was miserable. If he said it could be done, I should be able to do it. I finally understood what Laycher was saying when he preached about bringing the flesh under subjection. It must be the flesh that made you think about boys when you weren't supposed to. I still talked to Patrick about it all the time, and he would say that *our mutual friend* was concerned about me and wanted to know how I was doing and if I had been able to move on. I didn't think of Mateo as my friend. After all, I wasn't allowed to write to him, didn't dare speak to him, and if he tried to talk to me, I'd hide behind the closest person and wish I could become invisible.

I thought maybe I'd stop trying to fight it and just tuck it away somewhere until later. That seemed like a better solution. Maybe it would get easier with time. I had just started to believe that when Patrick, Laycher, and Mateo showed up on our doorstep and asked to talk to my parents. I knew instantly why they had come and knew there was nowhere to run. I was simultaneously shocked by their betrayal and consumed with guilt. My parents' faces were taut with the gravity of what I may have done. When Laycher showed up unannounced, it was a really big deal. My eyes found their way briefly to Patrick's with panic radiating from them, and he shifted his gaze away. I didn't dare look at Mateo.

My dad ushered my siblings to their rooms and told them to stay there, this did not concern them, but I knew they would have their ears pressed to the other side of the hallway door listening anyway, wondering what I could have possibly done to bring in the big guns. My accusers sat with my parents on the kitchen chairs in a half-circle around me, and I sat on the floor against the wall, my knees pressed up to my chest with my arms wound tightly around them and my face entirely hidden from view. I didn't move or utter a sound. I didn't look up, no matter who was talking. I didn't care if I'd be punished later; it was too unbearable—nothing I'd ever been through was worse than that. I listened as Patrick told my parents that he needed to bring something to their attention, something he'd tried to deal with himself but had later felt guilty about keeping it from them. I cringed as he recounted every last detail of what had happened in the weeks before.

He had promised not to tell.

Laycher sat quietly at first, and so did Mateo. I couldn't see my parents, but I imagined them shaking their heads in disbelief. Laycher had all of the letters I had written to Mateo, and he gave them to my parents. The three of them would continue the conversation separately and try to decide what to do about me. Patrick and Mateo stood to leave, their part was over, but first, Patrick addressed me directly. "We're so sorry, Sister Angie, but your parents needed to know. We didn't do this to get you into trouble; we did this to help you."

I knew he wanted me to look at them; there was a pregnant silence as they waited, but silence was my only power, and I wasn't going to give them the satisfaction of taking that too.

I wanted to screech, and kick, and punch; to yell at them that *friends don't do this*. I wanted to ask them why they were just like everyone else when I thought they were different. I wanted to shriek that I never wanted to see them again. I wanted to run out the door and never stop—but, as always, instead, I was frozen, quaking with shame, and horrified by how naked I felt. I wrapped my arms more tightly around my knees and sobbed into them.

Laycher came over to lay hands on me, and he and my parents prayed together. Still, I didn't move. They talked in hushed voices between the three of them about how my mom and dad needed to get better control of me and keep me as far away from the single brothers as possible, 'She's a young woman now," Laycher said, "and can be led into temptation."

I sat like a statue.

Laycher left, and my parents tried to pry my arms away—I didn't let them. I waited until they left the room and then raced out as far into the prairie as I dared and screamed into the empty expanse.

The next day was Saturday, and after church, I'd gone out to the outhouse, not really because I had to use it, but because I didn't want to hang around and have everyone check on me and try to pry information out of me. As I walked back toward the church building, I saw Patrick waiting for me. I tried to avoid him and hurry past. I was more crushed than angry. I didn't trust him anymore. He cornered me. I sidestepped, and he blocked me. We were outside between the church and the trailer that served as our school. We were alone. I trembled with anger and unease. Laycher had just told my parents to keep me away from the single brothers, and here was Patrick, choosing to be alone with me in broad daylight while everyone was right there inside the church. I stopped walking and studied the ground, dragging my foot back and forth in the dust. I wanted to lean into him, to break down, to swing at him and ask why, but I just stood there.

"You're really mad." He whispered.

I remained staunchly silent. What did he expect?

'Look, I'm really sorry. I made a terrible decision. I never should have betrayed you like that. I hated it the whole time, but I felt like my hands were tied. I didn't know what to do. I promise I'll never do that to you again."

I could tell he was sincere, but I was still crushed, deflated, and gutted. I wanted to stay mad, to make him feel worse, but I needed a friend so badly, someone on my side, so I reluctantly believed him, and soon after, I forgave him.

17 TWO WEDDINGS

Laycher sent Mateo away to Missouri, where we had a new church just barely established with three families living outside of Springfield. I knew he'd stay away until I managed free myself from my carnal thoughts. I tried to write him letters, but Laycher had instructed the family he was staying with to read all of his mail if it came from me, so I ended up causing a lot of trouble for both of us. I didn't know why no one understood that all I wanted was for him to be my friend. They would tell me I was too young to think about getting married, and I would furiously write about how stupid that was in my diary. I didn't want to marry him. I knew I was never getting married. I just really wanted him in my life, although I never could have explained why. When he left, I felt like I had been torn in two.

Patrick helped keep my head up. He was my lifeline in and out of school. I told him everything about the constant chaos dominating my world, and he kept his promise and never betrayed me again. But by that point, we were being watched by everyone because, in their eyes, I was no longer a little girl but a young woman who had *fallen in love* (remember when I said there was no nuance? It was either separate worlds for men and women or love and marriage, period, which left zero space for teenage crushes) with one man, so why not all of them? I was swimming in their fishbowl, bashing my head against its suffocating walls.

Now, they had to try to contain me by strangling every bit of normal development I was experiencing and placing the onus on me to be more than my teenage tempest. I wasn't supposed to have a man as a best friend and confidant; the single sisters could scarcely contain their disgust and superiority.

I began to hear whispers from the other kids about what the grown-ups were saying, mainly from Laycher's granddaughter, Anika. Laycher and Maxine never seemed to notice when she was lingering, so they would talk freely, she would soak it all in, and then she'd tell us. She told us what they said about Patrick and me one day on the way home from school. We were in our usual gaggle, orbiting around him. She whispered so Patrick wouldn't hear, but he heard anyway. "They said that they finally got you to leave Mateo alone, so now you've just moved on to Patrick, and that somebody needs to get you under control." I stopped walking and stood directly in front of Patrick, who was trying not to look worried. Everyone else stopped walking and turned to watch what would happen next. Anika smiled a self-satisfied grin, not maliciously, just pleased with the tasty little morsel she had just dished up. It was obvious that it had been a good one.

I looked him directly in the eyes, something we children rarely did with grown-ups. *"When is this going to end?"* I dared him to share my rage. *"It's absurd.* I'm sick of it, sick of being accused, sick of being mistrusted, sick of always trying to prove that I'm not a slut" (I wasn't sure what a slut was, but I had been called that by Maxine and thought it probably had something to do with liking too many boys, all the boys, which of course wasn't true). Then, more resignedly, barely holding back the tears that were desperate to come, I sighed, *"I'm. Just. So. Tired."* I dropped my head against his chest for a few seconds. I wanted him to scoop me up and tell me that everything would be okay, that he would fix it, that he would protect me.

I so needed a hero, a defender, but he stiffened and

pushed backward with a forced grin. One of the little girls giggled and asked, "Are you guys getting married?" He backed up a few more steps and then sidestepped to the other side of the road, farthest away from me. I felt a knife of shame and horror sink into my chest as if it were an actual blade—right there in the V of my ribs, pain radiated throughout my body ending in pins and needles in my fingers and toes. Somehow, I'd crossed a line, a line that even my rebel friend Patrick was determined to walk obediently.

What was wrong with me? I ran the rest of the way to our trailer, scolding myself, screaming at myself, blood-curdling screams that echoed around the hallways of my brain. I had managed to alienate the one man that I trusted. The distance between us grew. I knew he was afraid to be labeled, to be called out—rebuked from the pulpit. I knew that as soon as Laycher found out—and he most certainly would—that I'd *dared to touch* a single brother with my head, he would make Patrick leave the school. It was just a matter of time.

My friend Gwen was a teacher, too, and Patrick was still hopelessly in love with her. She tried to avoid him while he actively sought her out. For some reason, I hadn't told her about Mateo yet. To be fair, I hadn't told Patrick either; he'd just figured it out. She would talk to me about Patrick and how furious she was with him because he kept breaking the rules and finding ways to be alone with her. I was glad I was someone she could count on; it helped take my focus off the whirlwind that was constantly tearing through my own internal existence. One day, she pulled me solemnly into her bedroom and closed the door. She said she needed to tell me something important, "but I can't look at you while I tell you, come here." She held out her arms to me. I didn't know whether to be frightened or intrigued. She hugged me, breathed in, and then out with relief, "I'm getting married."

She released me from the embrace and stepped back to gauge my reaction.

I instantly knew who she would marry, and I wanted to bounce up and down excitedly. I wasn't sure how she'd expected me to react, but since she said she couldn't look at me while telling me, I concluded that it was probably because she thought I would be upset. I decided on the spot that if that's what she expected, then I probably should be upset, so I burst into tears. I was strangely skilled at deciphering the desired reaction from grown-ups and producing it on a whim.

"Oh, don't cry, Honey, this is happy news," she soothed, "It's a good thing. For him and for me, it's not a bad thing. Why are you upset?"

I sat down on her bed and covered my face with my hands, partly to emphasize my distress and partly to hide the fact that I was actually thrilled. I had to come up with *something*, a logical reason for my tears. So, I let my hands fall back to my sides, "I'm just afraid you're not going to be my friend anymore." I had to guess why I should be upset—that seemed like a plausible enough reason, but even as I said it, it sounded silly.

She sat down next to me and rested one arm on my shoulders. She smiled her gentle smile that always put me at ease. "Of course, I'll be your friend; I'll always be your friend. We both will, I promise. You can spend as much time with us as you want now because we'll be married, so no more rules about being friends with single brothers." She winked, and it dawned on me that Patrick had told her everything we'd ever talked about or been through together. I was strangely relieved. She knew about Mateo, and I didn't even have to tell her.

"Patrick told you about me." It was a question statement.

"Of course he did, but you don't have to worry. We'll always be here for you, and you can tell us anything. If you want to sit and talk about Mateo all afternoon, I'm okay with that, but I want you to remember that you're so young; you have no idea how you're going to feel in ten years. Just be a kid, go to school, hang out with us. These things tend to work themselves out."

I was so relieved I could finally talk to a girl about him.

I dried my tears. On the inside, I was delirious with delight. The two people I loved most in the world were about to marry each other, and I could barely contain my excitement. Married couples were the safest people in the church to be friends with. They had the most freedom, were the most respected, and were the pillars of the church, somehow more holy than everyone else since they had entered into a holy union. Within that union, they were strong; they could resist temptation, keep each other honest and be chaperones for the single brothers and sisters. There'd be no restrictions on the time I spent with them except from my parents.

I wanted to know all about how she'd finally decided to marry Patrick, so we settled in, and she recounted the details. "You've probably noticed how Patrick keeps dragging me into the library at school," (the library was in the non-functioning bathroom of the school trailer. That bathroom was also a study room, a punishment room, or the place you went to have a private conversation apparently.) "Well, I was getting really mad at him because you know how we're not supposed to be alone together, but he didn't seem to care about that. Finally, he pulled me in there to read me a poem he'd written for me, and when I told him that he really needed to cut it out, he retorted, 'Well, if you'd just marry me already, we wouldn't have to worry about the rules.'"

"And I said, *'Okay, I will.*'"

She continued to paint the picture of Patrick so overcome that he sobbed in the tiny bathroom, Gwen shushing him lest the entire school hear. "It was like he didn't quite believe me," she said. "He had to ask again, 'Really, you will?'" Then they had to tell Laycher and get his blessing. He gave it enthusiastically.

And that was it. I thought it was the most fantastic love

story I'd ever heard.

Patrick had to quit teaching school because he was going to be the head of a family, and so it was time to be the man and go work. No one who taught at the school was paid for their time, which is probably why the job usually fell to the single sisters, whether or not they were qualified or even wanted to teach. Because sisters weren't allowed to work, *they had enough free time on their hands*, and they were basically obligated to teach school, sew for the single brothers, and help the overwhelmed married women with household chores and childcare. I was sad to see him go but glad that Gwen was still at school. When school let out, our walks home were grown-up-free, so we made them last as long as possible, moving at a glacial pace and stopping repeatedly to sit in the dusty ditch in a huddled mass of giggly girls. Anika continued to be our fount of information, and she didn't disappoint. And when the gossip wasn't about me, I was happy to engage. Lately, it was about Jenna, the woman who had been living with us when my dad was sent away to Oregon and who we kinda despised. She was the lowest in the pecking order of the single sisters, and no one ever told me to be like her.

We knew she was weak because Laycher would rebuke her from the pulpit all the time and tell her she needed to free herself of her carnal thoughts. She cried a lot and begged for forgiveness constantly. But she was nasty to us kids and relished bossing us around and tattling on us. So, in turn, we shunned her and gossiped about her.

Oh, the cruelty of retrospect. Writing those words makes me cringe even though they are true. The poor woman must have been surviving in a living hell.

Jenna had rushed to Laycher to tell him she'd received a message from YHWH in a dream that she was supposed to marry Nathaniel. All the single sisters and some of the married ones, too, were in love with Nathaniel. Even as a kid, I could tell by how they talked to him, about him, and how they lingered around him, and went out of their way to get his attention. They all fell over themselves to sew his clothes, and he had to keep changing who sewed for him so they wouldn't think he wanted to marry them. He was the ideal of an honorable and devoted brother. He was kind to everyone, especially us kids, he was circumspect and humble, and he was the one person I would have been genuinely upset about losing if he got married. He was there when I was born, and long into my adult life, I'd often wished he'd been my dad.

'So, my grandpa says," Anika was explaining, with great fanfare and drama, "he'll talk to Nathaniel and let her know what he says. So, he goes and talks to Nathaniel, and then he comes back to Jenna and tells her that YHWH didn't speak to him and that he didn't want to get married. But my grandpa told my grandma that what he really said was *not a chance*."

Everybody giggled, but I let out a sigh of relief. Nathaniel getting married would have been bad enough; marrying Jenna would have been unforgivable from my perspective. We stood up from our huddled group in the ditch to continue our walk home.

"Wait, there's more," Anika pulled us back into our squat. 'So, Jenna comes back the next day and tells my grandpa that she's had a new dream from YHWH, and this time he told her that she was supposed to marry Antonio. My grandpa goes to Antonio and asks him what he thinks, and he said that 'What a miracle, YHWH had showed him the same thing. 'He said he had walked into a room just the other day and had seen her there, and she had the most beautiful glow around her, and right then, he knew that she was supposed to be his wife."

We all howled with laughter. We knew that Antonio had actually wanted to marry Delia for years, and she kept saying *no*. I ran into her in the church parking lot after hearing that Antonio was getting married to Jenna, and she was tucked in between two pickup trucks crying. I tried to comfort her and asked what was wrong, but she predictably told me I was too young to understand, even though I knew exactly what had upset her. I wondered why she had kept refusing him, and now that it was too late, she was heartbroken. She had kept saying *no* to Antonio because she was waiting patiently for Nathaniel. I figured she was crying because she knew that Nathaniel would never marry her and that Antonio had been her only hope, and now that was gone, too. I hugged her because that's all I could do, even as I wondered why grown-ups were, as Yahanna would have said, so dumb.

It wasn't long after Anika had filled us in on the gossip that Antonio decided to tell me about his engagement to Jenna, even though the whole church already knew. After my talk with Gwen, I knew exactly what kind of reaction he'd be expecting. He came and sat by me after church on the bench where I was lingering by myself. I looked at the floor and waited. He seemed nervous, just like Gwen had, and fumbled a bit like he didn't know where to begin. I braced myself; *here we go again.*

"I know you know that I'm getting married." He smiled with his mouth and his eyes but then grew serious again. "And I wanted to check on you and make sure you're okay."

Why wouldn't I be? I wondered to myself. But I quickly remembered what I was supposed to do and then teared up sufficiently to be convincing.

"Oh, don't cry," he said, giving me an awkward, one-armed hug, which he then quickly pulled back from. He used to be one of the brothers who could hug me whenever he wanted because he'd known me since I was little, but now that he was getting married and I was practically a single sister myself, those days were over. "Don't be upset," he cooed, "nothing is going to change, I promise. Now we can see each other more, now that I'll have a wife."

"You know that's not true," I insisted, "every time a brother gets married, he abandons us kids. You'll have kids of your own and then be too busy for us." I had to come up with something, and it was true; it had happened before.

"No way, not me; you are too important to me," he soothed. "In fact," he added, poking my ribs playfully, "If you were a little bit older, it probably would have been you." He smiled sweetly, triumphantly, sure that he had eased my mind. He put his arm around me again, this time without hesitation, and I let him, but I felt a twinge of discomfort and wiggled free. Had he really just said that he wished he was marrying me? I brushed it off, deciding it was just his awkward way of trying to make me feel better.

There had never been a wedding in the church that I had been old enough to remember. Now, there would be not one, but two weddings, only a week apart. I could sense that everyone was giddy for a couple of months. Jenna oozed relief that she was going to be more important than the other single sisters because she was getting married. She whiplashed abruptly from being nasty to being painfully nice to me and desperately trying to be my friend. I was amused but still didn't trust her. She was treating me like a grown-up, though, and to prove it, she asked me if I would help her sew some of the clothes for her wedding. She was frantically sewing all new outfits for her and Antonio, from the inside out—pants, a shirt, and a robe for him, and for her, bloomers, an undershirt, a wedding dress, and a veil. She was frantic and overwhelmed. "You've learned how to sew real good," she flattered. "If you could help me with some of this sewing, it would be such a relief."

She had suddenly become legitimate, visible, and respectable—she was about to be someone's wife—all of the waiting, torture, and unrequited longing had paid off. Now, if she wanted to, she could look down her nose at the other ladies who were still alone, waiting patiently for someone to choose them, or she could throw them a bone from her lofty perch, which is what I think she was doing with me. Now that she mattered, how could I say no? She wanted me to sew her nightgown for the wedding night.

I wondered why she needed a special nightgown for that particular night, but I didn't ask. Instead, I agreed to help her out. She chose a pattern with lots of tiny pleats all along the bodice and delicate buttons all the way down the front, by far the most intricate design I'd ever tried to sew. I hated making buttonholes, and those ones were itty-bitty, but I was determined not to disappoint her. Currying favor with married women was just as important as them lording over the singletons. The nightgown was sleeveless and had a deep V-neck. I'd never seen anyone in the church wear a V-neck, sleeveless dress, even to sleep. I concluded it must be something married people without kids did.

I was nervous. I couldn't bear the thought of making a mistake on something as important as wedding clothes. I was relieved she hadn't asked me to make her dress, even though *that* would have been the highest honor. Gwen had asked Karen to make her dress, which made me sad because I'd thought she'd ask me since I was her best friend. But it did make sense since Karen was married to an elder, and she usually got the honors. I cut the pattern pieces out carefully and checked and re-checked them all before cutting the slippery and unruly fabric. I had never worked with silk before, but it was smooth and lustrous, and I loved the feel. I was glad my mom was nearby and happy to help me if I got stuck. I breathed a sigh of relief when I presented it to Jenna, and she said, "It's perfect. You have no idea how much you've helped." *And in no time at all, you'll be wanting me to help with your babies*, I thought. I knew I would treat them better than she'd treated me.

After I finished sewing for her, I started on my new dress for the weddings. I had no idea that we were all supposed to have new clothes to attend weddings, but I learned that was the case when I found out that Karen was making all new clothes for her family for the weddings. I told Mom that I would sew all the robes for the boys if she and my dad could find money to buy the fabric. The idea of new clothes was so fresh and hopeful, just like the feeling that was all around those days. It was spring, and I felt like I was one of the brave flowers standing tall in the grass—desperate with the knowledge that it would only last a moment. I knew from experience that phases of lightness and spring would soon be overthrown by the scorching heat of Laycher's wrath as he felt himself losing control. Like those prairie flowers, we would die back to our roots, to the cool safety of the earth, until the season changed again.

I helped my mom make robes for my brothers first. Then I got to work on my dress. Gwen had made her dress out of cream-colored raw silk, a panel dress with buttons all the way down the front. She let me use her pattern to make my dress for Antonio and Jenna's wedding, even though it was easily three sizes too big. I bought some teal-colored, lightweight denim and made sure to draw the panels out a little straighter at the waist instead of curved in like the pattern, so the dress would not be form-fitting. Then I chose brass-colored buttons to go all the way down the front. It was the most gorgeous dress I'd ever made for myself.

18 PASSOVER

The weddings were one week apart. I had just turned fourteen a month before Antonio and Jenna's wedding. I will never forget that wedding, not because it was fun, or because the bride was glowing, or because I was sad or happy about them getting married, but because, one week before, I had come to the end of my rope of sanity and endurance. Although I've not focused much on my dad's abuse, that doesn't mean it had stopped. It had persisted throughout the years, throughout the move to Boone, on a weekly basis, sometimes more.

As I said before, I had learned to tolerate it, to accept it as a normal part of being a daughter. Sometimes I would timidly remind him, "You told me to stop you, to not let you be weak," but he would make some excuse, "Just tonight, then no more, I promise," or "I'll try harder next time." I would turn my back to him when he climbed into my bed, try to wiggle away, or pretend I was asleep, hoping that would prompt him to go away, but he would push his way in, pry my legs apart or take my hand and force it between his legs. I would comply, knowing that if I did, he would go away, and I would get a few nights 'reprieve.

I have always contended that the grisly details are unnecessary, but suffice it to say; I couldn't even get a piggyback ride without having a finger shoved inside me.

Somehow, no one ever seemed to notice. I didn't know what I would do, who I would tell, or if I would tell anyone, but I knew it had to stop; I knew I couldn't take it anymore. I'd had enough of pushing him away and trying to help him change. Patrick and Gwen were planning a trip to Missouri to see their families once they were married. I knew they would take me with them if I asked because they liked to give me any chance they could to get away from my family and the pressures of being the oldest girl. I figured that once I was there, far away from Boone, I could just disappear into the streets of Kansas City. It was a terrifying prospect, but better than the one I was living through.

I couldn't understand why I hated my dad so much. Since I had always assumed that what my dad was doing was simply what dads did, I concluded there must be something wrong with *me* because the other girls didn't hate their dads like I did. Why was I the only one? It had to be some flaw in me because when my dad would tease in public, I would glare at him and punch him in the shoulder. Then those people would tell me to be nice to my dad, and then I would hit him harder. He would joke about how strong I was and pretend I wasn't hurting him, even though I wanted to, and I was. I wanted to keep punching—harder and harder. Then they would say, "Aww, c'mon, Sister Angela, don't beat on your old dad like that." I knew they thought that I was just being a moody teenager. I figured that since I'd never make it to heaven anyway, disappearing someplace far away was as good as anything.

Because I'd made up my mind, it was easy to stop speaking to my dad, to simply act like he didn't exist. I knew I might be chastised, and I had no idea what the punishment would be, but I didn't care at that point. All of our friends from Oregon and Missouri were arriving for the weddings, and there were services every night, just as there always were during the two weeks leading up to Passover. We observed the New Testament version of Passover, consuming unleavened bread and grape juice to signify the body and blood of YHWHHOSHUA. It was a solemn time, one of self-examination, repentance, and abstinence (from sex). Laycher would hammer hard on the message of being worthy enough to *eat the body and drink the blood*, right down to the sister he chose to bake the bread. It was a heavy burden he would flop onto the shoulders of that woman, to be pure, to be perfect, to be free of all sin at the moment in which she prepared and baked the bread.

"The bread can't be made by just anyone. Examine yourself and your children; then, you won't have to be judged. If you take the bread unworthily, you will be in trouble with YHWH. This is why many of you are weak and sickly; you are unworthy and have been judged. If you can't clean your spiritual house, I wouldn't take Passover. Get rid of the leaven within and without before taking Passover. If not, you are in danger of hellfire. Make up your mind or get out. The majority of you are hell-bound."

Every April, there were two weeks of *Teachings*. Teachings were timed to coincide with Passover, and everyone from the other two churches was required to make the trip to Boone for two weeks of nightly worship, which usually turned out to be nightly rebuking, and the final night of bread, grape juice and foot washing.

"We'll have services till the fourteenth day, which is Passover, and I dare you to be here every night. Teachings start at 7:30 PM, not 8:00 PM. If we're late here, we will be last on that day. We should try to be early to pray. All schoolchildren should make 90% of the teachings, or they don't need to be in school. If you are obedient, I'll give you a big gift. If you ain't gonna obey what you hear, don't waste your time, stay home and go to hell free of charge—don't waste your gas."

Passover was the only time men and women were allowed to touch each other and only while washing each other's feet. We, kids, delighted in watching who would choose who, a topic that would be tacked on to our gossip agenda during our walks to and from school. Of course, the luckiest ones were the ones who got to wash Laycher's feet—he was usually the recipient of several foot washings within the night. However, if he chose to wash your feet, well, the only acceptable reaction to that was to cry tears of gratitude. I was never really into the foot-washing thing. When I was little, I giggled because it tickled, and we kids would make a bit of a mess with the water, but once I was older, like that particular year, I would mostly just wash my friend Yahanna's feet, and she would do mine. We would do it quickly and quietly somewhere off to the side where no one else was, dying of embarrassment.

That April, I was disoriented, desperate, miserable, and already checked out. I watched in disbelief as Yahanna's dad, Jerry, crossed the churchyard toward my dad and greeted him with a heartfelt embrace. I cringed at my dad's creepy smile and his self-absorbed swagger, and gay chatter, and I thought to myself, *how can they like him? Why can't they see? How can they be so happy to see him?*

A few days before the wedding, I could sense that my dad was growing anxious about the way I was behaving. He loaded all of us kids into the van and said he needed to talk to us. I knew he really meant that he needed to talk to me, but he was afraid to single me out—somehow, he must've sensed the new resolve I'd begun to cling to. He drove toward the town of Boone to a little pull-off by the Arkansas river, one of the spots we used for baptizing, shifted the van into park, shut off the engine, put on his holy, severe face, and gave us one of his big, important talks about rooting out evil in our household and *getting back to YHWH*. Then he looked right at me. I could feel his slicing gaze and knew exactly what his beady little eyes looked like all squinted up, but I didn't look at him. Instead, I studied the line of trees by the water, focused intently on the river's current rolling defiantly by.

Then he asked pointedly, "What's the matter with you, young lady? You haven't spoken to me in a week. Why are you ignoring me?"

Silence.

"I am your *father*. You will show me some respect. You

will look at me when I'm talking to you, young lady."

His attempt to command me failed. What he didn't know is that he'd surrendered his authority long before that moment.

"*I'm speaking to you. Answer me when I ask you a question.*"

I answered with a defiant, blank stare focused in every direction but his, feeling a power grow in me that I'd rarely felt before, the power of silence. But I had never been so rebellious on purpose, and I was barely balanced on that cliff, knowing that if I did look at him, my fear would be louder than my resolve. I knew he might threaten me, but he wouldn't dare punish me. We had long since moved past that option. I'd never threatened to tell anyone about him, but I could tell that he was afraid I would.

"Please, look at me—" His voice softened to nearly a whisper. My brothers and sisters were quiet, too, eerily so. He was begging then, and I continued to fight back the only way I knew how. Deafening silence. He could make me do a lot of things, but he couldn't make words come out of my mouth. I wanted to slap him right across the face, the way he'd done to us, but all I could do was stare at the river and *keep breathing*. I kept my gaze steady, funneling all my energy, concentrating on anything but that moment. I had never stood my ground so completely. I had never refused to back down. I shivered, exhilarated, and petrified.

We returned home. I hurried to the bathroom, and when I came out, he was waiting for me in the cramped hallway by the washing machine. His back was to the plastic door with the tiny window, the one that we never used because once you opened it, it was nearly impossible to close again, and, he'd never gotten around to building steps on that side of the trailer so it was just a three-foot drop to the ground. Plus, it had a sheet of plastic taped to the inside for several months of the year to keep out the cold air that seeped in around the edges. I rested my gaze on that window, determined to keep it there.

I had no idea what would happen next, but I wouldn't

give him the satisfaction of seeing the fear in my eyes as I repressed the shivers racking my body while my stomach churned like that washing machine. I heard the panic in his voice as he asked again, more entreatingly than before, "What's the matter? Why aren't you talking to me?" I glanced at him for a second. He oozed brokenness and hurt, and his eyes were teary. I almost felt bad, almost—for a moment. The war was real, the war between love and hate. And the fear, too, but at that point, the hatred and disgust won out, and there was no turning back. What he said next extinguished any inkling of pity that I had been feeling.

"Are you going to tell someone?"

I held my breath; my heart hammered with urgency. I had not considered that.

"Do you want me to turn myself in?"

Barely breathing, I wondered, *what did he mean—turn himself in?*

"Do you want me to go to jail? Is that what you want? Because that's what will happen if you tell, I'll go to jail."

I stifled a gasp but very nearly fell over.

I couldn't show my shock, couldn't let him know that I hadn't known that he was committing a crime. How could I have known when no one had ever told me? If he could go to jail, why was he telling me? If he was committing a crime, why did he think that telling me would make me less likely to talk? He knew me. I was the kid who always did the right thing. Did he think I would decide that the right thing in that case was to not send him to jail? I concluded the opposite on the spot. From within the fishbowl, all I knew about criminals was that they were bad people, evil people, the worst kind of people. I let that thought roll over in my brain a few times.

My dad is a criminal.

My dad is a criminal.

My dad is a criminal.

I'd never thought of my dad as bad, only me, because I didn't like him. I continued to ignore him, and after a few more minutes of pleading, he walked away.

The next day at the wedding, I couldn't function. I couldn't think, I couldn't speak, and I couldn't stop crying. It was like a dam had broken, and the entire reservoir was pouring out of my eyes. Alan, a single brother the same age as Mateo, wanted me to sing a song for everyone after the wedding. Alan and I had been friends since before he'd decided to join the church. The brothers met him on a witnessing trip to Texas, but he hadn't returned with them. Remus, who was one of those brothers, took me aside one day. "I think he hears the call, Sister Angela, I think he wants to repent, but he's afraid. Maybe if you write to him, it will help. Hearing from someone young might give him the courage he needs." That wasn't an unusual request for me. I'd been recruited to write to people more than once, some of them even in prison, hoping that the innocence of youth would persuade them. So, I wrote to Alan, and he wrote back more than once, and he *did* decide to join the church, although I had no idea if it was because of my letters.

We remained close, as close as was allowed in a place that forbade friendships between the sexes, and Alan asking me to sing a song was quite ordinary. But on that day, I didn't want to sing. Still, he kept begging, insisting, hounding me, until I finally snapped at him, "I don't want to sing the stupid song; I don't want to sing any song; why can't you just leave me alone?" I'd never spoken to anyone like that before, and he was stunned.

He tried to smooth things over, "No biggy, really, it's okay. You don't have to sing if you don't want to. I just thought it would be nice. We all love to hear you sing, but, another time, there'll always be another time. I'm so sorry. I had no idea it would make you so upset."

I had just filled my plate with food, decided there was no way I couldn't eat, and spun around to put the food down or give it to someone else. My plate flew from my hands, and its contents coated the front of his new robe. It was an accident, but I bawled. He was even more perplexed and tried to calm me, "It's really no big deal, so easy to wash; I'll go scrub it out right now. Please don't cry. I really don't care." He was backing away from me, both hands in the air in surrender, a reassuring smile pasted in place, while at the same time holding me in an intense stare that said, *what are you not saying?*

I stumbled away, not hearing half of what he said. The fog was so thick, the people around me so blurred and bizarre. I found my way to the women's bathroom inside the church and locked the door. I had no idea what to do next. Quinn jiggled the handle and knocked on the door, trying to get me to open it. I ignored her, her voice hollow and distant. Gwen knocked on the door and spoke softly into it, "Hey, it's just me, Sweetie. Alan told me what happened outside." She paused, waiting for me. When I didn't respond, she continued, "It's really okay; it's nothing to worry about. He's not mad." Another long pause, with nothing coming from my side of the door. "Why don't you unlock the door? Just let me in, and we can talk about it, okay? Maybe you can tell me what's *really* going on."

How could I tell her that *I* didn't even know what was going on with me?

"Come on, Honey," she pleaded. "I'm worried about you, and so is Alan. I told him I would come and make sure you were okay. Just let me in. I promise we can lock the door and stay in there as long as you want." After an extended pause, I finally let her in and rushed to lock the door behind her.

"What is it?" she asked, "this isn't like you. What just happened outside with Alan? You've never done anything like that before. You know you can tell me anything, right?"

I glanced at her for a second and then turned away. "Not this," I whispered, "I can't tell you this." I was shaking, and my breathing was shallow.

"Of course, you can, I promise. You know you can trust me." Her voice was soothing and gentle. I knew she was sincere, but I wasn't sure it mattered.

My brain was in a vice, my heart was racing, and I was trying not to cry. Things were not going as I had planned. I was going to disappear—not stay and tell. What would happen?

She was pleading, but I couldn't tell her, couldn't say the words; they felt like bile on my tongue. She wouldn't understand, and I was worried she'd think there was something wrong with me—like I was the problem. I knew I could trust her generally, but not with that. "No, I'm not supposed to tell anyone, ever. I'm never supposed to tell."

I glanced momentarily at her again. Her face had turned ashen, and her cheeks quaked. She began a sort of guessing game.

"Is it something to do with your family?"

I nodded.

"Is it your mom? I know she's strict; that can be hard."

I shook my head.

"Well, is it your siblings? Are they getting on your nerves?"

I shook my head.

"Do you have enough to eat? Are you hungry? Does your family need help with food?"

"No."

"Do you feel unsafe? Are you scared of something?"

I shrugged my shoulders. I didn't really know that I felt unsafe or scared. I just wanted out.

"Well—is someone hurting you?"

I didn't know how to answer that. What my dad was doing didn't hurt, specifically, but somehow it felt *hurtful*.

I shrugged again. By this point, my hands were covering my face. I couldn't bear to look at her because I somehow knew she would eventually get to *the question*, the one I *really* didn't want to answer.

It was like she was purposely avoiding that question—I'm certain now, gazing through my adult lens—the one she knew she was going to have to ask eventually. Only, sometimes, you don't want to ask it because the answer can be too cruel. You want to exhaust all of the other options first, and you want to hope, with everything you've got, that it's something else. Her voice faltered a bit when she finally asked that question.

"Is it your dad?"

My nod was barely perceptible.

She breathed a controlled breath, slowly in and very slowly out.

"Is he hitting you?"

Another tough question, both of my parents spanked me, so I wasn't sure what she was asking. Sensing my confusion, I suppose, she corrected herself. "I mean, like, besides spanking, like more than spanking."

I shook my head.

Then her voice wavered as if she was barely holding it together.

"Angie, is he touching you?"

I answered by collapsing in a heap on the floor. I couldn't look at her; it was too awful; *I* was too awful.

She gathered me in her arms, and we both cried.

I was suddenly aware of what I had done. The secret I had carried for all those years, the words from my dad echoing in my head—pounding, hammering their warning. I had just committed one of the gravest of sins; I had dishonored my father by doing exactly what he'd told me not to do. I had disobeyed him, by choice, on purpose, and I had no idea what would happen next.

I quickly backpedaled, "Please don't tell anyone, Gwen," I whispered frantically. "He always says he's sorry" (as if that would be enough to absolve him in her eyes). "He told me not to tell—not ever." It was a half-hearted plea. I said it because I was supposed to say it. I said it because I was sure I was overreacting, making a *mountain out of a molehill* like the Bible said. I was just being a drama queen, just trying to get attention, as my parents had often accused me of doing before because I cried so much. They called me the attention seeker and said I should leave some for my sister

Ruth who was much quieter than I. They blamed me for the fact that she was shy, insisting that because of my attention seeking, no one ever noticed her. I was certain that's what people would say about me telling. I said it because I thought that if I defended him right after I'd just accused him, then somehow, the two would cancel each other out. But I knew I never wanted to see him again, and I had no idea what Gwen was going to do.

My mom knocked on the door. I stumbled to my feet in a panic. I felt like I'd just been caught—like I was doing something bad, and she would take me home and punish me. I turned to Gwen and frantically shook my head. Neither of us made a sound, hoping she would just go away. I didn't want to see anyone ever again.

After a minute, Gwen whispered, "I need to go talk to Patrick. You lock the door when I'm gone, and don't let anyone in."

I locked the door the instant she closed it, afraid that if my mom was still there she would try to push her way in. The room was spinning. I sat on the floor and closed my eyes. My mom knocked a few more times and tried to talk to me through the door, but I didn't answer, and eventually, she went away. I knew I was crushing her, and I felt rotten about it, but I was afraid she was going to tell Gwen that it was a family matter and to let her take care of it. I was worried she would give me that look, the, *what have you done* look, and force me to go back home with them, and say that I needed to just learn how to love my dad and that nothing would ever change.

Gwen returned a few minutes later. "What did Patrick say?" I asked.

"I couldn't find Patrick, but I talked to Brother Laycher," she was still trembling, and her face was scarlet.

"*Oh no.*" Panic flooded me again. "Not him, he'll tell my parents, they'll make me go home—NO-NO." I paced the tiny bathroom like a caged animal, hyperventilating.

Gwen tried to calm me, "No," she stated firmly, "You

don't have to go home, not ever again, not while your dad is there. I told Brother Laycher that either he's got to do something about this, or Patrick and I are going to take you and leave."

I felt so guilty that I was relieved by the thought of not having to go home. What kind of person *wants* to desert their family?

"And he listened to you? What—what does that mean? What is he going to do about it?"

"I have no idea. Let's get you out of this bathroom." She opened the door a crack to see if anyone was hovering outside.

I yanked her back. "*No.* I don't want to see anyone." I, by no means, understood what I had just done, but I did have the sense that it was a bit like a bomb exploding, I had no idea what the fallout would look like, but I knew that it would be my fault.

"It's okay; we'll just go downstairs to my room, where we can wait without anyone bothering us." Gwen lifted her long veil and held it out like a curtain hanging from her left arm while keeping her right arm tightly around me. She shielded me from view as we hurried out the back of the church and down the stairs to the basement below the church where she, Patrick, and the single sisters lived. She and Patrick were living there in her old room temporarily while he worked and saved enough money for them to get their own place. The curtains were drawn, and the room was dark except for a small bedside lamp. We sat together on the bed, waiting—for whatever would happen next. I urgently wanted to do nothing more than to go to sleep. *I was so tired.* I curled up into a ball. Gwen covered me with her quilt and laid down next to me, and I closed my eyes and sank into a momentary bliss of nothingness because it felt like everything that had been inside of me had spilled out, and I was completely empty—hollow.

Minutes passed, but only a few before my mom and dad knocked on the door and then barged into the room without waiting for a response. I bolted upright and held Gwen's arm in a death grip. I knew what would happen next. They were going to tell me I had to come home. They were my parents, I would have to obey, but if they were going to take me, they were going to have to pry my fingers loose and drag me out kicking and screaming. My mom was mute, staring resolutely at the floor. I couldn't tell if she knew the whole story. My dad fixed Gwen in a challenging stare and said, with an agonizing dose of confidence and mockery, "I have a feeling that my daughter has told you something that was just supposed to be between me and her," he turned and glared at me, the fear and shame that had haunted his eyes before had been replaced with arrogance and provocation as if he was daring me to stick to my story. My mouth went dry and my palms clammy. He turned back to Gwen and asked, "Do I see hatred in your eyes, Sister Gwen?" He was trying to pull rank, man rank, the law of YHWH that said men should be subjected to YHWH and women should be subjected to men. He was daring her to call him out.

I was flabbergasted.

Gwen was shaking—her face, her hands, her voice, and she looked down at the floor, trying to regain some control—to steady herself. She held my hand tighter, and I knew she would never let me go back. Then, with eyes that pierced like daggers, she stared defiantly right back at him and said, "I'm trying really hard, Brother Bill."

I didn't know what she was trying really hard to do or to not do, but I'd never seen her so furious. I knew we were taking a big risk. There was no guarantee that anyone would listen. I expected my dad to say that I was lying or exaggerating—which I assumed would hold more weight since he was the parent—and for Laycher to tell me that it wasn't that bad and my dad would repent of his sin and I needed to honor my parents and submit to them.

Laycher soon found his way to us and whisked me outside to the school trailer. I was vaguely aware of people milling around outside. A heavy, somber feeling had descended; I saw grownups all around me hugging each other and wiping their eyes, but their silhouettes were hazy, and their voices muted, and I had a fleeting sense of regret; *I'd ruined the wedding.*

It was approaching dark, but no one had gone home. Laycher ushered me into the school and closed the door behind us. He held me while I sobbed, absentmindedly rubbing his hand up and down my back. "I'm so sorry, Jita," he cooed. "It's all over now. You don't have to worry anymore. I sent your dad away, and he is not welcome back here." He was quiet for a moment and then continued. "Why didn't you come to me, Jita? Don't you know you can trust me? You should have told me. I would have listened. I would have helped. That's why I'm here." Another pause, the only sound, my sniffling and hiccupping, and his breathing, and then he added, with the authority of someone who knows all. "You know what the Bible says, Jita? It says that if you know someone who is sinning and you don't speak up about their sin, then you are just as guilty. You should have told me so much sooner, Jita. You should have told me that he was sinning."

I stiffened and staggered backward out of his embrace. I sat down shakily at one of the desks, my thoughts a sucking vortex. *I didn't know, really; I would have told. I didn't know it was a sin until he told me.* But no words escaped my lips. Instead, they were trapped inside my head, swirling, swirling, tied to my doubt. Was I really just as guilty? Was this my fault, too? Were my dad and I actually in this together? The thought made me shudder as bile burned in my throat, but I knew that Laycher couldn't be wrong; he never was. If he said that I was vile and filthy and a sinner, then I was. And although he didn't say those exact words, he may as well have.

I spent the night with Patrick and Gwen. I had seen my mom briefly but didn't know what to say to her except that I was sorry. I saw Joseph momentarily, and still can't shake the image of him lying on the couch in that basement apartment of the church. He was deep in a whispered conversation with one of the single brothers, Rick, but he looked up as I walked in the door from my talk with Laycher in the school, turned to Rick, and said, "But that," pointing to me, "That's what hurts the most." They both turned to look at me, and then Rick stood up and left to give us a little privacy. Joseph sat up and reached out to me. I took his hand, and he pulled me down onto the couch beside him, held me desperately close, buried his head on my shoulder, and sobbed. My big brother's tears were falling on my neck, and he kept saying, "I'm so sorry, sis. This never should have happened to you; I should have protected you." I hadn't expected him to protect me, and I didn't know that he knew that there was anything to protect me from. I let him rock me while he promised he would take care of me and the family. Then he lifted his head, took my face in his hands, and made me look at him, "I'll kill him." His face shook like Gwen's, then it softened and twisted with grief. "Oh, sis, I want to kill him so bad. If it wasn't a sin, you know I'd kill him; I'd kill him with his own gun."

I rested my hand against his wet cheek, relieved that he wasn't actually going to commit murder but just *wished* he could commit murder. I wondered how he knew what my dad was doing and how he knew that it was so wrong when I had only found out a week before. Everyone seemed to know but me, and everyone seemed to think it was a much bigger deal than I'd ever expected.

I spent the next few days a sort of zombie, moving through motions without knowing I was making them. I was relieved my dad was gone, but felt sorry for him, too. He'd broken the shotgun, the one that he kept in the kitchen closet next to our five-gallon buckets of drinking water, into pieces, and we found it the next day when we all went home. It was surreal to go home knowing that my dad would never live there again. I knew that was true, but I still had difficulty believing that he wouldn't find his way back somehow, weasel his way back in; he was very good at weaseling. To this day, I still have weird nightmares that my mom and dad are back together, and I'm stuck living with them, even though I have kids of my own who are there with me. I knew that my dad was going to the lake of fire and that there was no way to change that. I felt a momentary twinge of regret that I was the one sending him there.

No one called the police. I hadn't thought about jail since the first time my dad had mentioned it. He was gone, and that's all that mattered to me. Patrick and Gwen moved into our tiny trailer with us. We girls gave them our room and moved into the back bedroom with my mom and my littlest brother, Samuel. She wanted it that way anyway. After everything that had happened, she wanted all of us close, and we were all feeling a bit clingy. The entire floor was covered in thin mattresses, with mounds of pillows here and there and stacks of neatly folded quilts.

A week passed, and we were sleepwalking through a new routine. Although unsettled, it helped to keep moving, keep going through the motions.

Then the phone rang on Saturday night, a week after my dad left. Gwen answered it.

"Who is it?" my mom asked.

Gwen covered the mouthpiece with her hand, "It's Sister Maxine. She says that the sheriff is at their house, and we need to go over."

"What on earth? What do you mean?" My mom's eyes widened in disbelief.

"The sheriff," Gwen repeated, "he's over there, and they're saying we need to come right away."

"Who called the sheriff?" My mom demanded, disbelief giving way to distraught displeasure.

"They did."

"But why?" My mom demanded. "We don't need them; we took care of it. He's gone."

Gwen whispered into the mouthpiece for a bit and then listened, "Okay, okay, yeah, I get it. I'll tell them."

She motioned for my mom to come closer, "they were worried about what might happen if word got out. If someone found out and reported it, the state could storm in and take all the kids and say we failed to protect them because we failed to report."

My mom closed her eyes and sighed in resignation and then looked up at Gwen, defeated.

"We don't really have a choice now," Gwen soothed. And then, speaking into the receiver again, "We'll be right over."

My mom's lips set in the thin, white line I was so familiar with, and tears welled in her eyes as they had so many times that week. "It's not supposed to be this way. Haven't we been through enough? Do we have to involve the law and the courts?"

I stood there witnessing this exchange, the gravity of it hitting me like a freight train. My dad's words echoed in my brain, "I could go to jail. Is that what you want? Do you want me to go to jail?"

Well, not exactly—at least—I wasn't sure. I knew I wanted him out of my life, but the idea of punishment or justice of some sort hadn't even crossed my mind. What I did know is that it had been hard enough to talk to Gwen, and *there was no way on earth* that I was going to talk to anyone else, especially not the police. It was a completely unexpected move, a decision taken by Laycher and Maxine without consulting my mom, Patrick, or Gwen. Gwen looked over at me and then at my mom. I knew what that look meant.

"No—no, *please, no.*" I begged Gwen, begged my mom. I sat down, determined to stay glued to that kitchen chair. If they wanted me to go, they'd have to drag me, chair and all. "I can't, not the police, I can't talk about it, not anymore, not to anyone else." We, kids, had always been terrified of the police. As in any social group that distrusts the government and insists that they'll only follow the laws of the land as long as they don't break the laws of their god, the police were a symbol of that law and, therefore, a threat. Police pulled us over for little things, like a broken tail light, and gave big tickets for driving without a license or insurance. If Social Services showed up at our house, we knew the police would be with them. Nothing good ever came from interacting with the police. I thought that the only reason someone would have to talk to the police is if they did something wrong. Laycher had said that I was sinning, too. Would the police think I was a criminal like my dad? "Please don't make me," I begged in one last half-hearted attempt to sway them.

"We have to go," Gwen insisted gently. "There's no way around it. You'll be alright. I'll be with you the whole time. I'll never leave your side."

I relented; I knew I had no choice in the matter. It was dark outside as we walked to the car and although it was late spring, I felt a dull chill and shivered down to the deepest part of me. The two-minute drive to Laycher's house felt eternal, and I kept hoping my mom would change her mind, that Gwen would change her mind, even up until the moment we turned into the driveway. I saw the two sheriff's cars in the yard, black and white with lights on top, lights that were not flashing, and sirens that were silent. I'd never seen quiet police cars before. My stomach turned inside out.

A sheriff from Pueblo County and his deputy were sitting on the flowered sofa in the dimly lit living room. Laycher and Maxine sat with them, and they all looked up and rose to their feet as we filed in the door. I stood like a statue.

The sheriff asked my name, and I just stared at the floor.

He said he was there to help and that he was sorry for what had happened.

I didn't move.

He promised there was nothing to be afraid of, that I could trust him.

I was mute.

Turning his attention back to the adults in the room, he

instructed that we all go to the station in town and continue the conversation there. The station was a thirty-five-minute drive away in the same building as the county jail. I had never been there before, but it sounded ominous. I still didn't understand why the police cared about what my dad had done or the fact that he was gone. Or why they had the power to tell the grown-ups what to do or why the grown-ups listened.

We made the drive in Maxine's sea green, antique Oldsmobile station wagon. I'd seen her drive it before, a self-satisfied grin on her face, a queen in her carriage, but I'd never been inside of it. I sat in the front seat, Laycher driving, Maxine next to me. They spent those thirty-five minutes cracking jokes, trying to distract me, trying to make me laugh.

I didn't think they were funny. I thought they were insane. I thought they were cruel and didn't care one bit about how I felt or what I wanted. How could they make me do this? I concentrated my attention on the dashboard. It was maroon leather and smooth, without any cracks. All our cars had cracks in the dash with crumbling yellow foam falling out. In that car, you couldn't feel the bumps; it was like we were floating above the street—I was floating, too, trying to escape that car, but the windows were all rolled up.

When we arrived, we were ushered into a little room, and a policeman named Carlos started asking me a ton of questions, questions that were specific and pointed. Questions that made my skin crawl, and my mouth go dry. Questions that made my face and ears burn red with shame. Questions like: "Did your dad ever kiss your breasts?"

Kissing is not how I would describe it, I thought, and then following up the thought in my head, *weird, is that something that grown-ups do? I thought that breasts were for feeding babies.*

"Did he make you touch his penis?"

What's a penis? I wondered silently while I continued to sit, frozen, staring—at the wall, the chair, the floor—anything but him.

Did he touch your vagina? I didn't know what a vagina was, so I had no idea if he had touched mine, although I was quickly beginning to surmise that all of those words that I didn't know were probably the body parts that were bad words that we weren't allowed to say or know.

"Did your dad ever stick anything inside of you?"

That question I understood. I nodded and whispered, "Yes."

When? Where? How? For how long? "We need as much detail as you can give us."

Everyone was prodding me to talk, telling me that it was okay, urging me to *just get it over with*, that it would make things better. I didn't believe them, and I still wasn't sure that I wanted to be the one to send my dad to jail. My lips were sealed, my hands were sweaty, and I was surrounded by exasperated grown-ups.

Carlos glanced around the room at the army of adults sitting with me and said, "I'm going to need to speak to her on her own."

Laycher oozed concern for me, but I knew he was really concerned about not being able to monitor what I said. What if the man started to ask me other questions about the church that had nothing to do with my dad? Everyone had been worried about it for years, that the state would somehow find a reason to take the kids away. Laycher rested his hand defensively on my head, determined to speak for me, "I don't think she wants that. You don't want to be alone in here with this strange man, do you Jita?"

Actually, I did. Answering the questions they wanted me to answer would be easier if no one I knew was in the room.

I looked up at him, "It's okay," I whispered, "You can go." They all stood up reluctantly and left. It was just me and two policemen in the room.

Carlos squatted down in front of me. Tears leaked from the corners of his eyes and rolled down his cheeks. He looked up at me beseechingly, his hands folded over one knee, the other bent beneath him. "I want to help you," he said softly, "that's why I'm here. No one is ever going to hurt you again. But I can't help if you don't talk to me. Sweetheart, please don't be afraid. This is my job. It's what I do. There's nothing you can say to me that would be wrong."

It broke my heart that he was so sad. I really did want to help him do his job. I worried that maybe he would lose his job if I didn't help. He was so sincere; it seemed like he really cared. I wanted to tell him it would be okay, that he didn't need to cry. I wanted to tell him everything, but the words were stuck somewhere below that lump in my throat, the words that I didn't even have, the words that no one had ever taught me. I felt too stupid and embarrassed to admit that I couldn't name the things that had happened to me.

Carlos eventually figured out that one of the reasons I was having trouble articulating was because I actually didn't know the words to say what needed to be said. "Sweetheart," he asked, "did anyone ever teach you the names for the different parts of your body?"

I shook my head and then quickly corrected myself, remembering that anything I said could make the church look bad, "well, yes, some of them, of course, the ones I need to know, like my hands and my head and feet, but...."

"But not the ones you need for this," he finished for me.

"No."

He contemplated what to do. "I can't put words in your mouth; I can't guide you what to say, the judge won't like that..."

I went cold again. *Judge? Was I going to have to go to court?*

Carlos continued, "Maybe it would be easier for you to do a written statement. Would you be okay with that? You could take it home with you and work on it for the next couple of days?"

"Okay," I squeaked, even though I didn't want to write it any more than I wanted to say it.

Carlos took me back out to the crew waiting for me. I

felt so bad about not being able to tell him what he needed that I must have said *I'm sorry* a dozen times. He kept assuring me that I had nothing to be sorry for, that none of what happened was my fault in any way. Laycher had said that it was my fault, so I wasn't sure who I should believe, but probably not Carlos because he wasn't in the church. I tried to believe him, but I know that I never really did. I believed Laycher for the longest time because he was supposed to be wise, and he was the mouthpiece of YHWH. For years I thought that I could never separate myself from my dad's filth, that because I didn't stop him, I must have been a willing participant. Laycher had said I was just as bad, and although I didn't understand why or how I trusted him against every instinct and every other voice to the contrary.

The drive home was silent. No jokes, no distractions. I knew the grown-ups were disappointed in me even though they never said it. I was disappointed in myself. Why couldn't I help that poor detective? There was a big cavern inside of me, dark and empty. I thought about my dad burning in the lake of fire, about how I'd never see him again and how he might actually go to jail, and for a fleeting moment, I regretted all of it.

19 THE AFTERMATH

The months that followed were a blur of meetings. Meetings with detectives, with lawyers, with guardians ad litem, and with doctors, both medical and psychological. I had never spent so much time with people outside of the church before and was caught off guard by how nice and decent they all seemed to be. Still, I mistrusted their kindness and concern, their basic goodness, because, of course, they couldn't be good, not if they weren't in our church. I kept my guard up. They all promised that what was happening, what I had to go through, was important, that it was necessary, that it would put my dad in jail.

Whether or not I wanted my dad in jail was beside the point. All of the grown-ups seemed to think that was exactly what was supposed to happen, so I did everything they asked me to do. "It's up to you," they would tell me, "only you have the power to put him away, to give him what he deserves." It was the right thing to do. I knew I had to do the right thing. I had to put an end to the whole ordeal. I was the only one who could end it, the one who could stop the chaos and pain that my family was going through, who could ease the tears my mom cried every night when she thought no one was listening. I did this to them; I had to end it. I had to make justice happen—I had to be the strong one.

Even when it meant that I would have to let a doctor

examine me. I had never been to a doctor, and I knew doctors were some of the worst of the blasphemous people. It would be fine, they told me, it was a woman doctor, and she would be very gentle. I couldn't bear the thought of taking my clothes off for anyone, woman or not, but it was the right thing to do, and I would do the right thing.

The hospital gown was cold and stiff. The room was too bright, too fluorescent. I sat on a skinny table covered in papery sheets that had been pumped up off of the floor after I'd climbed up. For the life of me, I couldn't figure out why it was okay to go to this doctor but not to other doctors. They told me it was because the State required it. We never usually listened to the State, but these days we seemed to be doing everything they told us to do.

The doctor entered the room, introduced herself, and instructed that I lay back and put my heels in the weird metal dips on either side of the table. I did what she asked, noting that it opened my legs wide. Involuntarily, I pressed my knees together like a vice. She asked me to open them. I resisted. There was only one other person who had ever made me do that. She rested her hand gently on top of the paper gown and looked over the peaks of my knees at me. "I won't hurt you," she soothed, "just breath, try to relax, and I will make sure it's over as quickly as possible." Her countenance was weary like she'd had to do that too many times. Silent tears escaped from the corners of my eyes and rolled onto the scratchy pillow. They said I had to be examined because sometimes kids lie. I couldn't believe they thought I was lying. Defeated, I pretended there wasn't a strange woman sticking a contraption inside of me, pretended I wasn't beginning to doubt myself, pretended that I wasn't beginning to wonder if I had exaggerated it all, that I'd imagined it was worse than it really was. Maybe I *had* created that world of chaos just to get attention. Maybe I never should have said anything.

The time between the doctor's exam and the sentencing was brief. My dad didn't deny the charges; he agreed to a plea bargain, one that would greatly reduce his sentence. He'd admit to one count of sexual abuse and could serve up to twelve years in prison.

One. Count.

I protested to the D.A. "There were hundreds of counts for years. He didn't just do it once; how can he just plead to one?" I assumed there was a *count* for every time he molested me. Only much later, while studying Criminal Justice in college and working as a victim advocate after college, did I learn that that's not the way it works. The criminal justice system often has very little to do with justice and a lot more to do with expediency and who is more skilled at the game.

"It's the best I can do with you unwilling to testify," The D.A. replied, her words pregnant with irritation. "The deal is done, but you *can* influence the judge's decision if you'd be willing to make a statement at sentencing."

I shook my head—not a chance.

She continued to stack her papers and files, regarding me as a minor annoyance, a single blip in her busy day of punishing bad guys. "There's really nothing to it. I've had very little kids talk in court with no problem at all, kids much younger than you." She was slathering on the guilt. "All the judge has to go on at this point is second-hand information from your mom and your friends." Then she stopped stacking and looked right at me. "Hearing from you would have a very big impact on him and make a huge difference in his final sentencing decision."

But it won't change the plea of one count, I thought. Her words echoed through my inadequate brain, *kids much younger than you have no problem.*

I had only run into my dad a few times since he'd left, but each time had reduced me to a crumpled, hyperventilating ball, and I could not expect that it would be any different in an intimidating courtroom full of people. But, I was determined, as I always was, to do the right thing, the thing that only I could do, so I agreed to make a statement to the judge, although I didn't have a clue as to what *make a statement* meant, nor what I would say.

My grandpa Gordon flew to Colorado for the sentencing. Grandma Jean didn't come; Grandpa said that she was still too furious to be anywhere near my dad. Years later, as she pressured me relentlessly to reconcile with my dad, I would grow to understand that her fury was not at my dad but rather at the church and my mom, who she presumed had turned my dad into the kind of man who would do such a thing. From where she stood, her little boy was a victim, too.

The courtroom was crowded. It felt like every grown-up in the church was there, and I wished they weren't. It was bad enough trying to say something in front of a bunch of people that I would never see again, but with them there, it would be worse. My confidence was quickly retreating. Every part of me shook, and my palms were sweaty. I sat in the back of the courtroom, Nathaniel like a statue at my side, while my dad gave his statement to the judge, pausing theatrically to sob between excuses.

I had believed him when he said he was sorry. I had actually thought that he would take responsibility for his actions. I never really considered him a bad person, just a weak one, like he'd always told me. My naive child logic led me to assume he would humbly accept what he deserved. I couldn't believe the words that were coming out of his mouth, words like *he had stopped long ago; he hadn't done it often; he had repented...*

"Judge, I'm sorry. I'm sorry to you, and I'm sorry to my family, and I'm sorry to my Almighty. I know I was wrong, I know I made mistakes, but the pressure and the stress that I've been under all of these years—I did something I wouldn't normally have done. That wasn't me, Your Honor; that was my weakness coming out because of the life I've been living...."

Mistakes? A mistake is something that you do by accident. What he did was to make choice, after choice, after choice, consciously and deliberately, secure in his assumption that he would never be found out. My throat tightened, and I knew that there would be no words coming out of my mouth. All those people counting on me, and I knew that when it came down to it, I would not be able to follow through.

"I have someone here who would like to make a statement to the judge," the D.A.'s voice reverberated off of the walls and impossibly high ceiling. I stood—and froze. My feet would not move. The judge's podium seemed miles away. Everyone was looking at me expectantly, and I finally understood the phrase, *so quiet you could hear a pin drop*. A ball of fury, fervor, and panic spread through my chest and throat, blocking off my voice, stymieing my determination and dedication to my only purpose for being in that courtroom—bringing my dad to justice. Someone urged me forward; I pulled back. "No, I changed my mind; I can't," I squeaked. More coaxing. I shook my head vigorously. My face was hot, my eyes brimming. The judge looked impatient. I tried to quench the water that was involuntarily squeezing out of my eyes.

I had promised myself I wouldn't cry, promised myself I'd be brave, and there I was, like a fool in front of the entire court, unable to utter a word. I hadn't even thought about what I was going to say.

Somehow, I made it to the judge's bench. He turned his attention to me impatiently. The D.A. gave me a nod. *You can do this*, it said. The stenographer's fingers hung expectantly above her keys, my dad's head hung against his chest—someone's hand held mine. I transfixed on the judge for a second and managed to mutter, "I just want justice."

He glared at me and then turned away like I'd wasted his time.

I spun around and raced down the aisle, out of the courtroom, and into my Grandpa's arms. His face was flushed and quivered with anger. He turned to the people from the church who were ready to surround me and comfort me and demanded, "What's wrong with you people? Hasn't she suffered enough? Why'd you bring her here? What on earth were you thinking?" I let him scold them. I didn't have the energy to defend anyone right at that moment.

20 DESPERATE MEASURES

My dad was sentenced to one year in jail and something like twenty years of probation (I don't remember exactly). He served that year in jail on work release because of *his special diet that was required by his religious beliefs*—a load of crap, but his lawyer knew how to work the system. Immediately after he was released, he filed for joint custody and visitation rights, and his parents filed for visitation rights. Grandma Jean said that she was afraid that because my dad was gone and we were isolated in the church, my mom wouldn't let them visit us anymore. I'm sure that was somewhat true, but my grandmother was also one of the smartest, fiercest, and most cunning women I've ever known. She saw an opportunity to move in for a last chance at forcing us out of the church, and she took it. My mom knew that, and I knew that, and at the time, I was one hundred percent behind my mom and worked tirelessly alongside her to keep both of the cases from turning against us.

It was to be a long battle, and by the time it concluded, I was sixteen. My mom was crumbling under the strain of hearings and depositions and court-ordered guardians who had to come out and inspect the house and the church. I knew I had to be strong, I knew we had to present a united front, or they may take us kids away. I was old enough to understand that the guardian ad litem would not care what the grown-ups said or did; he would only be focused on the kids. If the kids seemed happy and healthy and invested in the church, then they'd be more likely to leave us alone.

The court had also ordered continued counseling with the therapist I'd seen during the criminal case.

We fought it.

Laycher said that we couldn't look to outsiders for healing; we had to find our healing through YHWH, so we refused to comply with the order. I wrote a letter to the Judge to tell him that I didn't need outside help because I was surrounded by people who loved me and supported me. I wrote from the heart, utilizing the creative flair I'd learned from Patrick. It was dramatic and whimsical. Following is word-for-word, the letter I wrote, cringeworthy to me now, but a peek inside my fifteen-year-old brain:

"*Dear Judge,*

Each day we awake into the beauty of the morning. We emerge from our home into the warmth of the sun. As we go to school and study and learn, and as we go throughout our daily tasks, we are engulfed in the love and care of YHWH and of our brethren. No matter where we are, we can be assured that if we are in need, both physically and mentally, there will be assistance. There will always be a friend near. The goal I seek after each day becomes more clear as the healing of my mind and body becomes more complete. I feel the joy swell within my heart as YHWH gives me peace and sets straight the distortions of my childhood. I see clearly the path of life, the path I must walk. My love for this truth and for the brethren grows with each step I take as I'm learning to understand the reality of liberty. This is truth—this is life, and this is the healing and the relief which my wound needs. YHWH is my father, and my family are those who do the will of YHWH. I do not wish to be separated from this, my life, and the environment in which I've been raised, to be introduced to that which I have been taught is harmful to my flesh and spirit. My environment is pure. An environment in which righteousness is promoted, and dangers harmful to both our flesh and spirit are discouraged. My mother has taught me and brought me up from birth in truth. This is my home; this is what I've known. To allow anyone to talk or visit with me without the presence or consent of my mother would cause much confusion in my mind. Knowing in my mind and heart the truth that I've been taught, I would have a great battle to fight if enticed to do or partake of that which I know is wrong....

I rambled on for a few more paragraphs, but that's the general idea.

Karen assured the judge that our family was flourishing in spite of hardship and praised our musical abilities and beautiful smiles.

"They are a very talented family, especially musically, which I believe is wonderful therapy. They write many of their own songs, which enables them to express themselves and release their emotions. The other evening along with my children, they were playing instruments having a great time making beautiful music and singing songs. They were smiling, laughing, and happy, enjoying this simple pleasure."

She painted a heartwarming picture of a family wrapped in love and support. As did my teacher:

"Children, at home and in school, are taught the basic principles in life going back to the old ways. They are corrected for their wrong-doing...

...One of our biggest entertainments is singing. Almost all of the adults, as well as most of the children, play at least one musical instrument. The children write religious songs and sing them for fun, for school, and for church. When visitors come to hear their songs, they always leave deeply impressed...

...In school, our curriculum goes along with any public school with an additional subject of religion and excluding the anatomy of the human body, as well as of animals."

Remus (the one who made the paddle for the school), who liked to think of himself as the self-taught, self-appointed lawyer for the church, outlined our doctrine in painful detail, quoting scripture as reference. Remus was smart, arguably the smartest person in the church in terms of IQ. As I mentioned previously, he built guitars, violins, and mandolins from scratch, which he had taught himself how to do. He also built fine furniture, including tables, chairs, and kitchen cabinets. He spoke more than one language fluently and could, quite possibly, have taught himself the law by simply studying law books.

He even tried to write like a lawyer:

"We, the brethren of the Assembly of YHWHHOSHUA, being called forth by this court to issue a declaration of our religious doctrine (regarding this matter), wherein are committed the oracles of YHWHHOSHUA the Messiah; beseech the Holy Spirit, having all good faith in the Word. We ask for guidance in this endeavor. We pray that the heart of this court will be as fertile ground, allowing the seeds of truth and righteousness to flourish."

The document is fourteen pages long, and all of the references for every single quote come directly and only from the Bible, including Psalm 1:

"Therefore the wicked shall not stand in the judgment, nor sinners in the congregation of the righteous. For Yahweh knoweth the way of the righteous: but the way of the wicked shall perish—(We will become sinners if we do not separate ourselves from what the Almighty has judged as evil)."

It isn't clear whether he is referring to my father as evil and my grandparents, or the court, or simply all of them. He goes on to quote Romans, Matthew, Proverbs, and Leviticus, but also to add a great deal of his own wisdom along the way.

"Since the philosophy of Sigmund Freud was first expounded, there has been a steady movement toward liberalism in this country. This liberalism holds dear these covenants: people are greatly influenced by the parenting style of their parents; things that happen in childhood form lasting life views; through insight, a person can change. Thus people who exhibit odd behavior or who are psychologically imbalanced, or who commit criminal acts are seen as in need of rehabilitation. We of the Assembly of YHWHHOSHUA believe in these things as well. Parents should teach their children about the ways of the Almighty. We love our children deeply. Our community is small, and all the members are as one large family. Our commitment runs deep. Far deeper than that of the world. We understand that childhood is a vulnerable time. That is why we guard so closely the things to which our children are subjected."

He addresses the reasons we shouldn't be able to have

visitation with our grandparents:

"*The rod and reproof give wisdom: but a child left to himself bringeth his mother to shame*"—*Proverbs 29:15. Unsupervised visitation with the grandparents is also disapproved of. We do not allow our children to use or make any graven images. This includes television, movies, certain books, images on clothing, toys, and the like. We don't want them exposed to unclean foods. We have very strict diets. No fast foods, no caffeine, no white sugar, no additives, preservatives, or artificial colors or flavors. No pork. No fish without fins and scales. No eating in restaurants. The list goes on. Immodest clothing is not acceptable. Women in pants, short sleeve blouses, shorts, etc. No bathing suits. Haircuts and adornments are not allowed. No make-up or perfumes or colognes. No jewelry. Nor do we want our children exposed to such things.*"

Remus assured the court that his new wife, now my official counselor, was more than qualified to be my guide through the healing process. Remus and Lynn had met not even a year earlier when she first joined the church. He detailed that information in his letter to the Judge.

"*We don't want to take our children to any counselor of the world. We believe that through faith, we can be healed. We believe that when the Savior died, He died that we might have a hope in this life. All of the members of the Assembly have gifts bestowed upon them by YHWH, gifts that they can offer for healing....*

....As Lynn had recently joined with the Assembly of YHWHHOSHUA around the time she took up counseling the girl, we spoke of her interest in improving her own soul and agreed that in exposing her own soul to the light of the truth, that is, to bravely face her own fears and frustrations, she would exemplify for the girl the course that she would take toward healing."

And about me:

"*The purity and confidence of this young girl shine, as she increasingly savors the clarity to discern whether the love of the almighty is there within people and within herself...to take responsibility to communicate, to adhere to wholesome disciplinary standards and to positively solve problems as they arrive.*"

He sums up his letter to the Judge with this quote from

Matthew 7:
> *"Judge not, that ye be not judged. For with what judgment ye judge, ye shall be judged: and with that measure ye mete, it shall be measured to you again."*

We pummeled the State with a united front, and they finally backed down and agreed to let Lynn be my therapist as long as she submitted reports to the court on a regular basis, but not before the court-appointed therapist weighed in, submitting her own report to the judge about our final encounter: *"Upon arrival [the mother] announced that she would not let me see her alone, that she and Lynn would accompany her so she could tell me herself that she didn't want to be in counseling."* I am glad I have her letter because I have no recollection of the details of the conversation.

She continues: *"When we sat, [the mother] instructed—'Now tell her.' When Angela did not respond, I asked if she wanted to share the work she had done since we last talked. [The mother] interjected—'You just have to tell her what you want.' Angela then spoke, stating that she believes she is getting all the help she needs from the brethren and doesn't need or want outside help."*

I'm sure I meant every word, but I do remember going into that room with firm instructions about exactly what I should say. We were really only there to tell her that we wouldn't be back, consequences be damned.

"Lynn then took the opportunity to clarify their position. She spoke forcefully about their religious convictions and connected that to their decision not to allow any further involvement on the part of the 'world.' She explained that the Almighty is the only true counselor and heals all. She ended by emphasizing that their community is separate and wants to stay that way. She advised that they will not cooperate any further, that they will fight if they have to, and she made a reference to the appropriateness of dying for what you believe."

Evaluation:
"It appears to me that continued counseling may be perceived as threatening to the religious community, which perhaps depends upon isolation for survival. If this is so, it would be experienced by the adults of the community but could be filtered down to the children indirectly as

well as directly. The emphasis on separateness and isolation would serve to undermine treatment goals...I continue to be convinced that, were it possible, the treatment plan would provide counseling...It is difficult to perceive how this could be implemented in an environment of resistance and negativity."*

I didn't hate my sessions with Lynn because they were usually just girl talk, lying on our stomachs on her bed, or taking long walks in the afternoon. We barely talked about my dad; we mostly talked about Mateo and Remus. She was decades older than me, but we were just a couple of silly girls talking about boys.

She had married Remus within months of joining the church. Remus had been single forever and, like all the single people in the church, had wanted nothing more than to have a wife and a family. Lynn pursued him vigorously. I had never seen that before. The sisters usually waited to be asked to marry by Laycher or a single brother, or they went to Laycher first, like Jenna had. But Lynn had no shame and went straight to Remus herself when she decided she wanted to be his wife. I expected him to be angry because he was strict and obsessed with doctrine, but instead, he started spending all kinds of time with her, which was really weird. He was nicer when he was with her. And seeing as how I spent as much time as I could with her, it meant the three of us were together a lot. Her wedding dress was the one that I *did* make.

When she asked me to make her dress, I said yes without thinking. I had known she would ask—because despite our thirty-year age difference, I was her best friend. But when she dropped the fabric and the pattern off, my confidence faltered. More silk. Even finer than Jenna's and more tiny buttons. I managed to produce something beautiful but had I known how to curse, that dress would have been riddled with more than a few swear words.

When the day of their wedding came, I felt like I was dying. My eyes pressed against their sockets like they were going to pop out of my head, and my head felt like it was going to explode. Every part of me ached, and I was flushed with fever, and my throat was on fire. But there was no way I was going to miss it. I had spent way too much time preparing, being a part of every detail. Plus, Mateo had come from Missouri for the wedding, and there was no way I was going to miss seeing him. I was used to it, being sick that is; it always seemed to happen the same way. Every time I looked forward to a thing for months, something always seemed to happen—like me getting sick—to prevent me from being there.

The wedding went off without a hitch. Lynn's dress looked lovely on her, and I was relieved. After they said their vows, Lynn didn't wait for Remus to take the lead like the other sisters did. She reached up, standing on her tiptoes—at six foot six inches, he was more than a foot taller than her—and pulled his face into her hands and kissed him. I had never seen anyone do that before. Weddings were the only times couples were expected to kiss in public, but when Antonio had tried to kiss Jenna after their vows, she had pushed him away and burst into tears. But Remus smiled through his tears of joy and kissed Lynn right back.

After the line of congratulations and hugs had filed past them, Lynn took me by the hand, and the three of us walked out to their old truck to drive to the abandoned community hall five miles away for the fellowship dinner that followed. In spite of the flu wreaking havoc on my body, it was the newlyweds and me; they'd chosen me, and I was on cloud nine.

21 DAY OF RECKONING

Remus and Lynn were married barely a month after I turned fifteen. Those teen years were the busiest and, yet, the blurriest of my childhood, but a lot happened between the time my dad was forced out and when Remus and Lynn became my new couple of the moment.

Once my mom was single again, and since I was fifteen, our home was one that was restricted by the same rules as any other that housed single sisters. The single brothers weren't allowed to visit without a married couple, and they avoided us like the plague. Nathaniel was the only one who ignored that rule and stopped by nearly every evening on his way home from work, and it was supremely comforting. He would come inside, close the door, sit down in front of it, sometimes without saying one word for twenty minutes or so before he'd put his hat back on, walk back to his van, and drive away. It was weird, but it was reassuring having him there, even a silent him, checking on us, making sure we were okay. He kept getting into trouble because Maxine liked to sit out on her porch swing with binoculars and watch our house, but he didn't seem to care. I think that was the first time I saw anyone blatantly disobey Laycher.

Mateo was still living in Missouri, and although I probably thought about him on a daily basis, I was also sufficiently occupied with a life that had changed dramatically since my dad left. My mom was alone and needed to depend more heavily on me. She, in turn, allowed me a bit more freedom to spend time with friends. My friends were all grown-ups, so I suppose that didn't hurt. I spent as much time as I could with Patrick and Gwen. Patrick had stayed true to his word and never again betrayed my trust. He was the only one who didn't insist that I *just forget about* Mateo. He knew that it was ridiculous to ask a girl to simply stop feeling what she was feeling. He would tell me that he knew Mateo wanted to be my friend but couldn't because of the constant scrutiny. Mateo had been rebuked by the pastor of the Missouri church because of me. The letters I'd snuck into the mail to him had been intercepted by the pastor there, as Laycher had commanded, and that same pastor immediately demanded to know *what Mateo's intentions were*, whether he loved me and planned to marry me. Mateo was floored and aghast at the suggestion. He called my mom and told her that she had to stop me from writing.

I was furious, and I took all of the letters he'd ever written to my family and threw them into the outhouse hole right on top of that pile of poop. After that, I boomeranged between loving him and hating him. Patrick tried to help me past that by saying things like, "Just wait a few years; he can't love you right now, but maybe when you're older," or "I bet he wishes he could be here hanging out with us right now."

Gwen would get irritated with him and retort, "You shouldn't lead her on like that. There's no guarantee of anything. She's too young to concern herself with what he may or may not do. Don't give her false hope; she'll just get her heart broken." Although I appreciated what Patrick, the eternal optimist, was trying to do, I knew that Gwen was probably right, there was no guarantee, and I was most likely going to get my heart broken. They were my rock. They stood by me, with me, and let me say and think any damn thing I pleased. But good things never seemed to last in my world.

We were at church one Sabbath Day, and I could tell it was going to be a rebuking day; I could tell by the way Laycher's eyes flashed righteous anger, and his beard quivered with pent-up fury when he talked. He was at the pulpit, scanning the pews, moving from one person to the next, people who needed to be chastised, humiliated, and brought to their knees to ask for forgiveness. I sat board-stiff, as far against the edge of the pew as I could go without falling off, slumped down behind the bodies of my mom and my brothers, who sat on the bench in front of me. I thought maybe if he couldn't see me, he would forget that I was due for a lashing. I knew that he knew about Missouri and the intercepted letters.

The letters that I had been writing to Mateo, I had written with my mom's permission. She read them before I sent them, but I knew that wouldn't matter. Mateo never wrote back to me, he wrote to the whole family, and sometimes he would send us money. He knew we were barely scraping by on the income of Joseph's pay from working with Laycher. The minute my dad had been ordered to leave, my big brother, at sixteen years old, had been pulled out of school and forced to work five days a week pouring concrete. He would come home and lie in his bed and cry because his body hurt. I would go in and sit next to him, wanting to help somehow, but all I could do was massage his back and shoulders and wish he didn't have to be the man of the house. At the end of each week, Laycher handed my mom one hundred dollars, Joseph's pay. Sometimes Mom felt bad about Joseph working so hard to earn money but never having any to keep for himself. She would give him a few dollars (it was all she could spare, we needed the rest) and tell him to buy himself a treat, a candy bar, or ginger ale to cool down at work. And otherwise, somehow, she managed to make ends meet for a family of eight on four hundred dollars a month. That was why it was always nice to have the money that Mateo sent.

But the single sisters, who, as most unhappy people

often are, could be really petty, had been complaining to Laycher, whining that it wasn't fair that we were getting *extra money* from Mateo (even though there were eight of us and only three of them). They lived off of money from The Box at the back of the Church, and as *widows and orphans* (my dad wasn't dead, but he was *dead to us*), we were supposed to get our money from The Box, too. But we never knew how much money would be in there. The brothers put money in when the spirit moved them, and Laycher gave it to the people he thought needed it. We didn't need it as much because Joseph was supporting us.

That Sabbath Day, as Laycher made his way through the pews with his chastisements, I almost thought I would manage to escape his wrath again, until I heard my name spat out of his mouth in front of everyone and Mateo's name right after.

"Sister Angela."

It was happening. After all those years of dreading it, I was hearing my name from the pulpit—at fifteen years old, I was officially grown up enough to be rebuked in public.

"I've given you chances, too many chances. I've tried to be gentle with you, gentle like a grandpa should, but grandpas also have to chastise—no more chances. Get your carnal thoughts under control and bring your carnal desires under subjection."

His words were distorted and remote. Although I was still seated, board upright, and staring straight ahead, I was already gone.

"I've gone easy on you because you're young, and I'd hoped you'd learn. Course, it's not just you. Brother Mateo…"

Oh no, leave him out of this, I begged silently. *He doesn't deserve this.*

"You're not to send money to that family ever again. Send it to me, and I will give it to those who need it. Get your flesh out of here and get your wicked desires under control."

I sat through the whole thing, took my licking like I'd learned to do. I knew better than to challenge his right to pound me to a pulp in front of everyone. On some level, I thought that I deserved it.

Of course, I was swimming in shame and embarrassment. I had spent so much time trying to be good, trying to avoid the exact thing that had just happened. But there was something else pushing to the surface, too—simmering ever so briefly before quickly raging into a boil—and that thing was fury. I didn't recognize it; it was a new feeling for me, but to my surprise, because of that feeling, I didn't crumple there in front of everyone. I stood up, turned around deliberately, and walked the length of the building and out the door, looking straight ahead and not at all the eyes fixed on me.

Once outside, I caught my breath and began to tremble. I didn't know I could feel so many contradicting feelings all together—guilt and hurt, but also confusion and fury—because I had, after all, followed all of the rules when I wrote my letters. So, I knew, on some level, that I had done nothing to deserve it.

Gwen followed me outside and held me tight. Her face quaked, like when I told her about my dad. She was saying that what Laycher did was inexcusable, but I barely heard her. "It's just the last straw," she murmured as much to herself as to me. "We've had enough. We can't take it anymore. We're sick of the hypocrisy, sick of the double standards, sick of watching him beat everyone down, even you, even children, just to hold onto some idea that he's in control."

My blood ran cold as I snapped out of my stupor. Had I just heard what I thought I heard? Was she talking about leaving? Without them, I knew I would never survive. I suddenly wanted to go too, a completely unexpected urge that I'd never felt before, but I knew that my mom would never let me.

"Oh heavens no—please—no, you can't; I can't be here

all alone." I begged, my voice barely a whisper.

"I'm so sorry, Honey, but we can't do it anymore. It's killing us slowly, suffocating us. No one is ever going to stop him; no one ever stands up to him. Patrick has tried to talk to him, to call him out when he's being hypocritical, and he won't listen. He thinks he's infallible, but he's not, he's just a man, and he makes mistakes. But he won't admit it, he won't change, and we can't keep pretending everything is okay." She said so much more, but I may as well have been deaf. All I heard was that she was leaving. All I knew was that the only two people who were holding me steady would be gone. We had walked downstairs to her old room in the basement of the church. We were tearful but also defeated.

When the service ended, I insisted wearily that I absolutely had to say goodbye to Patrick. "Too many people have left without me being able to say goodbye, but not you, not Patrick—not this time."

"Stay here, and I'll go find him," she patted my hand as she stood, "no one knows where you are, so it'll be okay." But right after she left, I heard footsteps in the hallway, lots of footsteps, and I knew that it wasn't Patrick and Gwen and it wasn't going to be okay. Laycher and two elders burst through the door without knocking, encircled me, laid hands on me, and started to pray fervently to cast out the evil, carnal spirits that had taken control of me. I was mortified and horrified. Gwen came back, and they wouldn't let her into the room. "I love you," she yelled from the hallway, her voice broken by her own sobs.

"Let me go," I shrieked, "I just need to say goodbye. Gwen, they won't let me say goodbye." She tried to get in, but they blocked her. I tried to get out, but they held me back. I could barely breathe. I screeched and cried and struggled like a crazy person while they held me down and prayed harder. I kept saying, over and over again, broken and desperate, "I just need to say goodbye" until my voice grew hoarse from the screaming.

They didn't listen. Instead, in that basement bedroom,

with only a thin shaft of light slanting in from a tiny rectangle window, three grown men, each one with a hand on me and the other in the air, continued to pray fervently to rebuke the demons that were plaguing me while I screeched and struggled like a mad woman to free myself. That is, until I started to believe them, to believe I was possessed because I certainly *felt* possessed. There was a slithering python of anguish crushing my chest, panic cinching my throat, and tunnel vision causing the room to pitch and spin. My breath came in sharp gasps and hiccups as I begged, my voice raspy from screaming, "Let me go, please, let me go—I just want to say good-bye." Each time I struggled to rise, they pushed me down again and prayed harder and louder.

I was frantic—*they didn't understand*. I would sit there on that bed as long as they wanted and let them cast out *all* of my demons, past, present, and future *after* I said goodbye.

Gwen's voice sounded again from the hallway. "I love you," she yelled once more, "And I'm sorry, I'm sorry I have to leave you. I'm so sorry, honey." As her voice faded and I ran out of strength to struggle, the waves of grief, the kind that engulf you when someone dies, washed over me. I stopped resisting, collapsed back onto the bed and surrendered to the fact that I was possessed and that I was alone—I'd never felt so alone in my life.

I couldn't think; I couldn't move. I knew I would never see them again. As backsliders, they had to be dead to me—yes, that was the feeling—I was dying. As I gave up and collapsed in defeat, they released me and stopped praying. Then they tried to comfort me by telling me that if I was truly repentant, YHWH would forgive me. They brought my mom in to make me feel better. They reminded me that there were plenty of people who still loved me and would be there for me. I barely heard them, and I didn't believe a word they said. They'd broken me. I would do whatever they wanted because now I had no one to protect me.

I never saw Patrick again before they packed up their

pick-up and left a week later. It was torture to know that they were still there, just a mile down the road, but I wasn't allowed to see them or talk to them, no matter how much I pleaded and begged. I felt like my heart was being ripped out of my chest, emotional pain ripping through my physical body. I saw Gwen at Laycher's house by accident. Maxine was deathly ill with hepatitis, and I went to over give her a back and foot massage, which I had been doing several times a week at that point. As I rounded the corner in the living room, Maxine walked out of the laundry room, a room I'd never been in before, and jerked her head toward it, indicating for me to go in there. That was the weird thing about Maxine. For the most part, she was bitter, calculating, and vicious, and then out of the blue, she would do something completely thoughtful and unexpected. Gwen was hiding behind the door. We fell into each other's arms and wept silently for a minute or two. Once we were able to control our tears, I told her matter-of-factly that I knew what had been wrong with me that day in the basement. "I had demons, Gwen; I could feel them choking me and making everything black."

"Oh, Honey, no—no, that isn't true. Who made you believe that?" There was pain in her voice but also resignation, like she had no more fight left in her. Her eyes were sad, those of a person who's given up.

"They said when they came to pray for me, after you left me in the basement, that I had demons, and that was the reason I felt so frantic and why I haven't been able to stop loving Mateo. They told me that if I work hard enough and I really want it, I can be free of the demons and all of those feelings. They have to be right, Gwen; nothing else makes sense."

She sighed, tears gathering again in the corners of her eyes while she stroked my cheek. "I'm okay now," I told her, "You don't have to worry about me. I know I can be righteous. I'm going to try with everything I've got from now on."

Then we heard footsteps approaching. "You better go," she whispered. "I don't want you to get into trouble."

"Write to me," I pleaded, "even though you're not supposed to. Please, write." And with that, I released my grip from her hand and slipped back through the door.

Their departure sent me tumbling down a rabbit hole of doubt about everything. Nothing was exempt from my intense need to question, to demand reasons and answers. I spent a lot of time with Remus and Lynn at their house, driving to and from Pueblo to witness or to shop, or in their pick-up truck sitting in our driveway—Lynn in the driver's seat because Remus was legally blind and wasn't allowed to wear glasses. They seemed invigorated by my desire to understand the doctrine. My *why* questions didn't ruffle them. Remus, as I indicated previously with his letters to the judge, loved to dissect doctrine for anyone who would listen. Now, the fact that I was listening overjoyed him.

At first, Remus and Lynn were super supportive. Remus encouraged me to think and ponder and to write it all down. Lynn encouraged me in subtle, symbolic rebellions by being a part of them. I had so many itches that I needed to scratch and an intense urge to shake the boundaries all around me to see if they would hold. I asked big questions, and I asked small, seemingly insignificant questions, like "Why were the brothers the only ones who played instruments when we sang together in church?" They would leave their pews and walk to the front of the room with their guitars, violins, mandolins, and flutes and play while the rest of us sang. I had never heard anyone explicitly say that women weren't allowed; I'd just never seen a woman do it before.

Lynn laughed out loud, "I never thought about that before."

"We should go up there with them next time and just see what happens."

"I don't see the harm in that," she pondered quizzically.

"I'll only do it if you do it with me."

"Okay, let's do it."

The next night in church, I could think of nothing else. I kept glancing at the guitar rack to my right, where I'd carefully hung my guitar when we arrived, and thinking, *am I really going to do this?* Am I crazy? I worked myself up into quite a frenzy, just wondering and worrying about what would happen when I did.

When it came time to sing, it took every bit of effort I had to force my feet to take those few steps out of the pew and to the rack. It felt like the church was dead silent, and everyone was looking at me as I gingerly turned the guitar sideways to slide it out of its spot, careful not to bang it against the wall. I glanced quickly across the room to make sure that Lynn was standing up, too. She was already in place opposite me, and she gave me an encouraging nod and smile. My hands trembled slightly as I took the guitar strap and placed it behind my head over my shoulder. I had never stood to play the guitar before. There were a few surprised looks, some double takes, and some approving smiles, but other than that, nothing happened.

I was vocal when something didn't seem to make sense, no matter how much they explained it, and they encouraged me to keep asking and to keep trying to understand. Those intense conversations lasted for a few months, and I wish I could remember specifics, but I don't. What I do remember is how they ended, how I ended up adrift and alone—again. We were sitting in their truck in our driveway, talking about backsliders, forgiveness, and YHWH's infinite love. I was still mourning the loss of Patrick and Gwen and the rule that said that we could have no contact with backsliders.

"If YHWH is love, how is it that we aren't supposed to show love to people who have lost their way?" I asked. "Isn't it possible that staying in touch with them could encourage them to see that they've made a bad choice, remind them of what they had, and even lead them back?"

"They aren't innocent," Remus insisted. "They knew what they were doing, and they chose the world over the church. YHWH is love, but he also rains down his wrath upon those who reject him." I sensed more than a little righteous anger in his voice when it came to Patrick, something a bit closer to disgust.

"But that's *his* wrath, not *our* wrath," I pushed back. "Isn't it true that we are supposed to leave the judging to him, that it's not our place to judge, but just to show love and mercy no matter what?"

"Of course, that's true," Lynn piped in, "that's what we're all trying to do. If they came back, we would welcome them with open arms."

"But that's *not* true," I contended, "we've all abandoned them simply because Brother Laycher said to. Why do we always just do what he says? Why does no one ever refuse? Just because he's the pastor doesn't mean he can't make mistakes."

Remus's demeanor changed, and his brow furrowed. He looked at me, his eyes stern and dark. "I don't know how else to help you understand. No matter how much we talk, you keep pushing back. You're just a child, and yet you think you can ask all of these big questions without having any of the answers. If you think you're mature enough to ask questions, then you better be mature enough to come up with the answers. You can't just keep telling us about the problems; if you think there are problems but don't have any solutions, you should just shut up."

I had not expected the sudden about-face. In a single breath, he had told me I was just a child who needed guidance and then, at the same time, that I couldn't ask questions unless I had the answers, that I couldn't point out the problems unless I had the solutions. It felt like a complete flip-flop from what he had been telling me in the weeks before.

Confused, I said meekly, "I thought that's what we were doing together, coming up with answers."

22 WALKING THE LINE

Having been *put in my place* by Remus and Lynn, I drew back into myself again like those plants that close up tight when you touch them. The whiplash of the ever-tightening circle of acceptable behaviors for me closed my throat in a tight knot and deflated any balloons of belief I may have been trying to fly. And there, beating my head against the walls of the fishbowl, doubt, and gloom pushing into the furthest reaches of my suffocating psyche, I was presented with the gift of a new friendship and a new ally—Rick.

Rick was young, the same age as Mateo. He had a penchant for white robes—white symbolizing purity. His straight blonde hair settled in ringlets at the tops of his shoulders, and his red-tinged beard curled tightly against his face. He carried himself up the aisles of the church as if he was floating, embracing the image he'd envisioned for himself, the prophet he so wanted to be. He hung on every word during sermons, gazing at Laycher as if a man in love, his head slightly cocked, his blue eyes misty with devotion and rapture. He was trying desperately to prove himself to the leaders of the church; his ultimate goal—to be a leader himself. It was this man who stepped forward to try to fill the void left by Patrick and Gwen and help me move past my fallout with Remus and Lynn between my fifteenth and sixteenth year of life, seeing me as the perfect person to mold and save. He was my first male friend besides Patrick, although I always thought of Patrick not so much as a friend but as a teacher, a mentor, and an irreplaceable advocate. Rick was too young in my book to be either a teacher or a mentor—thus, it was easy for me to consider him a friend, an equal.

Rick listened intently when I spoke, didn't talk down to me or judge me for asking questions, and agreed with me that if there was to be any hope for the survival of the church, we kids needed a voice. Rick had decided that he was a perfect bridge between the two worlds; just barely an adult himself at twenty-three, he could commiserate with someone my age while still enjoying the power and privilege of not only being an adult but an adult brother. We agreed that we needed to challenge the status quo, to demonstrate that some things weren't black and white, that trust could be earned, and that change isn't always bad. We set out to show, by example, that men and women could be friends and confidants and could spend time together unsupervised without anything bad happening. He stopped in to see me at home often, ignoring the rules, to prove to me that he was committed to our cause. The first of many long talks we had took place in my bedroom with the door closed. My mom admired his zeal and trusted him because I wasn't in love with him, and so she didn't seem to care the way she did with Mateo. I think she also witnessed and appreciated my renewed zeal for the faith. I had been her rock throughout the duration of the court cases, and because of that, she had grown to trust me and respect me up to a point.

I was *all in*, just like always. I hung on Rick's every word, believed him with my whole heart, and gave one hundred and ten percent to our mission. I was so desperate for motion, for change; I so needed to believe that change was possible in that fishbowl because I had not yet begun to imagine a life outside of it. So, when the betrayal came, I was, of course, devastated and, for the second time in my life, livid.

But before betrayal comes trust.

Rick and I were both enthusiastic about breaking the rules, especially since we were doing it for a good reason. If we wanted anyone to take us seriously, we had to convince ourselves first. I felt invigorated, hopeful, and determined. My doubts about hypocrisy, double standards, and my inability to get through to anyone began to dissolve, and I had, however brief, a renewed surge of faith in YHWH and a revived dedication to the doctrine. Only, I decided to take it even further. I felt like I had to make some sort of grand gesture, some symbolism of my commitment. I had been baptized as a baby, so I couldn't do that again, but the devotion I was feeling was different than I'd felt in the past. It was *my choice*, and I had a deep need to memorialize it, a renewal of my vows, so to speak. For the first time, however briefly, I felt like I was in control.

Rick started teaching at the school, yet another way he was attempting to step into Patrick's shoes, and for two to three months, we got to spend the whole day together and then the walk home. We squeezed out every possible moment, walking as slowly as we could while my siblings rolled their eyes and hurried ahead. We talked about everything and anything and were completely honest; no subject was off limits. We knew that the only way to make our point was to treat our friendship like any sanctioned friendship with the same sex. We were inseparable, talking for hours, playing music together, spending our Saturday nights knitting together, playing games with the kids, and making popcorn and candy.

Knitting was a trend that had only sprouted in the previous months with the single brothers. It started off with one brother who decided that weaving wasn't too feminine, and if women could do it, then, of course, he could too, and probably better. He was a machine, pumping out ponchos and jackets one after the other and thoroughly enjoying himself. Then, since he was so good at weaving, he started knitting and was far more productive, much to his smug pleasure, than the sisters, who were also cooking, cleaning, managing households, and raising children. A handful of single brothers followed his lead, Rick being one of them (the brothers' knitting seemed to fall seamlessly into our assertion that men and women weren't so different), and before we knew it, there was a regular knitting frenzy buzzing through the congregation with both brothers and sisters carrying around half-finished sweaters, socks or baby blankets in quilted handmade bags. Most of our yarn we had hand-carded and spun ourselves (two activities that I found hypnotically relaxing) from wool from our own sheep. The atmosphere was downright euphoric during those few short months. In an environment that was determined on keeping the sexes apart and highlighting the stark differences, sharing a simple activity like knitting had signaled that maybe the lines didn't have to be so dramatically drawn, and that was refreshingly hopeful.

That is, until Laycher decided to shut it down—something he always did when he noticed that the congregation was finding joy, unity, and hope, and it had nothing to do with him or the fire and brimstone that he loved to rain down on us from the pulpit to keep us trembling in our Birkenstocks. He sneered and chuckled as he preached, "All you brothers who think you've found the answer with this knitting and sewing—women's work—you're just becoming effeminates, sodomites, (his word for *fag*—I use *fag* cautiously, knowing that it is an insult, but because that is how he meant it) and you're weak, and you're out of line."

Rick promptly gave all of his knitting supplies, including a half-finished sweater and skeins and skeins of yarn he'd spun, to me. I protested vigorously, insisting that it was a ridiculous rule. "We aren't following the rules anymore, remember? The whole reason we're pushing so hard against the rules is to prove that they can be changed—wasn't that sort of our mission?" I couldn't understand why he was caving so readily.

"I agree," he responded, without much conviction, "but change takes time, and it's better not to rock too many boats at the same time. If Brother Laycher is wrong, I'm sure YHWH will show him, and everything will work out." I wanted to believe him, but I didn't. In spite of my newfound zeal, doubt was creeping in again. I tried to quash it by diving in even deeper and closing my ears to the little devil (or angel, depending on how you look at it) sitting on my shoulder telling me that something was terribly off.

It was on one of our walks or one of our bedroom talks, I can't recall, that I told Rick about the urge I was having, the need for a re-dedication of sorts, a marriage to YHWH. It would be my own private moment; no one would know except him. I would dress in all white, like a bride, and dedicate myself, body and soul, to YHWH and YHWH only. Rick knew all about Mateo, I had no secrets from him, and we both knew that what I was actually saying was that I was finally free of my carnal feelings—they weren't gone; they were just no longer in control. He was so impressed and moved to tears by the idea that he gave me money on the spot to buy the fabric I would need to make a dress and veil. I was so excited that I leaped up and hugged him on impulse. *This is really working, I thought; I'm hugging a man, and the sky isn't falling. My mom doesn't care, he doesn't care, and we're just friends.*

"I feel so unburdened," I told him days later, ambling along in my new muslin dress and veil on our way to church. "I don't even need anything else or anyone else. I don't even need Mateo; I'm free—I barely think about him anymore. I mean, I still feel the same, but somehow it's not controlling me."

"That's wonderful, Sister Angela, really wonderful. I'm so happy you've found that freedom."

We lingered behind the group of people walking with us, savoring the moment in silent appreciation and reverence. The fact that no one else knew intensified it, and my head buzzed with the headiness of it, and my stomach fluttered.

After services, Rick convinced Mom to let me go witnessing in Colorado Springs. My mom never wanted to let me go anywhere alone, but she didn't hesitate when we told her that Antonio and Jenna were going—having a married couple along to chaperone made everything legit. Rick and I never left each other's sides and sat together on the long trip to the park and back again, and once or twice, he even looked at me the same way he gazed at Laycher, with that look of rapture and reverence. I knew it meant that I was finally holy, finally pure enough for him to believe in me the same way he did the elders and to respect me the same way he did the woman he was in love with, Anna. Anna was two years older than I, and we weren't really good friends, but she taught at the school, too. He didn't know I knew how he felt; somehow, I'd bared my heart to him, but he'd never done the same. It wasn't a difficult thing to figure out, though, because he talked about her non-stop and told me that she was a perfect example of purity and holy devotion, *I should try to be just like her.* That definitely stung a bit because I was trying so hard to be pure and devoted, and I thought maybe I could finally just be me. But as always, I wasn't enough; he wanted me to be more like Anna.

    I was so glad we were both in love with other people because it made our relationship simple and uncomplicated. Rick didn't last long teaching at the school, and not long before he left, I could feel him pulling away. I knew the feeling too well; there was no mistaking it. I wondered what I'd done, what rule I'd broken that I didn't know about. I'd conducted myself exactly how he'd told me to and truly believed we were on a crusade together. Before he quit, we were walking home from school one day, and he turned to me and said, "You know, as much time as we spend together, I almost feel like we're not separate people anymore. We know each other so well, you know, almost like boyfriend and girlfriend." Then he chuckled, trying to make light, but I could tell it was an uncomfortable chuckle.

I wasn't sure what he was trying to say.

No, no, nooo—not you too. I thought dejectedly. *You said it would be different for us, that we could make it different.* I ignored the alarms bells clanging incessantly in my brain and replied with the utmost composure, in an effort to reassure myself just as much as him, "All we need to do is make a choice to keep our friendship pure; it really is that simple. The thing that makes us such good friends is our zeal for YHWH and our commitment to make this place better for young people, nothing more, nothing less." But I thought about what he said for the rest of the day. Why? Why couldn't he just be my friend? Why did he have to make it into something it was not?

The next day before school, Rick ushered me into the women's bathroom and shut the door. He told me that he couldn't be my friend anymore because he was pretty sure I was falling in love with him. I couldn't believe my ears, and if I hadn't been practicing how to be meek and quiet so intensively over the previous months, I would have instantly challenged him, *what on earth are you talking about, you hypocrite? Just who's falling in love with who? You know exactly who I love, and you know that never changed because I told you, and in spite of your fake friendship, you never liked it. You always thought you could convince me to stop loving him, but you couldn't, so now you're doing this.* There were always so many words that ping-ponged around inside my head but never found their way out of my mouth.

While we were in the bathroom with the door closed, Karen showed up and wondered why the rest of the kids were sitting unsupervised in the front of the church (we started each school day in the church with a ten-minute prayer meeting, during which time most of the kids just fidgeted and sighed), found Rick and me in the women's bathroom with the door closed, and aghast at what she was witnessing, gave us both a tongue lashing. I don't recall what she said, only that Rick turned white and raced away, and I refused to leave the bathroom.

I sat in there tearful, but not because I felt guilty. I didn't. Rather, I cried because, after months of telling me that we were equals, and we were *in this together,* Rick decided that he needed to pull the man card and the grown-up card and *put me in my place* for something that was only real in his head. I didn't think I could take another blow. I felt like a fledgling bird whose wings weren't yet ready to carry me all alone. The wall of hope I'd built up around me was crumbling rapidly, and in that cloud of dust, in my moment of self-pity, appeared Anna's cherub face, sincere chocolate eyes, and a painfully humble voice telling me that *I had to give all my desires to YHWH and let him choose what was best for me.* She tried to hug me, and I half-heartedly let her, and then she cooed, "If it's meant to be, it will happen. Carnal desires are always painful, which is why we have to strive to purify our thoughts and give our deepest wishes to YHWH."

And, once again, I experienced that new emotion that I was growing to know well; I was livid. What in the world was she talking about? I knew she was also assuming that I was in love with Rick, which was stupid and made me want to punch something. I knew that she was obsessed with him, and it made her concern feel even more disingenuous. I wanted to lash out at her. *I'm so sick of this. Don't you people ever think about anything else? He was my friend, that's all. I trusted him, I believed him, but it turned out that he was just like all the others. You don't have to worry. I haven't stolen him from you; I never wanted to. You can have him. Pleeease, take him—keep him far away from me.* But, of course, like always, no words could get past the lump in my throat nor my all-consuming desire to be good. So, I freed myself forcefully from her embrace and left her standing alone, shaking her head, wishing she could get through to me. But at that exact moment, I'd finally realized that *I* wasn't the one who needed *getting through to.*

Rick left his teaching position abruptly and hopped on a Greyhound to Oregon. Shortly after he arrived there, a letter showed up in our mailbox from him addressed to both me and my mom, which was always ominous. I saw his handwriting and wanted to burn it without reading it, but Mom opened it and couldn't help but shake her head as she handed it to me. Rick solemnly revealed our friendship to my mom, which was silly because she already knew about it. He detailed the reasons that we could no longer be friends, including the fact that I was right, it had been he who had wanted more from our friendship, that he had given in to weakness, and we were wrong; men and women could not be friends. The rules existed for good reason.

When I finished reading the letter, I turned to my mom and rolled my eyes and then, with a sigh, "This makes me so mad. I don't know why I ever believed him." What I couldn't have felt beneath my anger at the time was that I was also really sad. Another loss, but I had grown so used to loss that it didn't even register.

"I know," she said as she patted my back. "People will always make mistakes and let us down; only YHWH is perfect." I'll never forget how grateful I was for her support in that moment. That she believed me was all that mattered. It wasn't the first time I had been accused of *falling in love* with the older men in the church, accusations that increased exponentially after my dad left. Each time it happened it was more irritating than the last until it was downright maddening and then so absolutely ridiculous that it was comical. The last accusation had come from a man who was old enough to be my father, who had told my mom I was flirting with him, *sparkling my eyes* at him, and *flaunting myself* at him.

"What's flirting?" I asked.

"When you try to get someone's attention because you like them and want them to notice you," my mom explained.

"Definitely don't like *him*—he's disgusting and old, and annoying," I exaggerated with a shiver. "And, he's a little bit coo-coo," I motioned a twirly sign next to my head, "If he thinks I'm trying to get *his* attention. The only thing I ever want from him is to go away." My mom repressed a chuckle and reminded me to not call people coo-coo, but her eyes danced, and I loved that I'd managed to amuse her.

I threw the letter from Rick into the outhouse, although now I wish I'd kept it, and decided on the spot that I'd tried and was done trying. It had all been a lie. He'd promised that he was different, but he was just like everyone else who'd told me one thing and done another, who said they'd believed me and *believed in me* and then turned on me.

A year later, when I'd decided to leave the church, he begged me not to. He promised that things would be different, that I would be taken seriously, that I would have a voice. He told me he'd convinced Laycher to let me go hitchhiking with them, something I'd begged to do before when I was having my very brief moment of faith, and which had been answered with an unequivocal *no—never—don't even ask—it's absolutely not an option*. But suddenly, once I'd had enough, everyone was okay with it, granting permission, offering a little more freedom—begging me to say yes.

I could feel Rick's desperation, hear it in his voice. And it gave me such pleasure, such satisfaction to say, "You're a hypocrite, and you're too late."

23 THE AWAKENING

I quit school on my sixteenth birthday. When Patrick was my teacher and, later, Rick, I looked forward to school because I felt like I was there to learn. After they had both moved on, Quinn simply stopped teaching me. She had her hands full with the younger grades and told me that I would just need to just *figure it out*, do my own work, and then correct my own mistakes with the teacher's editions. Functioning as my own teacher, I decided to skip ninth, tenth, and eleventh grade and instead pulled the twelfth-grade books that were covered in dust from the top shelves of the bookcase. No one had ever used them because no one had ever graduated from our church school. I planned to be the first. I was pleasantly surprised that the work in the twelfth-grade books was not beyond my abilities. However, working from those books while in ninth grade made me wonder how I was going to fill the last three years of my schooling. What books would I learn from after I finished those? As I considered the matter one day, I had an epiphany; I could simply ask for college books. The idea sparked an electric anticipation that pulsed to the tips of my fingers and raced around my ribcage like a kid out for recess. I hurried outside to where Quinn was watching the younger kids play. "I figured it out," I stopped to catch my breath, "when I finish the twelfth-grade books, you can just get me some college books. Then maybe I won't just be the first one to graduate but also the first one to go to college. Wouldn't that be good for the church?"

"Absolutely not. You're not going to college."

"I didn't say I wanted to *go* to college," I clarified, "I just want to use the books, just the ones that you guys think are okay."

"No. Nothing good ever comes from partaking of the Tree of Knowledge, you know that."

"*No schoolchildren should be coming to our school to get a G.E.D. and get to college or get a worldly job, especially the sisters. Their orders are to be keepers of the home and to love their husbands.*"

"But y'all have been telling me that you want me to be the first one to graduate. What am I going to do for the next three years without harder books?"

"That's why I told you not to skip ahead."

"But you know the books in my grade are too easy, and they're boring. Maybe we could just get college books about teaching. You know that Brother Laycher wants me to help you teach once I graduate. Wouldn't that make me a better teacher?"

"You don't need college to be a good teacher. I've been teaching all these years and doing just fine."

Debatable, I thought, but knew I should keep that to myself.

"Higher education breeds doubt and makes you question everything we've taught you," she continued. "The more worldly knowledge we get, the less room we have for clean knowledge and the word of YHWH."

"Then why have any knowledge at all? Isn't it all worldly? Why even go to school?" I knew I was pushing my luck with my tone, but I had been so excited by the prospect of college books that I wasn't ready to back down. Plus, I knew how desperate they were to have the church school appear legitimate to the outside world—having a teacher who had grown up in the church and then *gone to college* would have legitimized the hell out of it.

She was not going to back down. "We have a school

because we *have* to—the state requires it. And they require us to teach you certain subjects and to submit your grades every year; otherwise, they would take y'all away. Plus, it's good to know how to read and write; it helps us to spread the word of YHWH, and the brothers need math to do their construction work."

I had internalized the expectation to be the first graduate, but I also knew that, by law, I could quit school when I was sixteen, which was just a few months away. I couldn't imagine wasting one more minute locked in that tiny trailer learning nothing, my brain starving for more but being told I couldn't have it. I also knew that my time would be much better spent helping my mom at home.

I decided to have the last word. "Well, if I can't have college books, there's no point staying in school. I'm going to quit the second I turn sixteen."

"You would do that? You'll be a giant disappointment, not just to me but to everybody. Everyone who's believed in you, and encouraged you, and supported you. You know we've all been excited to have you complete all twelve grades. Don't you know how important that is, how important it is for the State to see our kids graduating from our school? You know you're the oldest, and you're supposed to set the example for the other kids. If you quit, then you're going to teach all of them that school isn't important."

"But it isn't, not really," I retorted. "I already know how to cook and clean and take care of kids. I don't need school for that. My mom needs my help. She's all alone with six kids. There's no point in me wasting my time here anymore."

Quinn told Laycher about my plans, and he echoed her irritation and disappointment, as did Anna, but I didn't care. I asked my mom about it, and she said it was up to me, and so, on my sixteenth birthday, in the middle of the school year, I walked out of that trailer with my head held high, knowing that no one could stop me because Colorado law said I could quit school at sixteen.

I felt brilliant and defiant and was flying high on having made my own choice against the advice and wishes of every adult in my life except for my mom. As if on cue, as we walked out of the church driveway, Mateo's bus floated by and stopped in front of us on Apple Road. Because he knew how thrilled the kids were every time they had a chance to ride in his bus, he always pulled over and opened the hydraulic door, the compressed air hissing loudly as he asked, "Anyone need a ride?" He had bought the bus when he lived in Missouri and began the process of converting it into a home on wheels so that no matter where he went, he had his own place to live. It was an old 1980s, thirty-five-foot Topeka, Kansas, city bus. My life had been so busy with mine and Rick's ridiculous experiment and my decision to quit school that I'd barely had time to think about him. But at that moment, my world felt nearly perfect, as I couldn't imagine a better ending to my day.

All of the feelings I had been avoiding instantly came flooding back, and my heart was in my throat. I was both giddy and petrified, feelings that morphed into dread when he stepped out of the bus, hugged all of the other kids, smiling with his mouth *and* his eyes like he always did; but when he came to me, he refused to even shake my hand and looked quickly away. We had never hugged when we saw each other, but he always shook my hand with a smile and a chaste, "How are you, sister?" This time, his eyes were cold, and I could see that he was in pain. I was confused. I thought he would be proud that I'd finally learned to forget him and focus on my life. I hadn't spoken to or written to him for nearly a year.

I crashed to earth. What had happened? What had I done? I wracked my brain but could come up with nothing. As soon as I could, I tapped into my reliable grapevine, Anika.

She tittered and then quickly grew serious, her eyes darted around, "You didn't know?" She almost whispered,

"My grandma told him about you and Rick."

"What about me and Rick? He was just my friend." My heart pounded.

"That's not what she told him; she told him yous guys were *in love*. She told him that you were just a stupid little girl who was desperate to get anyone she could to notice her and would fall in love with anyone who paid attention to you." Anika giggled again and then wandered off to join the other girls.

I felt like someone had kicked me in the stomach and wrung all of the air out of my lungs at the same time. *No. No, this can't be happening*, I thought. *I did what I was supposed to do, what everyone has been telling me to do, and now it's all messed up.* I wanted to take it all back, all of the devotion, the faith, the dedication. I was desperate, so I turned to my mom, not sure that she would be willing to help, but knowing that she was my only chance. I told her about Anika and Maxine, and Mateo. "I need to talk to him," I pleaded, "it might not help, but I have to at least try. You're the only one who can get him to agree."

My mom hesitated at first, but she knew I wouldn't take "no" for an answer. So she called Mateo and asked him to come over to our house. When he arrived, she instructed him to follow her to the back room, which was our sewing room, and also my bedroom and was where I sat waiting. When he saw me, he turned on his heels to leave. "Wait," my mom commanded, "just hear her out." The three of us sat in three corners of the room, all avoiding each other's gazes. Mateo shifted and fidgeted and made it desperately clear that he'd rather be anywhere else but there. No one was talking, so I just dove in, "I know what Maxine told you some things about me and Rick, and I really *need* you to know that they aren't true, not even a little. They are flat-out lies. She lies a lot, I've noticed, and no one seems to care or want to stop her. She just said it because, for some reason, she likes to hurt people, especially people she's mad at, and she's mad at me because I've been trying to change the church to make it better."

I waited for an answer, but for a long time, there wasn't one, and the silence was excruciating. Then he chose his words carefully and without looking at me, "The flesh is our worst enemy, Sister, and as for me, I'm only interested in bringing it under subjection. Whether or not the rumors are true is none of my business." Then he stood up and walked out.

My mom crossed the room and settled in next to me while I sat, crumpled over, holding my face in my hands. "It *is* his business," I murmured, defeated. "He has to know. I've never loved anyone else but him, and I didn't want to admit it before, but I don't think I can bear the thought of him never loving me." I had never asked him, and he'd never told me, but I had hoped against all rationality that maybe, someday, he would love me too. Now, there was little chance of that. Years of one-sided feelings, of wishing he would see me not as a kid but as a young woman—and now? Now all he saw was a whimsical girl, blown about by any whiff of wind that passed. That was what Maxine wanted him to believe anyway, even though it wasn't true.

I was gutted.

The rest of the summer and fall were pure torture. Mateo rarely acknowledged my existence, and when I walked into a room, he stood up and walked out. He left Colorado every chance he got, taking more road trips than usual, one of them with Rick and Anna, which made me furious.

By late winter of my sixteenth year, I decided to leave home and the church. My brother, Joseph, had left the day he turned eighteen, but I knew I couldn't wait that long. I missed him immensely, he hardly ever came to visit, and I went for months at a time without hearing from him. When he did show up, he never stayed long because my mom wouldn't let him into the house unless he put on one of his old robes. Sometimes, he'd slip begrudgingly into one of the robes I'd made for him that snapped up the front like a duster. He would leave it unsnapped. Then my mom would bark, 'Don't come into this house unless you snap that up.'" He'd defiantly snap two snaps in the middle and sit at the kitchen table, laughing and roughhousing with our little brothers.

Other times, he'd refuse to put on the robe at all and wait in his beat-up little truck for me to come out. My mom wouldn't let the other kids go out, but she trusted me, and I'd convinced her that maybe I could bring him back, so I'd walk out on my own and sit in the truck with him. He'd turn on the country music station and tell me about his girlfriends, brawling in saloons and bars, and how he was going to be a country singer. I believed him because he was a talented guitar player and had a great voice. Before he drove away, he'd always say, "Love you, Sis. If you ever need anything, anything at all, you call me." I'd walk back to the house feeling conflicted. I felt guilty for listening to the radio, but I missed him and really did believe that I could win him back by giving a little by not being so rigid. And that, I thought, was the problem with the grown-ups; they were never willing to bend, not even a little. I'd stay up late into the night wondering what would have to change in order to keep all of the kids from leaving the minute they turned eighteen. Then I'd remember that I'd already tried that, and it didn't work. So, I decided it would be best if I just left and went to live with my brother. Together, the two of us would be okay.

But everything changed in a moment. I was on my way to Karen's house to borrow some sugar for my mom. I decided to walk because it was a beautiful, sunny day, a little breezy but pleasant. I knew how to drive the car, but I needed the fresh air and the time to myself, time that was always in short supply. Mateo was parked at Antonio and Jenna's bus (yeah, they had a bus too—it was a fad right about then), right in front of our trailer, literally in our back yard, where they had moved to when the house they had been renting next door to us, was sold. They had decided that we could use a man around the house, and they built a shed in our backyard to supplement the space in the bus and to accommodate laundry and showers. I spent a lot of time in their bus when Mateo wasn't there but knew better than to show up when he was there. I'd made that mistake once, and he'd promptly got up and walked out without saying a word to me. That had ended with me in tears and Antonio and Jenna trying desperately to console me.

So, that day, I was aware of him in the driveway as I walked by, but since he'd been so distant, I purposely didn't even steal a glance in his direction. At that point, I had basically given up on any notion of *us*. I hadn't walked far before he pulled up next to me and stopped, or I should say, drove painfully slow, as I refused to stop walking. I couldn't imagine why he was even talking to me as he had made it abundantly clear that he wanted nothing to do with me for months.

"Where are you going?"

"To Karen's to pick up some sugar for Mom," I looked past him, determined to be indifferent, while my heart pounded in my temples.

"Want a ride?" I stopped and looked directly at him. Then, I hesitated, and glanced deliberately up and down the road to see if anyone was spying. I turned back to study his face for a moment. What was he playing at?

I opened the door, bewildered, and sat down in the passenger seat. He was choosing to be alone with me for the few minutes it took to drive to Karen's.

Why?

After months of pretending I didn't exist, why now? His brow was furrowed, his eyes worried.

He turned to look at me, "How have you been? You don't seem too well lately."

So, he *had* been paying attention.

"I'm not." I turned away from his gaze.

"What's up? Anything you want to tell me?"

Of course, I wanted to tell him—everything, always, but he had told me not to talk to him, ever. He had said that he couldn't be there for me, that we couldn't be friends because of the way I felt about him, that he had to draw a line. So, I didn't trust the sudden concern, his willingness to risk being seen, being rebuked from the pulpit just for being in the car with me.

I paused and held my breath for a second, then released it, and with it, the words that I had not yet uttered out loud to anyone, not even to myself.

"I'm leaving." My stomach lurched. It was suddenly real.

Silence.

"When?"

"Soon, I don't know for sure yet."

"Where are you going to go?" He'd skated right past concerned, and I could hear panic in his voice.

"I'll call Joseph, stay with him for a while. After that, I don't know. I'm pretty sure Michelle will let me work at the store and even stay with her if I need to." (Michelle was a kind, big-hearted woman who owned a health food store in Pueblo where we all shopped a lot).

I was tumbling through all sorts of confused and could barely believe the words coming out of my own mouth.

Longer silence.

Mateo let out a deep sigh.

We'd been creeping along at five miles per hour, trying to turn the two-minute drive into five. He opened and closed his fingers around the wooden steering wheel and stared straight ahead. I could feel him wrestling with what he was going to say next, like he wasn't quite sure he should, or wasn't ready, to say it. We were fast approaching Karen's house, and I was beginning to feel desperately uneasy. I could feel the eyes of all of the people in all of the church houses that we had to pass on that drive, burning a hole through the side of the car and right into our conversation. I knew they would be rushing to their phones to tell Maxine, who would tell Laycher, who would rebuke us from the pulpit again.

But, wait—why did I care?

I was leaving.

But I was so used to hiding that I didn't know any other way.

Mateo fumbled a bit more before he turned to look at me. It was one of the first times we made and held eye contact for more than a few seconds. We were stopped in front of Karen's house, and I was *dying* to get out of the car, but he was taking his sweet time. With tears glistening in his eyes he said with the utmost care, "It would really hurt me if you left, kinda the same way it would hurt you if I left. It's not easy out there. I'll try to be more open, more available to you when you need me. Please don't go, or at least, think about it some more before you do."

I was floored. I had thought that there was zero chance for us, and here he was telling me that he couldn't live without me. My brain hurt, and my heart thumped powerfully in my ears. All I could mumble was, "Okay."

I stumbled out of the car and up the driveway to Karen's, my world spinning. One little sentence from him and I'd just agreed to stay in the church, something I really didn't want to do. One little plea from him, and I'd abandoned my determined plans and walked away from a decision that had taken every bit of courage I could muster.

After that, things started to change rapidly for me and for us. At that point, I had been spending a couple of mornings a week cleaning and cooking for the single brothers. I had overheard one of them lamenting about getting home late at night and having to do all of the cooking and household chores *after* working all day. And since I'd been trained to be a perfect little housewife and knew that those men supported us financially, I decided it was only fair for me to do something nice for them. It was also a brilliant way for me to audition my housewife skills to any potential future husband. I knew that, my mom knew that, and I'm sure Laycher did, too, but we all had no problem pretending that I simply wanted to help. I had spare time, especially now that I wasn't in school, and I knew how to clean really well and throw a pot of beans on the stove and whip up some tortillas for their dinner, so why not let me do it a couple of times a week? Plus, I cherished the hours of quiet while I was in their trailer alone, quiet that was hard to come by in the chaos of our home.

Not long after the ride with Mateo, my cleaning visits became essential to both of us. We began writing letters to each other, leaving them in the top drawer of his desk for each other to find. I know this is probably where you're dying for something juicy, salacious, and titillating, and I hate to disappoint, but that's just not what happened. The letters were painfully virtuous, all about pure desires, perseverance and dedication to our faith, and following the path of righteousness that just maybe would lead us to each other. It was in one of those letters that he first wrote that he loved me. I was ecstatic, but I still didn't really believe him. Saying, *I love you very much, and I want you to be happy* at the end of a letter wasn't exactly the same as saying, *I'm in love with you, too*. So, while I was thrilled to have him in my corner, I didn't let my hopes run away with me.

We were still going to church, hoping and praying for changes, convinced that maybe we could shift the direction of the congregation by modeling open-mindedness and talking—a lot. Mateo didn't run away from me at church anymore, but he was still far more cautious than in his letters. We still avoided each other mostly, just to be safe, but he made sure I knew, with smiles and long, lingering looks across the room, any and every room that we were in together, that he was keeping to his word, that I was not alone, and as long as he was there, he would be there with me. At times the looks were so long and so lingering that I would begin to panic, willing him to turn away, certain that everyone would notice and all hell would break loose. I would look away to signal to him that it was time, but when I'd look back, he would still be focused on me with a laser gaze. Then my face would get hot and my stomach giddy, and he would smile gleefully as if he enjoyed that. It's remarkable how much a person can say with only their eyes.

24 TURNING POINT

I launched a final crusade of sorts, for the kids. I was in a sort of limbo, between leaving and staying, between the adult world and the kid world and I felt like I understood both. I was hoping I could build a bridge and bring the two worlds together. If the adults really wanted to know if they had built a foundation that would last, all they had to do was to ask themselves whether they had convinced any child to stay in the church beyond the age of eighteen. I knew for certain that the problem wasn't that every single kid there was bad and so, the minute they could, they left; there was something fundamentally wrong with the church. Not a single kid who grew up in the church had stayed (outside of Laycher's family who never followed the rules anyway and even they left and returned repeatedly). Some naive part of me still thought that I might be able to change the way things were, not necessarily in order to stay myself, but to make sure that the kids I was leaving behind didn't have it so bad. Having Mateo to back me up gave me confidence and so did having Jess there to crack my world wide open.

Jess was my newest, best friend. She was the same age as Mateo, had messy blonde hair and blue eyes that shone mischievously when she smiled. She was petite like me but had the presence of a giant and a mouth-wide-open laugh that would most certainly get her tossed into the *Jezebel* box. She'd met the brothers while they were witnessing in

Flagstaff and had come back with them. She was bubbly, she was fiery, and she was an unapologetic hippie. I had never seen anything like the clothes she wore. She was baptized within a week of arriving but didn't really change a single thing about herself. She didn't join the church out of longing, or a deep need for meaning; she just thought that it was something new, something she'd never done before, so why not? She bent a little, conforming to the rules requiring long dresses and long sleeves on her own terms by simply wearing a long skirt and a long-sleeved shirt under a sleeveless, short dress. Sometimes she wore a head covering; sometimes, she just wore a big Rasta hat with her hair tucked inside or a colorful Indian scarf. I was instantly in love with those fashions. Why had I never thought to do any of that? It made so much sense and I was enthralled by the thought of having some variety of dress in my life. I had never been a fan of the drab wardrobe that dominated my closet. The rest of the girls and I fell in line behind her like so many ducklings. Coincidentally, my options for clothes shopping at The Salvation Army expanded exponentially, because if I liked a short skirt or a short-sleeved shirt, I knew that I could make it work by wearing something else under it so my body would still be covered. We all went crazy with new, fifty-cent, and one-dollar-a-piece outfits.

I was awestruck the first time Jess sang in front of everyone at church. Sometimes, Laycher would *open the service for songs and testimonies*, which meant that anyone who wanted to, could go to the front of the church and share a song, or a dream, or an epiphany (although the brothers were the only ones who could testify because it was kind of like preaching and sisters *were not* allowed to preach). She had not even been baptized yet, when she leaped out of her seat, and swaggered to the front, shoulders back, head held high. I was certain she was going to try to testify and I found myself squeezing my eyes shut, willing it not to happen, and bracing for the backlash, but instead, she belted out *Natural Woman* (by Aretha Franklin, who of course, I'd never heard of). Her eyes were closed, her hands hung lightly by her sides and a bemused smile played on her lips.

My jaw hit the floor. I was swamped with giddy terror that someone was going jump up and stop her in the middle of it. *Lady, we only sing songs about YHWH here.* It was obviously a love song, but one that she was singing *to* YHWH. I waited, holding my breath, but no one did anything. I think they were all too shocked.

I decided that I needed to learn that song immediately.

Jess loved going for walks and she would pop over nearly every day to see if I wanted to walk *around the block* with her. It was a country block—probably at least three miles around, so I loved those walks because we made them last as long as we could and we talked the whole time.

My mom *did not* like Jess. She was everything she did not want me to be. The opposite of meek, she had no problem speaking her mind and encouraged me to do the same. It was on one of those walks that I vented to her about how my mom was making me *crazy* after I had barely squeezed permission out of her to leave.

"I'm not a kid anymore" I insisted adamantly, "I don't know why she keeps treating me like I am. I try so hard to please her in every way I know how, but even then, it's never good enough, and she hates to let me have time to do things that *I* want to do."

"Things like what, what kinds of things do you want to do?"

"Well, things like this, going for a walk with you. You know how hard it is to convince her to let me? There's always something—laundry to fold, cleaning to do, weeding the garden—sometimes I think she's coming up with things just so she can say *no*. But the worst is when she says *because I said so*. Doesn't give me any good reason, no explanation, no excuse, just—*because I said so*. Or sometimes it's, *it's just what I'm feeling right now*. What kind of reasons are those?"

"They aren't reasons," Jess stated matter-of-factly. "They aren't answers. You are your own person, a nearly

grown woman; you have the right to demand real answers."
Did I? I wasn't so sure.
"Oh, I don't know about that. I don't think I could. I don't want to make her mad, or probably she'd just be sad. Sometimes that's worse than her being mad."
"You've got to learn how to stand up for yourself at some point," she insisted. "You can't grow into a strong, powerful woman unless you put your foot down once in a while." And she stopped walking and turned to look at me, sincere and earnest. She smiled encouragingly and took my hand as we started to walk again—everything was so simple to her.
"You've got to expand your horizons, girl. There's a big, beautiful world out there and someday you're going to have to explore it. There are more than a billion people in the world," She stopped and turned to look at me again and then she asked, "Do you really think that we're the only ones who have all the answers, the only ones who know anything about what is right and what is true? How could *that* be possible?"
How *could* that be possible? It was the nagging question that was on my mind more often than not those days.
No one had ever told me that I could be strong and powerful, nor that what I wanted mattered. The next time my mom said, *no, not this time*, when I asked to walk with Jess, I plucked up my courage and asked why.
"Because, I said, *not this time*," she insisted.
"But that's not a real reason," I pushed back, "I need to know why".
"What do you mean? I said I don't want you to go this afternoon. That's reason enough."
"No, it isn't," I said forcefully, and then, a little more gently, "I've always done what you tell me to do and accepted what you want without question. I'm a good girl, and you know that. And I'm almost seventeen; I deserve a little more freedom. I've never given you a reason not to trust me. *Because I said so* isn't good enough anymore. If you

don't have a real reason, then I'm going."

Even as the words left my mouth, I couldn't believe I'd uttered them. And at the same time, I felt so invigorated to have done so. The look on my mom's face was pure shock—and then, in rapid succession, a shadow of anger, and then plain hurt. I had never defied her so blatantly before. I was tempted to apologize, to try to repair the damage and remove her pain, but I knew I couldn't because I'd meant every word of what I'd said. It took a mountain of determination to turn my back to her and walk out the door knowing that I was leaving her crumpled in tears.

Shortly after that, Jess decided she needed to go back to California to visit her family. Laycher insisted she take a couple of the single brothers with her to protect her from their wiles, but she easily dismissed that ludicrous idea. "They're my family," she retorted, "I don't need anyone to go with me. Why would I be afraid of my family?"

"Our unrighteous relations are our worst enemy", Laycher maintained, annoyed by her insolence, "and as a woman, you shouldn't be traveling alone. You need a strong man with you."

Jess laughed again. "I always travel alone. I am a grown woman and my family doesn't control me. I make up my own mind." It was a huge scandal. People were whispering, clucking their tongues, and shaking their heads in disapproval for days. *No one* talked to Laycher that way—it was like a kid backtalking their parent—and most definitely not a sister. Futile efforts of brother, after sister, after Elder, tried and failed to convince her to take someone with her. She stood firm in her decision and boarded a Greyhound bus back to California. After she left, I sensed a universal sigh of relief; most everyone around me was predicting that Jess was definitely gone for good—*the wanton woman.*

Imagine their surprise and displeasure when she defiantly reappeared a short time later in a gray 1950s pick-up truck with a camper shell on the back that she'd bought while she was gone. I knew she'd be back. I knew it because she promised me she would, and she wasn't the kind of person who would break a promise. Now, not only could we take walks together, but we could also *drive* places together whenever we wanted. I was no longer *asking* my mom if I could go. I was *telling* her that I was going and not waiting for an answer. Jess's friend, Sam, came up from Flagstaff to visit her, and even though he was a man and was supposed to stay at the single brothers' house, he stayed with Jess in the basement of the church with the single sisters. While he was there, Jess invited me to go hiking in the mountains with them. I cherished any time the mountains and we usually only went once a year, so she didn't have to ask twice. I wondered about Sam, we weren't supposed to be alone with a man, especially a worldly man, but I didn't say anything. As if reading my mind, Jess told me that she had asked Jenna, who, now that she was a married woman, was almost an appropriate chaperone (technically, we should've had a married couple), to go with us. Jenna was both flattered to be asked and then in an about-face, judgmental about the fact that three women were going to spend the day alone with a man. I wished to myself that Jess hadn't caved to the pressure. I knew I wouldn't have as much fun with Jenna there. When we parked at the trailhead, Jenna was so guilt-ridden by the idea that we were breaking the rules, that she was physically ill and decided to stay in the truck and take a nap.

 I was relieved that it would just be the three of us, after all. We hiked up the mountain for a while and then sat in the grass to eat some sandwiches. Jess and I settled into our usual routine of giving each other neck massages, and that time we did a massage train with Sam. I really had no idea what to think or feel about it, a man who we weren't married to touching our bodies, even if it was just our necks and shoulders over our clothes, but the two of them acted like it was the most normal thing in the world, so I just went along with it.

 It wasn't long after Sam went home that Jess also left. It

was the hate that drove her away. I knew it without her even having to say. "There are a lot of good people here," she said sadly, "but there are a lot of bitter, miserable, nasty people here, too." I knew she was right. She took my face in her hands, kissed my forehead, and smiled reassuringly. There were no tears at our parting, not from her and not from me. "Are you going to be all right?" She asked.

"Yeah, I'm gonna be fine." I smiled back. I knew I would be, and I knew that that parting was different than all the others had been. It wasn't a loss; it was a fork in the road. Jess would always be my friend. I didn't care about the rules anymore so I knew we would stay in touch. It wasn't an end to anything; it was just another phase.

The other girls and I kept wearing our hippie clothes, layers upon layers, nothing matching, colors, patterns, shapes, and textures all colliding. We were determined to keep Jess and every ounce of courage she'd given us alive and relevant. She had breathed inspiration into us and we were thriving on it. Our parents were annoyed and Laycher was furious. He preached at us; he preached about us; *YHWH's people weren't supposed to look like bums.* He forbade us from wearing hippie clothes. We complied, but I decided to start wearing two different color socks instead, and almost instantly all of the other girls did, too. I was quickly beginning to understand that I wasn't alone, that I had an army of kids who were ready for me to lead them. I was more certain than I'd ever been that with all of us, we might finally get the grown-ups to listen. We got bolder and bolder, and Laycher got madder and madder.

25 THE GATHERING STORM

I started to speak freely and forcefully, not only asking questions but *demanding* answers, first haltingly and then with more vigor. Like I had done with my mom, I was insisting on answers that made sense. If I was going to choose to believe something, blind faith was no longer an option. For example, our prejudice against the rest of the world. For people who were supposed to be humble servants of YHWH, the severe judgment and wrath against anyone who would not follow felt like a huge contradiction to me. If we were supposed to be beacons of YHWH's love, then how could we hate someone so much that we actually drove them away, like Jess? I spent a lot of time lying in my bed thinking, or walking across the prairie, thinking, asking questions, and then trying to answer them like Remus had said I should. If they wanted me to come up with solutions, I was confident I could do it. But I still wasn't convinced it would change anything or soothe the nagging doubt that was a constant thorn in the back of my mind. Some things I just couldn't reconcile or force to make sense.

Things like heaven and the lake of fire.

When I let myself lie there and actually think about them, it all seemed so utterly absurd and juvenile, like believing in a fairy tale. First of all, heaven was supposedly a place filled with angels in white robes blowing trumpets, somewhere right above us in the clouds, where we would all get white robes and trumpets and the ability to walk on clouds even though they're vapor. And for eternity, a thing that would never end—I couldn't imagine anything without an end—all we would do is walk around blowing trumpets saying, *holy, holy, holy is YHWH*, over, and over, and over again—Rick used to turn rhapsodic talking about it.

And that's it.

Nothing else.

After all the fear, all the pain, all the subjecting myself, all the beating myself up trying to be worthy—that was it; *that* was the reward.

If I'd known how to swear, I'd have said, *I call bullshit*. Because that's exactly what I felt. *Some reward*, I thought.

I could think of a hundred other things I'd rather have a chance to do, things that would feel like a true reward. The chance to grow up without the threat of the second coming looming over me. The chance to love and be loved, to live a stable life, and to have kids of my own. To go camping more than once a year, to eat good food and have plenty of it, to travel to places I'd never been, to feel the sun on my bare legs. I knew that I would choose those things a thousand times over, rather than the thing I had been promised my whole life.

And the lake of fire?

A big pit, full of fire and hot stones and a giant, angry god grabbing us by the feet and throwing us in? *That* suddenly seemed utterly ridiculous, too. It just didn't add up—none of it.

And yes, it took only a few contemplative moments like that for both of those things to lose the power they'd held over me all of my life—mostly, or at least for me to begin to release myself from it. I remembered that somewhere in the Bible it says that heaven is here on earth, and I began to understand what that meant, that we create heaven or hell for ourselves by how we choose to live our lives. It's difficult to convey the relief that that lightbulb moment brought to me, the relief of realizing that having a bad thought wasn't going to damn me to eternal hell. For the first time in my life, it was like I could actually breathe. I found the following in my old papers. I wrote it right after that moment. I had just turned seventeen.

This day I have received baptism into the truth of spirituality. I am an infinite soul seeking to be reunited with the Great Spirit of love and purity that created me. I choose my hope; I choose my sorrow; I choose my laughter.

With that weight off my chest, it was so much easier for me to keep trying to unravel the puzzle of doctrine and I became relentless in my pursuit of real answers. I began to corner every adult I could and bombard them with the epiphanies I was having and try to shake them free of their stupor. My mom got to hear most of it because she was right there. I can't say she agreed with me, she often didn't, but she made sure to tell me that she was proud that I was trying to find a way to reimagine the church into a place where the kids would want to be. Nathaniel was always supportive, much in the same way. He listened, mostly, but, to my surprise, he agreed with me sometimes as well, especially when I tried to address the persistent hypocrisy. He never wavered, even when Laycher commanded that I was no longer allowed to talk to anyone but him. "If you have a problem, you come to me. If there's something you don't understand, ask me and I'll explain it. But this, this thing you're doing right now, talking to everyone all the time, stirring up trouble, it's just sowing confusion and discord, and it's got to stop."

I told Nathaniel what Laycher had said and he shook his head in disgust. "That's not right," the war inside of him was written all over his face, "Why can't he see that that's not the way to do it? He's got to understand that he's just pushing people away," he closed his eyes and sighed. "You keep talking to him, and you keep talking to me, keep talking to your mom and to anyone you want. It's the only way."

But soon after, Laycher got his wish for me to talk to him. He was preaching a particularly nasty sermon about his flock losing the faith, getting sloppy and lazy, and giving in to temptation, and the cherry on top—backsliders—his favorite topic. Whenever Laycher wanted to scare us back into submission, he always preached about the backsliders, in detail, whether he was recounting their lives in the church or how miserable and unfortunate their lives had become once they left. One man had gotten cancer and died years after he'd left, which, of course, was the wrath of YHWH, punishing him for slandering Laycher. *"He cursed me when he left,"* Laycher said matter-of-factly, *"he cursed me and he cursed YHWH, and he died."* It was as simple as that to him and he believed every word of it.

That night he started with Jess since she was the most recent who had *fallen from grace*. He raged against her and her "gay" friend, Sam. Even though Sam wasn't gay, it didn't really matter; calling him gay somehow proved, from Laycher's point of view, that Jess was also perverse. Then he came around to Patrick; he always came around to Patrick eventually. Patrick was his favorite person to lash out at when he was really losing control. He was Laycher's kryptonite. Patrick had always defied him, right until the end and Laycher was consistently furious about it. I didn't write about it previously, because it's not really my story to tell, but I will now only because it's relevant. About a year before they left, Patrick and Gwen had suffered a tragedy, the loss of a pregnancy, one that could have been saved had they gone to the hospital. And that night as he condemned the backsliders, Laycher recalled that experience to prove his point.

"You know," Laycher admonished, "YHWH doesn't let things happen for no reason. That baby died because Patrick was weak and submissive and refused to command his own home. He was swayed by any wind that blew—he defied me, he defied the word of YHWH, and YHWH decided to chastise him. And in the end, it didn't matter. Instead of repenting, he lost his faith and turned away from salvation. He got bitter against YHWH and against the church and he and Gwen left after leading many of our young people astray." I knew he was talking about me and the other kids. We all adored Patrick and to this day, many of us are still in touch with him.

I was livid. So angry that I was shaking. I felt the fire start in my belly and spread up my body until it burst out onto my flushed cheeks and sweaty palms. The minute the sermon was over, I rallied the troops, the other girls and I who had become a pod of rebellion, and we sat in a huddle trying to decide what to do.

"We have to confront him," I said to them. "He can't keep doing this. He has to know how we feel. He has to know that his hatred and his lack of compassion are not making us want to stay here. He told me that if there is something I don't understand or something that makes me upset, that I shouldn't talk to anyone else, I should come straight to him. So, let's do that. Instead of sitting here being mad and wondering why or how he could say those things about Patrick, let's go up there and ask him. Let's tell him about the real Patrick, the one that we remember. I can do the talking but I need you all to come with me."

The girls all agreed with me without a moment's hesitation. Laycher sat at the front of the church as he often did after services, waiting for people to come in turn to seek his wisdom and cry about their struggles and fears, or to ask him to lay hands on them. We girls took each other's hands, trembling with fear and anger, and marched up that long aisle to where he was sitting, a wall of freshly birthed feminine power that would no longer be repressed.

"We need to talk to you," I began, my voice wavering. It sounded small and uncertain. Laycher motioned for us to sit, but we chose to stand. He looked weary; his face drooped with disappointment, and his shoulders stooped even more than usual as he struggled to keep a grasp on a fleeting sense of control. "It's about the things you keep saying about Patrick."

His expression changed in a flash and his eyes crackled

with fire, daring me to challenge him even as his voice dripped the false sweetness of a grandfather beseeching his granddaughter, "What things, Jita?"

"Everything—all of it. Nothing you say about him is true, and the worst part is that I think you know that. You didn't know him like we did. He was the best teacher we ever had. He was a loyal friend. He cared about us. He listened to us; *we mattered to him*. He was kind and gentle and never made us feel like we weren't important. How can you keep telling lies about him? And why now, why talk about him now, when he's been gone for years? What good does that do anyone? You preach for us not to lie, and we get into a lot of trouble if we do. Why are you allowed to lie?"

A shadow came over him; dark rage shook his face and turned it scarlet as he unleashed on me a slur of righteous anger that I'd only see him reserve for the very worst of sinners, backsliders, or devils he was casting out.

"You are out of control, young lady. I've let it slide; I've let it go; all this time that you've been stirring up trouble, but now, now you've crossed a line, and *I won't sit here and let you disrespect me like that. I won't stand for it.*" His voice was raised enough to draw the attention of everyone there.

I continued to tremble from my head to my toes and I felt like I was barely breathing, but I stood my ground, forcing myself to look him straight in the eyes, daring him to dismiss me, while I mustered all of my strength to keep the tears at bay. The girls stood beside me and behind me; they were my strength, and they were the only reason that my mouth continued to form syllables and string those syllables into words. "You said I could talk to you. You said you were the *only* one I could talk to. You promised you would listen. But now, here I am, trying to talk to you, and instead of listening, instead of admitting for once that you might be wrong about something, you're trying to shut me down and shut me up. How do you ever think you are going to get through to me, to any of us kids, when you won't even let us speak, and when, if we do speak, you won't listen?"

"That's enough!"

"Shut your mouth, young lady. Shut up before I make you," He spat viciously.

"But, can't you..."

"I said, *shut up*. All of yous—I don't want to hear another word."

"No. I won't shut up—can't you see we're trying to help? We're trying to help you understand. We're trying to make this work for all of us."

"The only thing you're helping is paving your way straight to the pits of hell and you're taking all of these poor girls with you. You go around defending backsliders, may as well be one yourself—far as I'm concerned, you are."

I'd had a sense that the whole ordeal would be futile, but I'd hoped that I was wrong. I took one last look at Laycher. His face was still pulsing with rage, the veins popping out on his forehead, but his eyes betrayed him. They reflected the terror of a man who was losing his grip on a power that he'd come to depend on; they reflected defeat. And at that moment, I saw him for what he was, desperate, bitter, and lost. I turned my back to him, motioned for the girls to follow, and headed for the door. "We're done talking," I said to them and to anyone else within earshot, "they're never going to listen."

We left through the back entrance because it was closest. We sat outside in the warm, spring night on the accessible ramp, holding each other's hands, pain, and fear, and rage all mixed together in the tears on our cheeks and the lumps in our throats. The door squeaked open and then slammed shut. We looked up to see Maxine walking down the ramp towards us, the outside light behind her like a halo, a halo dotted with dancing moths and mosquitos. She stood over us, larger than life, her skin and the whites of her eyes tinged with yellow from the Hepatitis that was slowly killing her. The light, the night, the yellow in her eyes somehow made her more foreboding than usual, made her seem more like the monster that she very often had been. That being said, we weren't always sure what to expect. Sometimes she would try to be consoling or to make us think she was siding with us, playing the good cop to Laycher's bad cop, her voice dripping with artificial sweetness. But this wasn't going to be one of those times. I could tell by the flash in her eyes and the sneer on her face that she was there to put an end to our rebellious behavior once and for all.

"Yous girls think you're so smart." She paused for effect, regarding us like a cat does its prey before it pounces.

"Yous think that because you finally got brave enough to back-talk Grandpa, that you're suddenly big and important." She shook her head, "Idiots. I won't sit here and let you treat him like this. What's wrong with you? How can you be so nasty, and ugly, and ungrateful? Grandpa has done nothing but take care of you and love you and this is how you repay him?" She was talking to *us*, but she was glaring at *me*.

"You really think you have any right to strut around here doing the things yous guys been doing lately? Questioning everything he says and does, making him out to be the bad guy? YHWH hates little children who disrespect their elders, especially when those elders have been anointed by the Holy Spirit."

I didn't quite understand her sudden piousness—we all knew she did whatever she wanted, whenever she wanted. Her anger mounted as we sat silent.

"Grandpa puts up with you because he believes you when you say you want to understand, but you can't fool me; you're just a bunch of bratty little kids who need a good whipping."

She wanted to bait me, to draw me into a fight that I was neither vicious enough, nor cunning enough to win. I knew that, and I also knew that there was no use trying to talk to someone who wasn't going to listen. Instead, we silenced her with our silence and eventually she huffed, turned on her heels, and walked back inside.

26 ENGAGED

It's become apparent to me as I find my way through particular moments in my past how much time I spent in a sort of limbo, ping-ponging back and forth between wanting to leave and wanting to stay, clinging to the things I'd been taught and then rejecting them with fervor. I was genuinely torn, but the following events sealed the deal, so to speak, and infused momentum into the inevitable path to my future.

Not long after my seventeenth birthday, my friend and pen-pal, Tammy, who had been visiting for a couple of weeks, was heading back to Missouri with one of the married couples who lived there. Tammy was three years older than I, and we had been joined at the hip for about a year after Patrick and Gwen left the church and before my brother did. I wanted to go with her back to Missouri because I missed her terribly, but also because Mateo was going to Missouri for a couple of weeks at the same time. My mom said *no*, without a second's hesitation. She also asked Laycher's opinion on the matter, and he echoed a definitive *no*. That didn't stop a steady stream of people from popping in and out of our house to ask her again. People who were taking note, it seems, of my discontent and frustration and thought it better to give me a bit of a longer leash and keep me than to tighten it up and send me scurrying after my brother. That stream included my friend

Tammy, the couple she was going to Missouri with, and Nathaniel. But it was Mateo who finally convinced her. Unbeknownst to me, he had popped in and told her that he was really worried about me. "You're gonna lose her, just like you did Joseph, if you don't give her a little freedom. Some time away from this place and everything she's been through here would do her some good."

I had given up on the idea of going anywhere when my mom appeared in my doorway unexpectedly and said, "Pack your things; you're going to Missouri." It was early in the morning, and I hadn't yet crawled out of bed. "They'll be here to pick you up in an hour," she added as she turned to walk away. I was surprised but wasn't going to waste any time wondering what had changed or asking too many questions and risking her changing her mind back. I packed quickly and bounded out the door when the van pulled into our driveway.

The drive was brief, taking just the day, twelve hours to be exact. We stopped only for the restroom and once to eat sandwiches in the concrete shade of a rest-stop picnic table in the middle of Kansas. We arrived late at night and went straight to bed, the couple disappeared into their bedroom, and Tammy and I laid quilts down on the floor to sleep on. I was buzzing with the thrill of being on my own as my eyes grew heavy. It was such a relief to be far away from my mom's rules, out of reach of the prying eyes of Laycher and Maxine and every other busybody in Boone. Churches are a great place to refine the art of gossip. It's usually disguised as sharing, helping, or as cautionary tales, but it's really just pure, unadulterated gossip. I had been the subject of much of that gossip and was suffocating.

I was awakened in the tantalizing light of early morning by heavy footsteps on the porch, and I groggily opened my eyes to see Mateo's face in the window. Every cell in my body exploded with warmth and anticipation. I shook Tammy awake, and she screamed and hid under the covers. I couldn't fathom why.

"Don't be so silly," I prodded her.

"But I'm in my nightgown." She was aghast at my ignorance—*you don't greet brothers in your nightgown, ever, may as well be in your underwear.*

"But it looks just like a dress," I shrugged, "made out of flannel with a few extra ruffles." The guys were still outside the door, peering in at us. I bounced up off the floor where the two of us were curled up with piles of blankets, and while she leaped to her feet and ran to the kitchen to hide, I went to open the door. I hugged Alan easily, just like I always did, my face squashed squarely into his chest and then stopped abruptly in front of Mateo, expecting the usual cold handshake. To my surprise, he opened his arms, and I fell easily into them. It was a brief hug, lasting only seconds, but I knew what it meant—no more hiding, no more running, no more denying.

Tammy and I got dressed while they waited, and then Mateo proposed a walk over to the neighbor's house where, he suggested, I could call my mom and check in. The house belonged to the Elder who was in charge of the Missouri church, and the brothers were helping to fix it up before he and his family could move in. There was no phone at the house where I'd spent the night. We walked the short distance, all four of us together, chatting and laughing easily as if it was something we always did—but it was absolutely *not* something we always did, and I had a hard time convincing myself that it was real. We said good morning to the brothers who were working there, and Mateo and I continued into the house, into what would be the living room. It was empty except for a short wooden bench and a telephone that was attached to a long cord that stretched the length of the wall. We sat down on the bench together closer than we'd ever sat before, and Mateo lifted the receiver and dialed the number, using his dad's AT&T calling card for long distance. When he heard the ringing on the other end of the line, he handed the phone over to me, and I waited while it rang a few times before my mom picked up.

"Hey, Mom," I said, "I'm just calling to let you know I made it. Sorry I didn't call last night; it was late."

"Well," she said, "Praise YHWH that you made it safe. I imagine it's beautiful there. Is it so green, and fresh, and ....?"

She kept talking, but I didn't hear a word. My breath caught in my throat as I felt Mateo's fingers slide easily between mine and close around my hand.

What?!

He was holding my hand.

There were people right outside.

What if they walked in? What if they saw?

How in the world was I supposed to talk to my mom while he was holding my hand?!

I tried to return my focus to my conversation with my mom, tried not to look at his face, grinning like a fool, his eyes mischievous. I tried not to look down at our hands, resting so naturally together on the bench.

"Wha...what? Sorry, Mom, I didn't hear that last thing."

"I said, who are you with?" She repeated.

Could she see me through the phone? How did she know?

He wouldn't let go of my hand. I turned to look at him and then lied, "Oh, I'm with lots of people. Tammy and I walked over this morning to see the house and how it's coming along, and Mateo was here, so he let me use his calling card to call you. But I need to go now. I'm not sure what we're doing next, but I'll call you again soon."

"Okay, have a good day, and remember to behave yourself—conduct yourself with virtue," she reminded. "You know what's expected of you. You went out there to help; I expect you to do that." The final decision back in Colorado had been that I could go to Missouri, but only to help out one of the moms there who had eight kids under the age of twelve.

"Okay, Mom. I love you."

"I love you, too."

There was no way I was going anywhere near all those kids.

Not because I didn't like them or their mother, but because I was free. I had spent the last ten years of my life helping moms, mine and others, with kids, and for the most part, I didn't mind—I loved kids. But Mateo was holding my hand and seemed terribly pleased with himself, and I was a young woman who was finally far away from home and free, and I was going to do whatever I felt like doing. And what I wanted to do was to go stay with Michael and Judith.

Michael and Judith were, and continue to be, like a bonus set of parents to me. They were always a quiet, loving, consistent presence in my life—although from far away, in either Oregon or Missouri—but unconditionally kind and encouraging. When I was topsy-turvy with frustration and frantic that someone should listen to me, they did. Michael came up with a way to help me put my ideas for change on paper. He would write me a letter designating a topic or asking me a question. I would answer the question and send him my reply. He would then analyze my reply and ask follow-up questions. He was trying to teach me how to articulate myself so that maybe I could get through to more people. Luckily, I managed to save one of those letters. It goes like this:

Dear Angela,

Thank you for your freedom letter. I wish I could express myself as well.

Freedom. What it means to me! Freedom is the opposite of bondage (oppression); carnal freedom is, again, bondage. Spiritual freedom is to worship YHWH and to follow the truth. The truth is YHWH, and my conscience is my communication with YHWH. The church and the brothers are vehicles toward salvation. Their main function is to encourage me, <u>not</u> to discourage—towards my journey to salvation. Freedom is to follow my convictions from YHWH. We can lean on our Pastor or brothers and sisters, but later on, we have to stand on our own feet and look to YHWH for guidance and freedom. To help set those free who are still in bondage (oppressed) is my calling, I feel.

As it says in the Bible, "I have no greater joy than to hear that my children are walking in the truth!" Then love can come in, and trust and real unity, and we will have a better church.

May YHWH bless you.
Brother Michael
P.S. How about a letter subject: Unclean Fear

So I knew that staying with them would be uncomplicated and natural. They would treat me like the young adult that I was and allow me the freedom I deserved as someone who had always really done everything the grown-ups had asked of me. They weren't going to always be breathing down my neck or lying in wait, dying to discipline me.

When he heard my plan, Mateo thought it was a perfect plan and said he'd drive me over to their house. For the sake of appearances, Alan would ride with us. Tammy urged me not to, "Your mom trusted you. You know she only let you come to help out." But I decided that I wasn't listening to anyone anymore, not even Tammy, and I could tell she was more than a little hurt and annoyed by that. Mateo, Alan, and I grabbed my things, popped them into Mateo's car, and followed the winding road a few miles to Michael and Judith's.

Missouri was beautiful, I thought, so green, so lush; the rolling hills on every side of the road and lazy, slow-moving rivers, brown and green, were pleasant enough to gaze at through the car window. But I could not understand wanting to live there. There were bugs, endless bugs, chiggers, ticks, mosquitos, and spiders, lots of them poisonous, *and four types of poisonous snakes.* How could anyone ever relax?

When we showed up unannounced on her doorstep, Judith enveloped me in a warm hug and invited the men back for dinner that night. Then I followed her inside and deposited my small bag in the kids' room; she poured us each a cup of iced tea, and we walked out to sit in the rocking chairs on the porch. Her voice was gentle and sweet as she asked about my family, how my mom was holding up, and how big my brothers were getting to be. "I'm glad she let you come out to visit," she said. "I've been trying to get you out here for so long; it's a real blessing." Then our conversation turned to the ever-present topic of the now-persistent turmoil plaguing the church. Her face grew solemn and sad. "Michael isn't going to last much longer," she said, "we're tired, you know, just real tired. And all of the back-biting and hypocrisy—we've reached our limit. And it's so good that you are speaking up, my dear. Your voice and those of the other kids are so important."

We stood up to go inside. "I'll help you with dinner," I offered.

"Oh, now, aren't you sweet," she cooed, her voice dripping with that Tennessee accent that persisted after a lifetime of living all over the world. "Let's get started then."

And we set about peeling potatoes and chopping cabbage for coleslaw. She punched down the dough that had been rising for bread, and we formed it into loaves to put into the oven. Judith was the only woman in the church who made her bread from sourdough starter instead of yeast, and it was delectable. I savored the subtle, tangy flavor, especially fresh out of the oven with homemade butter.

When the men arrived home and had cleaned up from work, we set the table (something we rarely did at my house) and sat down to eat. Judith had chosen our seats, and when we found our places, I noticed, with not a little trepidation but also a subtle thrill, that Mateo and I were seated next to each other. *Judith, you sly woman,* I thought, and then, *what an angel.* The meal was savored and appreciated, the conversation circulated effortlessly, and no one's head exploded because Mateo and I were sitting next to each other. In fact, it seemed like no one even noticed except Alan, who kept glaring at me as if to say, *what are you playing at?*

I chose to disregard him as I had Tammy and to stay

present in the conversation but did so with great difficulty because, under the table, Mateo's feet had bumped mine. I froze, expecting him to instantly pull back, but he didn't. He let them linger and then moved them closer. I remained frozen while trying desperately to appear as though everything was normal. He layered his feet over mine, where they settled in and remained for the remainder of the meal. They were charged with a current of electricity that ran from my toes up to the back of my skull. The conversation around us prattled on uninterrupted, but my world was at a standstill, and I could barely breathe, much less eat.

When the meal was over, Judith stood to clear the table, and I followed suit, but she protested, "No, you stay right where you are. The kids can help me with this." They cleared quickly, I remained seated as instructed, and Mateo didn't move either. Alan eyed us suspiciously again; I couldn't tell if he was worried or irritated, or both.

Judith sent the kids outside to play and then suggested definitively, "Alan, why don't you play us a song?" Motioning for Michael to follow her, she led them both to the living room and left us there at the table alone. Again, I knew it was not by chance, and I also knew that there was to be no explaining this away. My heart was pounding out of my chest, and Mateo had locked his eyes to mine and was smiling like a fool again, which made me painfully uneasy. He had the most piercing gaze and could easily have won a staring contest if that's what we were doing. But instead, he looked down at the table and took my hand that was lying there. It was clear he had something to say but was having a tough time saying it. I looked down at the table, too, thinking it might make it easier. Then I heard the words, the ones I'd been waiting for so long to hear.

He squeezed my hand, "I'm in love," he said, and then with his voice catching briefly, "and it's madness." We looked at each other then, our eyes glistening, silent for a moment. "I love you," he continued, "and I want to spend my life with you. I want you to be the mother of my children. I want you to go with me wherever I might go, to be my partner, wherever we may end up." I was bursting with joy and relief and overflowing with all of the love I'd been trying to hold in for so long. Then, his tone turned serious, "You're young, you have a lot of growing up to do, you're going to change a lot, so we can't get married any time soon, but just knowing makes things better, doesn't it?"

It did. I didn't care how long I'd have to wait. I felt the pieces fall into place, and it felt right. In spite of cliches, or theories that like to debunk true love as nothing more than brain chemistry, I knew that we were two pieces of a puzzle that were meant to fit together, and without him, my puzzle would never be complete. I could tell from his voice and the way he looked down at the table when he spoke that he wished he could control the way he was feeling but couldn't, and I was glad because it made me feel a little less crazy.

And just like that, we were engaged. He never officially asked me to marry him, and I never said yes; we just knew.

Alan and Mateo said goodnight and left, the kids had gone to bed, and Michael and Judith, and I were alone in the living room. We were mulling over the now-tired topic of change and growth and whether that was even possible in the church, but I couldn't focus on a single word. I was having an out-of-body experience, floating somewhere up near the ceiling, their voices muted and far away. I needed something to bring me back down to earth, so I blurted abruptly, "Mateo and I got engaged."

That did it.

I was deposited firmly back down in my chair. I had no idea what to expect. They had always been so kind and supportive, but this may have crossed the line. I braced myself for all of the reasons why it was a bad idea—I was too young, there was no way I could possibly understand what I wanted right now, marriage was a lot of work—better to wait a while until I could fathom the weight of such a decision.

But they never came. They were both smiling from ear to ear, and Michael said, "Wow, just wow. Congratulations. That's just wonderful."

"I knew you two were up to something," Judith added as if she was not at all surprised, "You two belong together; I just knew it."

It was a perfect ending to a perfect day, and as I slept, my head barely touched the pillow. It was our secret, just the four of us. I had no idea how many years it would be before we could marry, but until then, no one else needed to know.

But gossip works in mysterious ways, and of course, somehow, my mom found out, probably from Tammy, or Alan, or any number of people who'd seen me drive off in the car with Mateo. When she did, she hurried urgently to Laycher, and he handed over a wad of cash that Rick eagerly added to when he heard about the rescue mission. Antonio lent her his van, and she loaded up the rest of the kids and raced out to Missouri.

Meanwhile, I was pleasantly oblivious to the emergency unfolding in Boone on my behalf. I spent my day canoeing with Alan and Mateo. They asked Judith's permission, and she'd happily given her consent. I had never been in any kind of boat before, and I was totally *petrified* about being on the water. I didn't know how to swim, and being in a tippy canoe didn't help. The river was swollen with recent rains, and I sat like a statue in the middle of the canoe while the guys dodged branches and navigated the fast-moving current. I inadvertently held my breath for most of the trip, but Mateo and I were together, and that's really all that mattered.

Imagine my surprise later when, back at Judith and Michael's, I watched Antonio's van pull into the driveway, and my mom step out. I had been gone all of three days, and she had to come to check on me. I was *not* pleased. She climbed up the stairs to the porch and greeted everyone enthusiastically as if she had just randomly decided that the family needed a road trip. She gave me a kiss and a smile as if everything was normal.

But I knew better.

Later, as we dressed for church, I told her so. "Tell me why you're really here," I demanded.

"I told you. After you left, I decided that we could all use a little road trip."

"You expect me to believe that? You couldn't even give me one week on my own before you came rushing out to check on me. It's because Mateo is here, too, isn't it?"

"I told you. I thought we could all use a break," she wasn't going to budge, "and Laycher agreed."

"Oh, and he just suddenly had enough money to send you on vacation?" I was growing more sarcastic by the second—I was so sick of the lies.

"Yes, well, he gave me some, and Rick helped out, too."

"Of course he did," I muttered.

"What did you say?"

"Nothing."

I tucked my hair into one of the floppy hats that Jess had given me that I had been wearing to cover my head the whole time I'd been in Missouri and walked out to the van. I had asked Michael and Judith if it was okay, and they agreed that it was sufficiently appropriate since it covered my hair as the Bible commanded, and Mateo, when I asked his opinion as my future husband, said that he had no problem with it. My mom was a different story. She walked out to the van and, without missing a beat, drew her lips into that thin line that oozed disappointment and said, "Go get your head covering."

"My head is covered," I insisted.

"That's not a head-covering. Now, I'm not fooling around, *go and get it*," she commanded.

"All the Bible says is to cover our hair; it doesn't say with what. Tell me that my hair isn't covered." I stayed defiantly where I was.

"We're not going anywhere until you get your head

covering."

    I lost my nerve and did what she demanded, deflated and diminished from the strong, independent woman I had started to become back to the chastised child. I was miserable and ready to walk away from it all. Michael and Judith had reminded me just the night before that if I needed to leave home, I always had a home with them. It was time I took them up on that. When it was time to leave, I would simply tell my mom that I wasn't going home.

    But that didn't happen. Mateo convinced me that my mom depended on me too much, plus he was headed back to Colorado to work on the bus, our future home, and he wanted us to work on it together. "She's fragile right now; her world is falling apart; she needs you." I knew he was right. "We'll stick together," he promised. So I climbed behind the wheel of the van, my mom in the passenger seat, and followed him out of the driveway and onto the long, straight, black ribbon that was Highway Fifty West, back to Boone, Colorado.

    When we arrived home from Missouri, everything had changed. Word got out that we were engaged, and Mateo found all kinds of strange little reasons to come to the house and check up on me. Once, it was because he needed to borrow our vacuum cleaner; the one at the brothers' house was broken. Although he had no less than six other houses within a mile radius to borrow a vacuum from, he came to ours. I was relieved that my mom was out grocery shopping, and she had the other kids with her. I met him in the driveway, and we fell into an embrace before he even closed his car door.

    Sparks and zings pulsed throughout my body, like static on a dry winter's day, only stronger. I wanted to push back; I knew it was wrong, knew we shouldn't be standing there in the open, in my driveway, clinging to each other. I knew I should let go, but like grasping an electric current, I couldn't, and I didn't want to. I held on, waiting for a signal from him, a signal that never came. So we just stood there, without saying a word, scarcely breathing for what felt like forever.

27 THE LAST STRAW

We had agreed that we would wait for a few years to be married, but after returning to Colorado, I had grown more certain than ever that I didn't want to be in the church. I was itching to go but Mateo was still clinging to a fragile hope that something would change and that the church could be salvaged. I stayed because I loved him and knew that he would have to come to his own conclusions. In the meantime, he didn't insist that I go to church and I didn't insist that he not go.

"I promise you, if things don't get better soon, we'll leave." he soothed. "But if we do, we'll need to get married. We can't live together if we aren't married." I could have cared less if we were married or not, but if he thought we should be married, I'd marry him, since I knew I was going to someday anyway. I knew nothing was going to change at the church and waited patiently for the thing that would put him over the edge.

That thing reared its ugly head one day while we were both working on the bus, he, building cabinets, and I, sewing covers for the couch cushions and curtains for the windows. I found my sister Ruth hiding between the bus and the trailer, her head in her arms, tearful. I sat down next to her. "What happened?" I asked, draping an arm around her.

She shook her head—which meant that she didn't want

to talk; she rarely ever wanted to talk, preferring to tough it out and figure things out on her own.

"Tell me," I pleaded, "maybe I can help." I was painfully aware that I would soon leave her and the urge to protect her for as long as I could was overwhelming. I also knew that given that she was a tough-it-out kind of girl, the fact that she was so upset meant that whatever had caused her pain was important.

"Trust me, please."

She lifted her face slightly, tear-streaked and crestfallen, and looked at me.

"Anika told me that Maxine has been telling everyone that I'm a slut just because Jesse (Anika's brother) and I like each other. She said that she's not going to allow her grandkids to be anywhere near me anymore."

Ruth had always been Maxine's favorite. She was quiet, soothing, and sweet, and not prone to making trouble like me. She liked to keep the peace and wasn't inclined to defend herself. Ruth was devastated and betrayed and I was furious.

And so, yet again, I felt the fire boil and rage and spill right out of me. The injustice of it all had long since reached a crescendo. The nerve and the sheer cruelty of that woman devoured every last bit of tolerance I had. To attack someone who had never fought back, who had never caused anyone any trouble, to turn her rage on Ruth just because she could no longer hurt me—that was the last straw. It pushed me past the point of my own misgivings about going up against the two most powerful people in the church. I wasn't going to let them get away with it, especially since I knew that when I left, Ruth would have to stay and I wouldn't be there to protect her.

I took her by the hand and marched her into the bus where Mateo was working. She hid her face while I told him what happened. My voice was shaking, and the tremor went all the way deep down into the pit of my stomach. "I'm not going to let her do this to Ruth," I told him, "She knows she has no power over me now, so she's turned her rage onto my sister. I won't let this happen. I'm going over there right now to confront her." At that point, I was used to being badmouthed and belittled by Maxine. Although it still stung a little, I had started to just ignore it. But that was different; it was my little sister, and I wouldn't stand for it.

Mateo put down his tools, "I'm coming with you."

We sent Ruth inside to my mom, climbed into the Honda, and drove to Laycher's house. I trembled the whole way and continued to quake as we walked up the concrete path, knocked on the door, and pushed it open without waiting for an answer. Confronting them was still terrifying no matter how justified I felt, but I was getting better at it.

Mateo let me do the talking and just stood next to me for support. Laycher and Maxine sat on the couch and I planted myself in front of them. "I'm here to talk to you about what you said about Ruth. I found her crying just now because you called her a slut and said that she wasn't allowed to play with your grandkids anymore." I waited a beat for my words to reach their mark. Then I surged ahead.

"Did you really think I wouldn't find out? Anika tells us everything you say; she always has. You can't hide anymore—you can't expect us to just sit and take it. I know that you think you can get away with it because you've been talking about me like that, but I won't let you do that to my sister. She doesn't deserve it, and you know it."

"That's absurd; I would never say a thing like that. I love Ruth. She's always been my girl. She's not a trouble-making, smart aleck like you." Maxine's top lip curled into her signature sneer, and she turned to look out the window.

"You're lying and we both know it. *That's exactly the kind of thing you would say.* It's the kind of thing you say about lots of people all the time, only no one ever stops you because you're married to *him*," I pointed to Laycher, "And you get to say and do whatever you want."

Not anymore.

I, for one, am not going to just shut up when everyone

around me is so hateful and hypocritical."

Her sneer turned to sheer disgust and her eyes dilated with fury. Laycher's face began to twitch as he spat words of condemnation my way, "You wretched, wicked, shameless, loudmouth young lady. How dare you speak to us that way?"

"I can speak to you however I want and I'm not sorry because I'm telling the truth. It's *you* who has been lying to us this whole time, and not once have you tried to make things better, not once have you tried to hear what anyone else has to say—so now, I'm not going to listen to what you have to say."

I was on a roll.

We were screaming at each other; none of us were going to back down.

"You're lying, you filthy little lying whore," Maxine was spitting daggers, "and this, after all the times you've said that you love me and how much I mean to you. Judas love, that's what your love is. You with all your fake sweetness and loyalty."

"I *do* love you, Grandma. *That's why I'm here talking to you.* Don't you get it? I just want you both to *listen* to me." It was a last-ditch effort to appeal to her humanity.

"Oh, don't *Grandma* me." She flipped her hand in that dismissive gesture that I knew so well, confident that it would shut me up.

Before I had a chance to prove her wrong, Laycher, in an effort to take control of the situation as a man should, turned to Mateo and blurted point-blank, "And you, where do your loyalties lie? Are you staying or are you leaving? It's time to decide, right here, right now. No more wishy-washy, no more sitting on the fence. Are you with us, or with her?" I guess he'd noticed Mateo at church without me.

My heart skipped a beat and I silently begged, *please don't say that we'll stay, that you think we can work this out, that we can make it better.* I had made my mind up over and over again that I was going to leave; I was just waiting for him to catch up. In spite of that, the truth is that, if he said we were staying, I would have stayed, at least for a while. As his betrothed, I would be subjected to my husband, and the final decision would be his.

Mateo took my hand, and Maxine scoffed. "We haven't decided that yet," Mateo replied. "We'd like to stay, but it's stuff like this that makes us want to go."

"Well, you can't leave here today without making a decision. YHWH or the devil (Laycher glared at me), what's it going to be?"

I squeezed Mateo's hand, summoned up all of my courage, turned to look at him, and asked, "Can we talk about it together first?"

His eyes met mine and I could see the weight of it all and the pain in his face. I could feel the war raging inside of him. "Of course, we can," he said gently.

Laycher was disgusted. "What do you need to talk to *her* about it for?" He was shouting now, spittle flying from his mouth as he spoke, and his face was beet red. "Aren't you the head of the household? Aren't you the man? Don't you decide?"

"We're one," Mateo replied defiantly, "Our decisions affect both of us and we're going to make them together."

"Oh, you're one, are you?" Laycher sneered. "So I guess that means you've already *had relations and everything*. I should have known; of course, you have." It was both a question and an accusation. He was sure he had caught us, had shamed us, and that he'd won.

It was Mateo's turn to spit daggers, but he was eerily steady as he retorted. "Actually, no, we haven't. Not that it's any of your business." Usually, *everything* was Laycher's business, and it was thrilling to hear those words uttered without any shred of apology or regret. "But, thank you, you've just made up my mind for me—we're out."

"Good, the sooner, the better."

Laycher turned away, pretending that he didn't care, but his fear was written all over his face. His empire was crumbling. We'd just blown the first major hole into it and I felt light, relieved, and vindicated as we let the metal screen door slam behind us and walked hand in hand down that concrete sidewalk and out of the squeaking metal gate for the last time. Once inside the car, Mateo leaned over and gave me a long, smoldering kiss in full view of those two bitter people we'd left behind.

We were finally free.

28 VOWS AND GOODBYES

I didn't spend a lot of time thinking about my wedding when I was young. I knew I'd marry, that my husband would work in construction, and I'd have lots of kids, that is, if YHWH didn't destroy the world before I had the chance. The fact that he might made me feel swindled somehow. What I did think about though, was how I wanted to get married in the meadow we used to hike to when we went to camp in the Huerfano Mountains, instead of getting married at the church. It was the most breathtakingly beautiful place I'd ever seen and that was the one thing I had my heart set on.

The meadow was nestled at the foot of Mount Blanca, a peak in the Sangre de Cristo Mountain Range. Blanca rose high above the tree line and was adorned year-round with a veil of snow, not unlike a bride herself. The meadow was pristine, the birthplace of the Huerfano River that flowed into the Arkansas River barely a mile from our home in Boone. There in the meadow, it was not roiled and sandy; it was crystal clear and icy cold, no wider or deeper than a creek, flanked in the wide expanse by columbines, Queen Anne's lace, and luscious, green, mountain grasses. A magical place for what I knew would be a magical moment.

After our run-in with Laycher and Maxine, Laycher had issued a decree—anyone who came to our wedding would be cut off from the church—excommunicated. It was his way of trying to cling to some semblance of control of a congregation that was very swiftly choosing to go their own way, and he was confident there would be few people who'd choose us over the church.

He was wrong.

At first, Mateo and I weren't going to have a wedding at all. We had talked about just hiking to the top of a mountain, saying our vows to each other, and calling it good. But it was soon clear to me that that was going to be really hard on my mom. When I told her about our plans, she protested. "You're leaving me," she said, her voice weary with grief, "too soon. Don't I get to be a part of the day that's taking you away?" She was also adamant that we couldn't really be married unless we had a ceremony that was blessed by YHWH. All I cared about was that I was finally getting out of there and that Mateo and I would be together, so it was easy to acquiesce to the things that mattered to her. It was the least I could do.

The other thing I conceded to my mom was wearing a white dress. I was determined not to do anything the way I was *supposed* to and had bought some slate blue, gauzy, crinkled cotton for the dress she was going to make for me. When she pulled it out of the Joann Fabrics bag, her face fell. She looked up at me, "You're not wearing white?"

"Why should I wear white?" I asked.

"Because you're my pure, beautiful daughter," she said, but in her eyes, I saw it, the desperation and the determination. She was thinking about my dad. He may have taken my virginity from me, but she was not going to let him take my purity. It had been weighing on my mind, too, a bit. I had been trying to push it away, but it was persistent. Was I really still a virgin in spite of my dad?

My heart broke for her. "It's okay mom, I'll buy some white if you want me to, and some lace, too—to make it special."

"It *is* special," she said, kissing my cheek and blinking back tears. "Thank you, my dear little girl."

"Mom, I'm not little."

We chose a date in early August, which gave us only weeks to prepare, and sat down to make a list of things we needed to accomplish before then. The first item on the list—who would marry us? I suggested that we ask Yahanna's dad to marry us because he was also a pastor, and even before we'd walked out on Laycher, we had decided that there was no way he was going to be the one to marry us. Jerry agreed to perform the ceremony after cornering me in the driveway to make sure that it was really what I wanted, that at my age, I knew for certain I could take such a huge step. I leaned heavily against the open door of Mateo's, soon-to-be-our little car, impatient—the wedding was bearing down on us and there was still so much to do. I'd gone there for a quick answer, not an interrogation. But Jerry wasn't going to let me off that easy. He was determined, not so much to change my mind, as to be convinced that my mind was made up. He started off like everyone else—*you're so young; it's a huge decision; you have no way of knowing how you'll feel in ten years; how can you be sure*—but shifted quickly into what he really wanted to know. *Was I really so mad at Laycher? Had I really lost faith so completely in the church? Did I really think there was nothing left to save?*

Yes, Laycher was a hypocrite and I was furious with him, but also betrayed by him. Yes, I did think there was nothing left to save, and whether I'd *lost* faith or never really *had* faith in the first place was up for debate.

After nearly an hour of grilling me hadn't succeeded in changing my mind, he said, "Well, if you know that this is what you want, I'm happy to do it. Brother Laycher will probably throw us out, but that's kinda bound to happen at this point anyway." He had the same weariness in his eyes that I had been seeing in most people's those days. He hugged me and let me climb back into the civic and drive away, but not before a tear or two ran down his cheeks. He, too, knew that it was the end of something even if it was also the beginning of something else.

Our wedding prep was frantic by our standards, but relatively low-key by most. There was no rehearsal, no caterer, no photographer to organize. There were no hordes of guests to manage—aside from church members, the only other people coming were Mateo's father and step-mom, his mother, his brother, Jess, who drove back to Colorado to be there, and Michelle and her husband. There were no seating charts to agonize over, no hotel rooms to book— we would be camping—and no wine to pay for. Instead, my sisters, Yahanna, and her sister, Mercia, spent an entire day in the kitchen with four juicers, turning a hundred pounds of carrots into a sweet, nutrition-packed drink for our reception. The juice did end up fermenting slightly, so I guess there *was* alcohol at our wedding after all. Our main course was salmon filets shipped in by Mateo's father who was farming them in Southern Chile, and the sides— macaroni salad, potato salad, and tabbouleh, were prepared ahead of time and packed away in Tupperware to be transported to the mountains. Karen, who surprised me by showing up in spite of Laycher's warning, made watermelon boats for dessert and sang *The Wedding Song—He is now to be among you, at the calling of your hearts…*as we sat around the campfire to eat. It had become the custom; I can't remember one church wedding when she didn't sing that song. Her husband and children did not come.

Karen was a bit of an oxymoron, because, although she was a stringent, doctrine abiding, Elder's wife, she was so committed to her faith and to raising her children to believe like her, that she actually took me aside to ask me point blank, 'Do you think all of the children here are going to leave like you are? Is this our future? You were the last one we expected this from. Do you think we have failed so completely that none of them will want to carry on with the teachings?"

My short answer was, "Yes."

I went on to explain that if you don't make room for kids to question and have their own voice, they will have no choice but to run. Also, the lying and hypocrisy were certain to make them reject *everything* they'd been taught and not only the things that didn't make sense. She was the only parent who ever approached me to ask, basically, *how did we get it so wrong?*

On the morning of our wedding, I opened my eyes to find Mateo's face peering through the fogged-up window of my family's station wagon. I'd slept in the car the night before, my last night as a single woman, even though all of my things were already packed in the bus. My mom had wanted me to sleep with her and the other kids in the tent, one last night as her little girl, but I wasn't her little girl; I was a woman about to be married. I couldn't help but smile back at Mateo's beaming face, his eyes laughing like always, his wild hair falling onto his shoulders. My stomach fluttered and then a slight panic gripped my chest—I was really doing it. I was really getting married—and it was for life.

I was quite possibly insane.

The day was a blur, mostly. I'd thought that it was supposed to be one of the most memorable of my life, but more than *images* of the day, I have a *sense* of the day. Silhouettes moving around me like wisps, suggestions of people, but no solid forms. I dressed in the bus with the girls and Jess. There was nothing complicated about my bridalwear for them to help me with, no makeup to do, no champagne to sip, so mostly we just giggled and chatted, the roiling in my stomach growing more intense by the minute. I ate a spoonful or two of yogurt to settle it, but it didn't help much. I had wanted to leave my hair hanging long and wear a wreath of wildflowers, but Mateo preferred to have my head covered, so, rebel that I was, I wore a white turban instead of a head covering.

The girls, my two sisters, and our two best friends, Yahanna and Mercia, were each one like a wildflower in their own right. They had sewn their dresses themselves. Yahanna, who was far more brash than I and had been forging her own way, plowing through the mire for a while by that point, not giving a damn about what anyone thought, defiantly chose a dress pattern with a V-neck. She hissed like a steam engine when her mom made her sew a triangle of fabric into the V to close it up.

    To say I was feeling a bit of the jitters would have been an understatement. I was making a lifelong pledge at an age when I was old enough to understand that I was *very young*. Unlike most people thought, I *did* grasp the gravity of what I was doing, but somehow, I just *knew* that it was what I was supposed to do. Marrying Mateo was simply solidifying a commitment I'd already made in my heart, that I knew was going to happen someday anyway. I knew that I could be his partner. I also knew that it would be years before I would be ready to be a mother—I told him so, unequivocally, and made him promise that we would wait for a long time before having a family. He had agreed without a moment's hesitation. So, I wasn't so nervous about the marriage, it was a combination of the marriage and leaving the only life I'd ever known.

    As I descended the steps of the bus and saw him there waiting for me, the flutters quieted a bit—taking those massive steps into the unknown with him would be so much better than doing it alone. His smile nearly split his face and his eyes were misty, "You look so beautiful." The flutters quieted a bit more, and I took his hand and walked to the waiting van that would drive us the forty minutes to the trailhead. I was a little bummed that I had to ride in the van. I had assumed I'd hop into the back of Antonio's pick-up truck like usual and enjoy the ride in the open air, but my mom and the other moms insisted that the back of a pick-up truck was no place for a bride.

    During the ride, I had time to relax even further as I watched the people around me chat and laugh and sing. As much as that day would be the end of the life they'd known for most of them, they didn't seem to mind; they were choosing to stand with us, whatever the cost, and the truth of that brought me to tears. A sharp pain began to take the place of my jitters. Those people had been my family and I was walking away. There was a rendering taking place as much as there was also a joining on the horizon.

By the time we arrived at the trailhead, I welcomed the fresh air, sunshine, and intoxicating smell of pinon pines and moist earth. I wore hiking boots with my wedding dress and navigated easily over the rocks and through the mud. The meadow opened up around us, just as magical as it had always been, Mount Blanca rising above us, a goddess (yes, I had fully embraced the idea of Goddess thanks to Jess) blessing our day with her grounding presence. Halfway across the expanse, we came to an abrupt stop and my stomach flip-flopped again. Mateo's mother tapped me on the shoulder and handed me a small bunch of wildflowers, "Every bride needs a bouquet," she whispered and gave me a quick pat on the back and a small smile. I knew that our choice to marry was without her approval, so the gesture was comforting.

"Does this work?" Jerry chuckled what I recognized as an uneasy chuckle and rubbed his hands together. Mateo and I glanced at each other and nodded in agreement. We were standing next to the river and everyone suddenly grew eerily silent; the only sound was the babble of the water.

"Please face each other and hold hands," Jerry instructed. I handed my wildflowers to Yahanna and turned to face Mateo and he took both of my hands, breathed in deeply, sighed, and closed his eyes. When he opened them again, he fixed me in a gaze that did not shift and that said, *there is no place I'd rather be.* I breathed in turn and felt strangely certain and grounded.

As I said before, we'd not rehearsed at all. We both turned to Jerry as he chuckled again and then started to speak. I don't remember the exact words, but it went something like this:

"We're here today because the two of you have decided that you want to spend the rest of your lives together.

You've chosen to give yourselves to each other fully and to love and trust each other. You have chosen, in spite of many of us trying to change your minds"—soft laughter circled round—"to take this step to become man and wife in the eyes of YHWH and of this assembly. Is that about right?" He asked, with a twinkle in his eye.

"Yes, it is," Mateo and I responded together.

"Let us pray." Jerry placed a hand on each of our heads and bowed his head; we, in turn, closed our eyes. His voice echoed across the meadow and bounced off of the steep rocks of the surrounding peaks. The prayer lasted longer than the first part and I couldn't keep my mind from wandering. *Is that it? Am I married?* It seemed too simple. I got my answer soon enough when Jerry ended his prayer, removed his hands from our heads, and smiled good-naturedly, "Well, how's it feel?"

I couldn't tell. Five minutes before I was just me and then abruptly, I was Mateo's wife, and he was taking my face in his hands and kissing me in front of everyone. People began milling around and the sound of voices drowned out the panic that was rising again. Mateo was somewhere out in the crowd, but I was feeling heavy with the truth of what came next. The crowd seemed happy, they were singing, and talking and smiling, but all I knew is that the kids were crying—no—sobbing, and it wasn't because they were happy, but because they were sad, and even mad, that I was leaving. They clung to me, a huddled mass, my little brothers and those beautiful girls, and we cried together. I was heartbroken too. I was abandoning them, I knew that, but I saw no other way. I needed to get away, far away.

I'll come back for them, I told myself, as the waves of our grief washed over me. *Once I'm settled, once I've found my solid place, I'll come back for them.*

And the rest of the day played out, as such days do, but I moved through those moments oddly numb, automatic—my extreme happiness swishing around with a sense of shame and guilt for walking out on all of those kids at a time of such tumult. I was suddenly extremely tired, and I think I even took a nap before the reception.

29 UNFURLING

"You know one of the things I've missed all these years?" Mateo asked.

"No, what?" We were circling the block around Acacia Park in Colorado Springs, looking for a parking spot. There was a tiny basement record store there, and he couldn't wait to buy some Bob Marley cassettes and pop them into the tape deck in the car.

"Vinegar...and *mustard*. If you've never had a sandwich with *really good* mustard," he closed his eyes and smacked his lips, relishing the thought, "You've missed out."

I'd never had either and I had a sense I'd *missed out* on a lot. Mateo was almost giddy to be introducing me to things that I'd never tasted, done, or could even conceive of. (Tragically, Jerry Garcia died just a week after we left the church and he never got to take me to a Greatful Dead concert, which he had really been looking forward to.) After years of following rules, adhering to a doctrine that was both erroneous and irrational, and changed at the whims of a delusional man, a simple thing like vinegar was intoxicating.

So was music, recorded music.

There were two tapes that we purchased that day, Bob Marley's *Babylon by Bus* and *Survival*, and when the lyrics and beats burst out of the speakers in that tiny Civic, Bob's music exploded into my soul and spoke to me on a visceral level. *Tell the children the truth,* Bob demanded, and I thought, *yes, this guy gets it; for once, tell the children the truth.*

We didn't dive into the outside world headfirst, *throw the baby out with the bathwater* as people like to say, although months later when one person begged me *not to throw the baby out*...I said, "fuck the baby." We didn't leap from the cliff of restrictions and embrace every facet of the world instantly. We took it slow. Partially because there were rules that I grew up with that seemed rational to me, like eating healthy food, distrusting the medical establishment, not drinking alcohol or coffee, and dressing modestly, but also because it wasn't only me who had turned my back on the church. There were two of us leaving that world together, and I was instinctively aware that we were both leaving with a very personal point of view and cumulation of experiences. Additionally, I still embraced the idea that my husband was the boss, and during those first months, I took my lead from him.

After our wedding, we drove the bus to West Cliff and parked it at the site where Mateo and Antonio were finishing up a remodeling job. They would complete the work before Mateo and I left to drive cross-country down to Florida and then fly to Chile where Mateo's dad and step-mom lived. I cherished that month because I knew it was the last I would have with my siblings and my friends for a while. My sisters, and Yahanna and Mercia, took every chance they could get to come to stay with us in the bus. I would drive the hour back to Pueblo to pick them up and then we would use every convertible bed in the bus to have room enough for all of us to sleep. Each one of those trips zipping down the mountain—or back up the mountain, switchback after switchback, Yahanna in the seat next to me, or all of the girls stuffed into the car—would find us with windows rolled down, volume cranked, and Bob singing:

Tell the children the truth...

We'd smile at each other, nod in agreement, and join in at the tops of our voices.

Tell the chi-il-dren the truth.
Tell the children the truth right now,
Come on and—tell the children the truth.
Cuz we've been trodding...
We'd be bouncing along in our seats, bopping our heads. REBEL, Bob commanded; we pumped our fists in the air, REBEL! Until I'd quickly remember—*two hands on the wheel.* I still had no driver's license or insurance.

Jess's friend Sam came from Flagstaff to visit, and one evening, just as dusk settled in, we implored him to teach us how to dance. I'd never danced before, only *swayed with the spirit* which never involved actually moving my feet or *heaven forbid,* my hips. I'd only reached my arms to the sky in praise and glory of YHWH and the thought of flinging them into the air to pump out the beat of a song—I wasn't sure I could even coax them to do that.

So, with all the doors of the Honda flung wide open, we cranked the stereo as loud as it would go. Sam bounced, first on one foot and then on the other, arms spread wide like a bird, a playful, bashful smile on his face as we all stared. I could feel the music in my chest and a stirring in my soul, I felt every drum beat and pluck of the bass, but I stood planted firmly in one spot; my feet had grown roots. The reverberations coursed through my very cells, but moving my hips felt vulgar, releasing my arms from their positions glued to my sides—flaunting.

Bob Marley urged us to *stir it up...little darlin'.* Sam opened his eyes and held out both hands, beckoning to me. He swept me up in a quick spin and, holding tight to my hands, pushed and pulled, first one arm and then the other, causing my shoulders to sway this way and that. I flushed bright red and thought I would die from shame. He released me and continued to bounce, turning in circles, laughing good-naturedly at our stupor and then coaxing, "C'mon, it's not hard; you just have to let it flow." *Like water, like the breeze,* I thought.

I closed my eyes; it was the only way; if I wasn't watching then maybe no one was watching me. I let the notes, pauses, and beats find their way, first to my heart, which began to glow and fill my chest with giddiness, and then from there, out to my limbs. I grew wings, small ones at first, baby steps, hips side to side—just a little, shoulders released, swaying slightly, but it would be a long time before I ever lifted my arms to the air for a song or a cheer. And although I've since come to understand the dogma that is inherent in much of Marley's music, I still appreciate and relate to the uprising, the revolution, and the rhythm, that to this day never fails to get me on my feet and bouncing. It is an integral part of my coming out and coming into my own.

That month in West Cliff was a honeymoon in the truest sense of the word. Not so much for my new marriage, but rather for my new life. The feeling of being *free*, of being able to make my own choices, of being allowed to go through my day without the sense of being under a microscope, without fear of reprisals. The lifting up, the release of years of weight was like flying. I was in a constant state of tingling excitement, devouring every new taste, smell, texture, and feeling.

But even amidst all of the freedom, discoveries, and ability to breathe, our new life was making demands of us, asking us to define—*who are we now, what do we believe now that we'd rejected the only system of belief I'd ever known*? What would that look like moving forward? For example, would we still pray? To whom, God? The Great Spirit? The Goddess? None of the above? Sitting cross-legged in a field early in the morning before Mateo left for work each day, facing each other, eyes closed, holding each other's hands meditatively, was all we could come up with. Those questions were too big for the first month of marriage, too big for the first month of navigating outside of the suffocating doctrines of the church.

During that time of opening up and expanding our lives and minds beyond the confines of the church, I tried briefly to reconcile with my dad. I was submersed in a process of reevaluating everything I'd ever believed or been taught, and that included cutting him out of my life, because what was forgiveness, *true forgiveness,* if it wasn't giving someone a second chance? Laycher loved to preach forgiveness, but he never liked to give second chances. I was trying to do most things opposite of what Laycher had taught me. I couldn't have known at the time, that I'd already given my dad too many second chances. That knowledge would come much later, after years of wrestling with those demons.

There would be a myriad of hurdles in front of me, not the least of which would be to simply interact somewhat competently within the larger culture. To say I was unrefined would be an understatement. Basic manners were lost on me. I had been taught to say "yes, sir" and "yes, ma'am"—respect of grown-ups was of utmost importance, but I had also been trained to *be seen and not heard,* which often rendered me speechless, as in, I could not coax words out of my mouth. I had to learn to shake someone's hand and say, "Nice to meet you," instead of shrinking behind the nearest object or person, usually Mateo. I learned that it was rude to sit with my knees pulled to my chest at the table, how to put my napkin in my lap, and how to use a fork *and* knife instead of just sawing away at a chunk of food with the dull side of my fork. Those were brutal moments for me because they seemed to confirm to my damaged psyche that no matter the world I inhabited, I would always fall woefully short.

But I muddled along, weeks, months, and years propelling me forward, until being *in the world* was much more natural, although, to this day, I still wrestle a bit with imposter syndrome. It didn't take me long to throw out the bathwater *and the baby,* as layer after layer of dysfunctional thinking fell away. My grandma Jean bought me my first pair of pants only a month after I left the church, khakis from Target, paired with a white button-down shirt, a western-style vest, and a fake leather belt. Even though I tried them on time and again while in the privacy of my bedroom, it would be six months before I finally wore pants in public. Somewhere around the one-year mark, I went to JC Penny's and had my ears pierced, and barely a year and a half after leaving the church, I got my first pixie cut. Before that, my hair had reached my butt.

I was giddy in the hairdresser's chair, and irritated when she kept asking, "Are you sure you want to do this?"

"Yes."

"What if I just cut it to your shoulders first?"

"No, I want it like the picture."

"How about I cut a bob and let you see that? Then you can decide?"

"Thanks, but I've already decided. Just cut it all."

"Does your husband know you're doing this?"

Exacerbated, "Why would that matter?" I couldn't believe that that lady, who was not anywhere near the church, was asking me if I had my husband's permission.

As she put the final touches on my hair, Mateo walked into the same salon and sat down to have his first haircut and beard trim since leaving. He was just as surprised to see me there as I was to see him. But while the whole salon seemed to hold its breath to gauge his reaction, he only smiled sheepishly and said, "Looks like we had the same idea." Afterward, we grabbed a sandwich from a nearby diner, hiked our brand-new selves up a short mountain just outside of Pomfret, Vermont, and watched the sunset together. Shedding that hair had felt like shedding something old and heavy, something we needed to release.

It was time to move forward.

EPILOGUE

Years passed and I never went back for them, those girls in the meadow, my little brothers clinging to my legs. Life has a way of traveling miles away from the path that you've plotted. When I finally did go home for a visit a year after my wedding, all of those kids had found their own way out of the church, with or without their parents, and were powering along, sustained by their own wells of courage and determination. I always felt like I had abandoned them, although logically, I know that there was really nothing I could have done differently. I had naively assumed that Mateo and I would settle in Pueblo, get a big house, and take in any kid who wanted to leave the church. I had never once discussed it with him or stopped to consider what that would mean for him because it was simply what I thought I had to do. Needless to say, that didn't happen.

Laycher did not excommunicate everyone who came to our wedding, just the ones he didn't like. My mom and Karen managed to survive the cut, but still, the church disintegrated quickly, with over half of the congregation making a mass exodus less than a year after Mateo and I left. Within the next couple of years, it was further reduced until only four people remained, one of them being my mom. Laycher and Maxine have both passed on; she not many years after we left and Laycher more recently. I had hoped to be able to send him a copy of this book, but, alas, it wasn't meant to be.

Leaving the church wasn't the end for me; it was the beginning, the first rung of a very tall ladder out of the mire. Nothing about it was easy, but years have passed, and life has progressed as life tends to do, and now I'm here, at the end of a journey I've so longed to take—of writing this story down.

I've grown into a woman I am proud to be—a mother to two beautiful and inspiring children and I continue to be a wife to the man I pledged my heart to in that meadow so many years ago. I have no bow to tie on this messy package, just my story to share. I hope that it will inspire some, empower others, and give comfort to anyone who has found themselves climbing out of a similar mire.

Made in the USA
Middletown, DE
23 January 2024